# THE MOST DANGEROUS PLACE

## PAKISTAN'S LAWLESS FRONTIER

### IMTIAZ GUL

PENGUIN BOOKS

PENGUIN BOOKS
Published by the Penguin Group
Penguin Group (USA) Inc., 375 Hudson Street, New York, New York 10014, U.S.A.
Penguin Group (Canada), 90 Eglinton Avenue East, Suite 700, Toronto, Ontario, Canada M4P 2Y3
(a division of Pearson Penguin Canada Inc.)
Penguin Books Ltd, 80 Strand, London WC2R 0RL, England
Penguin Ireland, 25 St. Stephen's Green, Dublin 2, Ireland
(a division of Penguin Books Ltd)
Penguin Books Australia Ltd, 250 Camberwell Road, Camberwell, Victoria 3124, Australia
(a division of Pearson Australia Group Pty Ltd)
Penguin Books India Pvt Ltd, 11 Community Centre, Panchsheel Park, New Delhi – 110 017, India
Penguin Group (NZ), 67 Apollo Drive, Rosedale, Auckland 0632, New Zealand
(a division of Pearson New Zealand Ltd)
Penguin Books (South Africa) (Pty) Ltd, 24 Sturdee Avenue, Rosebank,
Johannesburg 2196, South Africa

Penguin Books Ltd, Registered Offices: 80 Strand, London WC2R 0RL, England

First published in the United States of America by Viking Penguin,
a member of Penguin Group (USA) Inc. 2010
Published in Penguin Books 2011

1  3  5  7  9  10  8  6  4  2

Published in India as *The Al Qaeda Connection* by Penguin Books India

THE LIBRARY OF CONGRESS HAS CATALOGED THE HARDCOVER EDITION AS FOLLOWS:
Gul, Imtiaz.
[Al Qaeda connection]
The most dangerous place : Pakistan's lawless frontier / Imtiaz Gul.
ISBN 978-0-670-02225-0 (hc.)
ISBN 978-0-14-311921-0 (pbk.)
p.  cm.
Originally published under title: The al Qaeda connection. New Delhi : Penguin Books India, 2009.
Includes bibliographical references and index.
1. Qaida (Organization)   2. Taliban.   3. Terrorism—Pakistan—Federally Administered
Tribal Areas.   4. Terrorism—Religious aspects—Islam.   I. Title.
HV6433.P18G85 2010
954.9105'3—dc22          2010001898

Maps by Jeffrey L. Ward

Printed in the United States of America

*To my parents*

*and Sameena, my extremely caring better half,*

*and my sons, Faraz and Saad*

## Preface to the Paperback Edition

Since the publication of this book in hardcover, four major events have deepened Pakistan's internal political and economic crisis and added to the complexity of its relationship with the United States. In the summer of 2010, catastrophic floods inundated almost 20 percent of the country's landmass. Terrorists took advantage of the ensuing chaos to intensify their campaign of violence, launching homicidal attacks on major Sufi shrines in Lahore, Sahiwal, and Karachi. In July and again in November, Wikileaks released thousands of pages of classified memos sent by American diplomats and military officers in Afghanistan and Pakistan. And in December, Richard Holbrooke, Obama's Af-Pak envoy, succumbed to a fatal heart attack. Holbrooke's sudden demise shocked everybody in Pakistan, where he had emerged as a strong supporter since his appointment in January 2009.

The floods wrought havoc from the north to the south, devastating standing crops and shanty settlements along the Indus River. The World Bank put the losses at close to $10 billion. President Asif Zardari's credibility was a big stumbling block to marshaling a quick international response to the floods: the United Nations garnered only about $600 million when it launched an emergency appeal for $1 billion in late August. A few meetings of the Friends of Democratic Pakistan (FoDP), a forum set up to help Pakistan in Tokyo in April 2009, concluded without solid commitments. Meetings in mid-November in Islamabad similarly bore little fruit. Here, Holbrooke loomed large, though appeals to his sixteen Af-Pak colleagues to appreciate Pakistan's double crisis (floods and insurgency) fell on deaf ears. Many feared a misappropriation of funds by Zardari's government.

Holbrooke was cheerful and witty when I met him for a panel interview at the state-run Radio Pakistan. One could tell how seized he was with the mission of mobilizing funds for Pakistan. "We are trying to do as much as we can but a larger contribution will have to come from within Pakistan," he told me, pointing to the simmering debate as to why the country's ruling elite evaded taxation. He minced no words when he spoke of a "long battle ahead for Pakistan and us all."

As Holbrooke tirelessly pointed out, the insurgency that has taken hold in Pakistan and Afghanistan is a long-term challenge that will require Pakistan, the United States, and Afghanistan to work together closer than ever before. Nothing could have dented this edgy trilateral relationship more than the release in November 2010 by Wikileaks of thousands of classified cables sent by American diplomats working in Islamabad. Hundreds of confidential cables sent to Washington by Ambassador Anne Patterson provide an insightful analysis of Pakistan's military and civilian leadership and reveal that while publicly the leaders lambasted American interference in internal matters, privately they confided almost everything to American officials.

One of the most damaging things to emerge was news of a "silent coup" proposed by Pakistan's army chief, Ashfaq Kayani. In early 2009, General Kayani discussed with Ambassador Patterson the possibility of "persuading" President Zardari to resign and replacing him with the Awami National Party leader Asfandyar Wali Khan, an ethnic Pashtoon nationalist. Kayani said that he would keep Prime Minister Gilani in place. In another cable, Vice President Biden told Gordon Brown, who was then Britain's prime minister, about a conversation with Zardari sometime in 2009 in which Zardari told him that General Kayani and the ISI "will take me out."

These revelations inflamed tensions between Kayani and Zardari. Their poorly disguised antipathy stemmed from a disagreement in

December 2008 over how to deal with the fallout of the Mumbai attacks that November. Following a meeting with Senator John Kerry in mid-December, Zardari had proposed to Kayani, in the presence of Prime Minister Gilani, that one way of pacifying the Indians would be to allow them a couple of symbolic aerial strikes on Lashkar-e-Taiba camps in Kashmir. A shocked Kayani instantly opposed the proposal. A high-placed official told me later that Gilani backed the general, saying that such an act would trigger irreparable political damage. He added that Kayani had then driven straight to his office, called the air force chief, and asked him to send fighter aircraft to patrol over Islamabad and Lahore.

That bad blood existed between the army chief and his supreme commander was no secret. What surprised many in Pakistan was Kayani's candid admission to the U.S. ambassador that "he might, however reluctantly, have to persuade President Zardari to resign if the situation sharply deteriorates." He said this on the eve of a wave of protests in March 2009, when Pakistani lawyers were set to march on Islamabad to press for the restoration of several judges, including the chief justice Iftikhar Chaudhry.

Another cable from October 2009 showed that a small U.S. Special Forces team had been allowed to deploy alongside Pakistani soldiers in the tribal belt, the zone on the Afghan border that Washington considers an Al Qaeda and Taliban sanctuary. It was only the second time such permission had been granted, the cable said. Senior cabinet ministers were also shown to privately support U.S. drone attacks in the tribal belt. Publicly, both General Kayani and Gilani had reiterated their opposition to drone attacks and ruled out "American boots on ground" but the diplomatic cables betrayed these pronouncements, embarrassing them inside and outside the country.

America's drone wars escalated exponentially under President Obama, and Wikileaks revealed that this escalation happened with the government's tacit approval. On August 21, 2008, Prime Minister Gilani told Ambassador Patterson in the presence of Interior Minister Rehman Malik that he didn't care if drones struck, so long as they got the right people. Around 124 strikes in 2010—a 130 percent increase over the previous year, 91 on targets in North and South Waziristan—killed some 1184 people, *The News* reported on January 1, 2011. Ten groups were the top targets: Al Qaeda, Tehreek-e-Taliban Pakistan, the Afghan Taliban, Islamic Jihad, the Islamic Movement of Uzbekistan, the Islamic Army of Great Britain, Brigade 313, the Haqqani Network, Lashkar-e-Islam, and Lashkar-e-Jhangvi.

From an American point of view, the Wikileaks dispatches reflected positively on the Pakistani army for "ever-improving cooperation." They revealed how closely General Kayani and his men had been working with the U.S. military and diplomats. Domestically, however, they weakened Kayani by depicting him, contrary to his public image, as a man who was "in sync with American objectives."

The cables also exposed U.S. frustrations at Pakistan's refusal to cut ties with Afghan militants and Pakistani extremists such as Lashkar-e-Taiba. Ambassador Patterson confided that she believed the government and military were both likely to remain immovable on three key points of American policy: taking on the Afghan Taliban, launching a military operation in North Waziristan to disrupt the Haqqani network, and taking on Lashkar-e-Taiba. It is clear from the cables that despite its progress tackling militants in the tribal areas, the Pakistani military still considers India its principal enemy.

The timing of the Wikileaks document dump couldn't have been worse. Released only a few weeks ahead of the Afghanistan and Pakistan Annual Review scheduled for December 16, the cables kicked up a storm in Pakistan, where the public at large was incensed over the closeness of their civilian and military leaders to American diplomats and officials. General Kayani went on a public relations offensive, publicizing his visits to various troubled spots in the northwest in an attempt to salvage his tarnished image.

The news also severely damaged Pakistan's fragile government. Several leaders of Zardari's ruling Pakistan People's Party alleged privately that the Wikileaks disclosures had paved the way for two key allies—the secular Muttahida Qaumi Movement (MQM) based in Karachi and the faction of Jamiat Ulema-e-Islam led by Mullana

Fazlurrehman (JUI-F)—to blackmail their coalition partner. The MQM and JUI have been part of nearly every government since 1988, when civilian rule was restored after a long period of military dictatorship. Both have been used by the military to manipulate civilian governments.

In mid-December, the JUI-F dropped out of the coalition, complaining that its ministers were being mistreated and suddenly viciously opposing any amendment to a controversial blasphemy law that General Ziaul Haq had enacted in the late 1970s. Until the Wikileaks disclosures, the issue of the blasphemy law had been largely missing from national discourse. Its revival raised many eyebrows, prompting politicians and analysts alike to suspect that the embarrassed military establishment was manipulating the campaign to deflect attention from the Wikileaks disclosures.

The controversy surrounding the blasphemy law tragically triggered the murder of Salman Taseer, governor of the Punjab, on January 4, 2011. Taseer had earned the ire of the religious right by demanding a parliamentary review of the law to prevent its misuse. He was visiting Islamabad when one of his special guards, Malik Mumtaz Qaderi, pulled out a Kalashnikov and emptied two magazines. It was only a few seconds before the killer smilingly surrendered to his stunned colleagues, saying that the governor had committed blasphemy and deserved to be killed. The incident sent shock waves across Pakistan, where, alarmingly, those hailing Qaderi as a hero far outnumbered Taseer's sympathizers.

Political volatility in Pakistan obviously runs contrary to America's objective of defeating Al Qaeda and bringing the insurgency raging in Afghanistan under control. The number of attacks on Afghan and foreign security forces almost tripled in 2010. Most outsiders join the Afghan government in attributing this spike to Al Qaeda–affiliated Afghan and Pakistani militant groups based in North Waziristan, including the Haqqani Network. That is why the U.S. Strategic review in mid-December described Pakistan as "central to our efforts to defeat al-Qa'ida and prevent its return to the region."

A string of reports out of Washington accompanying the review suggested that the Obama administration was close to approving a major expansion of ground raids by special operations forces into Waziristan. The plan, reported by the *New York Times* and Pakistan's *Express Tribune* on December 24, flowed from the review's conclusion that Pakistan wasn't doing enough to eliminate terrorist safe havens in the tribal areas.

"Pakistan does not expect the U.S. to complicate matters," a government spokesman told the *Express Tribune*, adding that the U.S. mandate was restricted to Afghan territory only.

Vice President Joseph Biden's tough talk during his six-hour visit to Islamabad on January 13, 2011, reflected a growing impatience with Pakistan. Soon after meeting with Prime Minister Gilani, Biden promised before the press that U.S. troops would not "impose a war on Pakistan in the name of expanding counterterrorism efforts beyond Afghanistan." He reiterated at the same time Washington's desire for a full-fledged military offensive in North Waziristan. Biden declared that the "real threat" to Pakistan and the United States came from Al Qaeda and Taliban fighters hiding in Pakistan's remote tribal regions, reflecting the view of the Obama administration that the road to peace in Afghanistan will come via Pakistan.

Soon after taking charge following General McChrystal's firing in June, General Petraeus embarked on an aggressive new approach to tackling the militants in the tribal areas. On September 30, an American helicopter chased militants who had darted across the border into Pakistani territory. They ended up killing two soldiers guarding a post in the mountains of Kurram. Pakistan reacted by sealing a supply route into Afghanistan for ten days, bringing crucial food and fuel supplies for NATO troops to a grinding halt. Hundreds of tankers were burned, with suspicions falling on hard-line elements in the security forces. "Militant" attacks on NATO cargo transiting through southwestern Balochistan left at least 135 containers and oil tankers destroyed. The Torkham border was eventually reopened after Ambassador Patterson offered a public apology a week later, but this episode exposed the limits to which America could arm-twist Pakistan.

Reconciling the conflicting long-term interests of Pakistan with short-term U.S. policy objectives poses a formidable challenge. Most Pakistani analysts believe that General Petraeus has shifted the focus of war from Afghanistan to their country in an effort to pave the way for a phased withdrawal from Afghanistan. But it is highly questionable whether a frontal assault by the Pakistan army on militants in the tribal areas would bring stability to Afghanistan. Pakistan is keen to avoid antagonizing Afghan groups inhabiting its border regions and feels it has already paid a high price for America's war with Al Qaeda.

Pakistan today is battered and wobbling under the impact of skewed policies it clung on to even after the Soviet withdrawal from Afghanistan. Its future is threatened by a growing network of radical Islamist groups that declare allegiance to Al Qaeda but are rooted within conservative segments of Pakistani society. A significant number of silent supporters and sympathizers who are inimical to the West—apologists for the Taliban and Al Qaeda—support these militants and lend them the social space they need to survive and thrive. The fact that millions of Pakistanis hailed Salman Taseer's killer as a heroic defender of the prophet Mohammad is an alarming reminder of the dramatic radicalization of Pakistani society over the last four decades.

Financially, Pakistan is almost on its knees, living off borrowed money from the IMF. Politically, it is reeling under the blows of jihadis whose attacks have shaken its fragile coalition government. It needs to indulge in a cost-benefit analysis and to look with a cold eye at the alliances and partnerships that once constituted an important part of its defense doctrine but have in recent years only brought it discredit abroad and mayhem at home. The Pakistani establishment must weigh the cost of its deference to groups like the Haqqani Network and Laskhar-e-Taiba. Short-term fear of a backlash holds it back from a permanent divorce but the price Pakistan has had to pay for this decision has been astronomical both in political and economic terms. The United States and other friendly countries hope Pakistan will turn the corner and work with the international community to minimize the threat emanating from its border regions. So far, it has refused to do so. The military establishment still appears to underestimate the threat posed by Islamic militants, viewing them as "manageable" and little appreciating the fact that murderous ideologies can neither be managed militarily nor contained politically.

If the military's divorce from these groups were to transcend verbal commitments, mainstream political parties might then be inspired to refrain from cutting deals based on expedience with religious parties that provide political support to the Taliban and other militant groups. A big impediment flows from the way the establishment has shaped Pakistani society in the last forty years. "Public sympathy has made it difficult for the state to isolate and destroy these groups," argues Ejaz Haider, a noted Pakistani columnist and a visiting fellow at the Brookings Institution. "The menace doesn't have any defined center of gravity now." Haider believes that the media has made "the task of correction for the state more difficult."

There is little doubt that the only long-term remedy lies in undermining the appeal of these militants with better governance, improving the economic conditions of the millions of Pakistanis living on subsistence wages, and ensuring quick justice for the marginalized poor, including the roughly five million inhabitants of FATA. It would also help to put Kashmir on the backburner, to improve relations with India, and change Afghan strategies.

Pakistan's biggest challenge comes from the transnationalist militant groups that have rooted themselves in its tribal areas. Al Qaeda and its affiliates—spread from Afghanistan to Somalia and Sudan—rely on roughly four dozen auxiliaries to enlist foot soldiers for their 'jihad" against the United States, propagating a narrative that is enveloped in self-pity and denial and projects Muslims as the victims of American and Israeli imperialism. Containing these groups will not be easy. Military means alone are neither a match nor a solution to politically and ideologically driven conflicts.

Quite instructive, in this regard, is a statement that General David Richards made in an interview with the *Telegraph* in November 2010, soon after taking over as the chief of the UK Royal Army. "First of all you have to ask: do we need to defeat it in the sense of a clear-cut victory? I would argue that it is unnecessary and would never be achieved," Richards said when asked whether Al Qaeda could be defeated. "But can we contain it to the point that our lives and our children's lives are led securely? I think we can." General Richards proposed that the threat posed by Al Qaeda and its affiliates meant that Britain would be at risk for at least thirty years.

Only a combination of force and political engagement will gradually neutralize and marginalize the religiously motivated forces sheltering in eastern Afghanistan and Pakistan's border regions. It took Sri Lanka twenty-seven years to overpower the Tamil insurgency on the tiny Jaffna Island. The challenge in Afghanistan and Pakistan is much bigger in scale and transnational in nature. Seeking to address it with quick fixes and military strikes will only further inflame the problem.

# Preface

"In the nearly eight years since 9/11, Al Qaeda and its extremist allies have moved across the border to the remote areas of the Pakistani frontier. This almost certainly includes Al Qaeda's leadership: Osama bin Laden and Ayman al-Zawahiri. They have used this mountainous terrain as a safe haven to hide, train terrorists, communicate with followers, plot attacks, and send fighters to support the insurgency in Afghanistan. For the American people, this border region has become the most dangerous place in the world."

This conclusion, drawn by President Obama in a speech he gave on March 27, 2009, sums up Pakistan's journey in the past few decades—from a launching pad for the U.S.-led anti-Soviet jihad in the early 1980s to a "safe haven and sanctuary for international terrorists aligned under the Al Qaeda flagship."

While announcing his new strategy for Afghanistan and Pakistan—now called "Af-Pak," an indication of the administration's new focus on Pakistan—Obama said the forces holed up in the tribal areas were "not simply an American problem—far from it. . . . It is, instead, an international security challenge of the highest order. Terrorist attacks in London and Bali were tied to Al Qaeda and its allies in Pakistan, as were attacks in North Africa and the Middle East, in Islamabad and Kabul. If there is a major attack on an Asian, European, or African city, it, too, is likely to have ties to Al Qaeda's leadership in Pakistan. The safety of people around the world is at stake."

This pronouncement underscores a bitter reality for Pakistan: from

Afghanistan the war theater has now shifted closer to home, with
Robert Gates, the secretary of defense, and Richard Holbrooke, the
special representative for Pakistan and Afghanistan, threatening a hot
pursuit of Al Qaeda "wherever found."

Within two weeks of Obama's policy announcement, Pakistan experienced a dramatic surge in violence. From Waziristan to Peshawar
to Lahore to Islamabad, dozens of people perished in suicide attacks
or drone strikes. Statistics on the spiral of violence are mind-boggling.
In 2009, militants staged almost ninety suicide attacks and carried out
another five hundred bombings and ambushes, killing over three
thousand people. This is all the more striking given the fact that, until
2002, Pakistan had experienced only one suicide strike.

The deadly attack on Islamabad's Marriott Hotel on September 20,
2008, which killed more than sixty people, underscored a new reality:
after hitting targets inside FATA, in Swat and Peshawar, the insurgents
were now knocking at the heart of the capital. Within four hours of
President Asif Ali Zardari's avowal to "eliminate terrorists from the
face of Pakistan," a suicide bomber rammed a six-wheel dump truck
into a barrier outside the hotel. The truck was loaded with six hundred
kilograms of TNT and RDX explosives, including mortars, artillery
rounds, mines, and aluminum powder—the sum total caused a massive blast, followed by a rapidly spreading fire that reduced the entire
hotel to a concrete shell.

The closed-circuit video system of the hotel froze as a result of the
huge impact, but the shots taken before the explosion showed the attacker blowing himself up after the truck had become entangled in the
steel barrier. As he vanished with the explosives strapped around his
waist, the ensuing flames ignited the ammunition at the back of the
truck within a couple of minutes.

I was in the hotel at that time, dining with two friends at one of the
restaurants by the pool in the rear. About three hundred people,
mostly women and children, were enjoying dinner after breaking their
Ramadan fast. As many as 22 foreign nationals were injured; four of
them died, including the Czech ambassador to Pakistan and his Viet-

namese partner. Two American soldiers assigned to the U.S. embassy also lost their lives in the incident. I was among the 350 or so lucky ones who escaped unhurt. Once safely out, I looked back to see the inferno spreading over the building. Hell had arrived in Islamabad, the leafy capital of Pakistan.

Thus far, the attack on the Marriott Hotel, which reopened in December 2008 following massive and speedy restoration work, was the most consequential; the planners chose the high-profile hotel in an obvious attempt to scare foreigners and dent the country's image abroad. Stay off Pakistan, was the message delivered through this strike, the third on the hotel in three years. The tactic worked, with the United Nations forcing the evacuation of dozens of families, followed by many diplomats and their families.

For the first time, signs of a political war in Pakistan became visible. Prominent Pakistani analysts, including Talat Masood, Rasool Bakhsh Raees, and Dr. Hassan Askari Rizvi, declared that the attack had been on the "symbols of a functional state." This war knew no social values, no tribal tradition, and carried no religious trappings, they suggested in various interviews to the print and electronic media. Nor were attacks on innocent locals and foreigners morally justifiable. The chickens had come home to roost; religious zealots whom Pakistan's security apparatus had used as proxies for missions in Afghanistan and Kashmir had turned on their erstwhile mentor.

Two months later, ten gunmen held Mumbai, India's commercial capital, in the grip of terror for almost three days, going on a killing spree that claimed 179 lives. India, backed by the United States and Britain, blamed a Pakistani group, Lashkar-e-Taiba, for this act that sickened the world. Once again, my country was being held to account.

By the end of 2008, more than a thousand civilian and military officials had been killed across all the tribal agencies, including a number of those who were dubbed "U.S. spies." More than four hundred maliks, or tribal leaders, also lost their lives because they were viewed as "government collaborators." By December the militants were knocking at the doors of Peshawar.

Peshawar, which is surrounded on three sides by tribal agencies, served as the headquarters and staging post for Afghan mujahideen following the 1979 Russian invasion and occupation of Afghanistan. The nerve center of international jihad and the world's biggest spy capital, it was torn apart by tit-for-tat retaliation between Soviet and Afghan spies. The city appears to be under siege again, this time as a consequence of the war against a new generation of jihadists who oppose the United States and abhor all its allies.

The latter half of 2009 saw a bloody surge in terror strikes in the city, beginning with a suicide attack on its lonely five-star Pearl Continental Hotel in June, resulting in a dozen deaths and widespread destruction. One wing of the hotel that adjoins the official residence of Peshawar's corps commander was completely destroyed.

A dozen suicide attacks within the space of four weeks in November 2009 killed more than 250 citizens and officials. In one incident alone, about 150 lost their lives to an explosives-laden car that blew up in the heart of the city. Another strike took more than 40 lives. In one of the suicide bombings on November 8, terrorists eliminated Abdul Malik along with a dozen others. Malik, the mayor of a Peshawar subdistrict, used to be a militant sympathizer but had turned against them, raising his own army to defend his area. He did not last long in his new role. Militants from the tribal areas are clearly determined to terrorize Peshawar, the largest and busiest commercial hub in the region. So far, the Pakistan army has been unable to keep them in check.

On March 3, 2009, a dramatic commando-style attack in the heart of Lahore, Pakistan's second largest city, left the entire security establishment stunned and badly bruised. Shortly after 9:00 in the morning, a dozen or so heavily armed young attackers ambushed the convoy of vehicles carrying the Sri Lankan cricket team to Gadaffi Stadium. As the escort police engaged the attackers, the driver sped the bus away from the scene and rushed into the stadium, so most players escaped unhurt.

The police were still grappling with the aftermath of the attack when terrorists struck at the police academy in Lahore. A day later, Baitullah Mehsud, the head of the Tehreek-e-Taliban (the TTP), the association of militant outfits that forms the core of the Pakistani Taliban, stunned many in- and outside the country by owning responsibility for the commando raid and the ensuing bloody siege of the police academy.

"We did it as a retaliation for U.S. missile strikes off drones inside the Pakistan territory," said Mehsud in his first such admission. But he did not stop there. "Soon we will launch an attack in Washington that will amaze everyone in the world," he said in an interview with the U.S.-funded Dewa Radio. He identified the White House as one of the targets.

"He sounded unrepentant and pretty cool," the journalist Alamgir Bhittani told me of his conversation with the diminutive Mehsud. "He was cutting jokes, offered me blessings, and vowed to kill more."

Only a week before the Lahore attack, the United States had announced a $5 million bounty on Mehsud's head, describing him as a clear threat to American interests in the region. It thus finally lay to rest a long-standing concern among Pakistani military officials, who openly expressed their surprise that the U.S. never targeted Mehsud.

Between January 2006 and March 2010, CIA-operated Predators and other drones conducted some 213 cross-border strikes, with a staggering escalation under President Obama. In a February 24, 2010, report titled "The Year of the Drone," Peter Bergen and Katherine Tiedemann of the New America Foundation pointed out that President Obama had significantly increased the number of drone attacks in his first year in office. "In 2009, there were 51 reported strikes in Pakistan's tribal areas, compared with 45 during the entire administration of George W. Bush," they wrote. In 2010, the Obama administration would quietly up the ante again, launching as many as 118 drone strikes—more than twice the previous year's total.

The report touched on the killing of civilians in drone attacks, something that generates massive resentment and stokes anti-

American sentiment. Most Pakistanis view these attacks as a violation of their national sovereignty. The numbers of civilians killed by drones are highly contested. Some Pakistani commentators claim that "the civilian death rate from the drone attacks in Pakistan is 98 percent." At the other end of the spectrum, an anonymous U.S. government official told the *New York Times* in early December that "just over 20" civilians and "more than 400" fighters had been killed in less than two years. Bergen and Tiedemann's own assessment is that civilian casualties make up 32 percent of those killed in drone attacks.

"There exists a big gap on the issue of drone attacks which impinge on our sovereignty," Foreign Minister Shah Mehmood Qureshi told media at the Ministry of Foreign Affairs on April 7, 2009, as a displeased Richard Holbrooke and Admiral Mike Mullen, chairman of the Joint Chiefs of Staff, looked on. Moments before this press stakeout, officials told me later, the U.S. visitors and Qureshi had exchanged words that were certainly not pleasant.

The Obama administration has intensified its use of drones on targets in Waziristan and the adjacent tribal agencies. On September 3, 2009, American forces even carried out their first ground offensive in Pakistan, entering Zawlolai village in South Waziristan. This operation failed to achieve its goal: the killing of top Taliban or Al Qaeda leaders. It did, however, provoke countrywide condemnation, prompting the army chief, General Ashfaq Kayani, to issue a warning that such attacks were unacceptable, a move that considerably boosted his popularity.

Military officials and highly placed government officials, however, privately sound quite happy about the success of the recent drone strikes. "As long as they take out the guys who are a threat to us all, why crib about it," remarked a very senior general recently, when asked about the drones. "We don't have the technology, nor does Pakistan have a satellite to guide these drones, so why keep asking for it?"

Despite the public objections to such strikes and the protests over civilian deaths, a dispassionate analysis does lead one to conclude that drones are probably a more effective tool for hunting down wanted Al

Qaeda operatives and their local supporters than a full-blown military operation. This approach also allows the United States to circumvent or avoid legal procedures involved in capturing, detaining, and trying militants. Guantánamo Bay and Abu Ghraib are pertinent reminders of the risks to American values and prestige of holding onto alleged terrorists.

United States–Pakistan military cooperation appears to be entering a new phase, and both military establishments are now coordinating drone attacks and army campaigns better than ever before. Both Pakistani leaders and Afghan president Hamid Karzai seem to be helpless in the face of the U.S. conviction that drone strikes do offer an effective tool for eliminating bad guys on the ground.

American pressure on Pakistan's tribal areas has sent militants on a rampage across Pakistan. Their boldest challenge to the authority of the state took place in November and December 2008, when followers of Maulana Fazlullah, a reactionary cleric, stormed through the Swat Valley, killing and displacing hundreds of thousands of people, set up a parallel government, and imposed sharia law.

Fighting between militants and government forces has been a feature of daily life in Swat since 2003, punctuated by periodic truces during which the militants have generally disregarded their promises and cemented their control. The offensive in November and December 2008 caught the government of Asif Ali Zardari off guard. By the time Obama was sworn in as president, militants were less than a hundred miles from Islamabad.

When a desperate provincial government agreed to a cease-fire with the elderly Maulana Sufi Mohammad, Fazlullah's father-in-law, one of the terms of the agreement was that he could impose Islamic law in Swat, a demand that has resonated in the region since the mid-1990s. No one seemed to be bothered by the fact that this agreement was against the constitution of Pakistan. In April Pakistan's national legislature, the National Assembly, recommended that President Zardari sign what had come to be known as the Nizam-e-Adl Regulations and thus sanctify the agreement.

Most civil society organizations and foreign governments opposed the deal, calling it a "surrender to militants." In Washington, White House spokesman Robert Gibbs criticized the regulation as "against human rights and democracy. . . . Solutions involving security in Pakistan don't include less democracy and less human rights," Gibbs said. Yet the provincial government insisted the deal must be honored to bring peace back to Swat and to protect lives. On April 13, President Zardari signed it into law.

Days later Maulana Fazlullah's men began establishing checkpoints and went on a fresh drive to recruit young boys in Swat. (Fazlullah had had a falling out with his father-in-law and did not consider himself bound by the agreement.) They targeted military convoys and kidnapped civilians for ransom. Mingora's central Green Square became known as "Killer Square," as terrorists used its lampposts to hang the executed. TTP vigilantes began taking up vantage positions in the hilly region and embarked on a march southward, attacking the army and the paramilitary forces. Some captured and executed soldiers, including a group of four young commandos who had been air-dropped in on a reconnaissance mission. Their execution sent shock waves across the country. Once it had recovered their decapitated bodies from a roadside, the military high command made up its mind that the time had come to bring the beast under control.

"When the puppy raised at home begins biting its own people, he must be put to sleep," Major General Ejaz Awan, the commanding officer in Swat, said when I met him in Rawalpindi in late April 2009. Only hours before, the top brass, led by General Kayani, the army chief of staff, had decided to take on the militants in Swat and the greater Malakand region.

For the first time, Pakistan's mighty army complex has begun to view their former wards as "an existential threat to the country." This marks a new chapter in Pakistan's history: for decades these nonstate actors were an essential element of the army's security paradigm for its eastern and western borders.

Faced with the violence and brutal oppression of the TTP, and the increasing irrelevance of the peace deal, the secular Awami National Party, the ruling party in the North West Frontier Province (NWFP), which had advocated a political solution to the militancy in Swat, asked the army to move against the militants. "As the army prepared to launch the operation code-named Rahe Rast ("The Right Path"), we began working on plans to protect the civilians in the thickly populated towns such as Mingora, Dir, and Buner," Owais Ahmed Ghani, governor of the NWFP, which was renamed Khyber Pakhtoonkhwa on April 8, 2010, in a bid to placate Pashtoon nationalists, told me in his office in Peshawar.

The plan involved baiting militants away from populated centers to strategic locations in Upper Dir, Shangla, and Buner, which the security forces had vacated in a calculated way. By May 6, the army and the Frontier Corps had begun advancing on militant positions from four directions. On May 12 commandos from the Special Services Group landed in the mountains surrounding Peochar, Maulana Fazlullah's headquarters and the main training center of the Swat chapter of the TTP. They came across tough resistance and discovered elaborate training facilities, explosives, and a number of tunnels connecting homes to escape routes. From ridge to ridge, security forces cleared the area after intense engagement at every step.

As the army advanced, a humanitarian crisis was unfolding. Beginning with the first signs of mobilization, scared residents of Swat, Bruner, and Dir began leaving their homes for safety. Within days, the road between Peshawar and Mingora was overflowing with tens of thousands of people. By late May, this exodus had turned into one of the largest internal displacements of people ever witnessed in history; over two million people had left their homes.

Governor Ghani told me the massive displacement was part of a military strategy that aimed at keeping the militants guessing as to where to entrench themselves. Until then, they had easily hidden behind the population, preventing the security forces from attacking them. Now, with hordes of families rushing out of towns, the fighters found themselves exposed to all possible tactics by the army. The strategy was to depopulate the towns, locate terrorists' hideouts, pound and bomb them, clear the areas, and hold them. Simultaneously the military gave up many of its best positions, baiting militants into taking control of them only to be bombed and pounded. Several hundred militants were eliminated within the first few days of the operation.

Anticipating the mass exodus that the military operation would cause, the government had instructed all educational institutions to close down weeks before the actual summer break was due to start. Schools and colleges were turned into camps where thousands of refugees were taken in. Meanwhile, the army began a double-pincer movement, closing in from four directions on areas that the TTP had held in its control for over a year.

By early July, security forces had cleared almost all of Swat, Dir, and Bruner—an area spread over 3,360 square miles. This gave people the confidence to return home before the monsoon rains began in August. Although conditions remained volatile and the civilian administration fragile, the government and international relief agencies helped them resettle refugees and with the dawn of 2010, life had returned almost to normal in most towns in and around Swat.

The disruption of the Pakistani Taliban's network in the Malakand region, and the vigorous military campaign in neighboring Bajaur begun in August 2008, marked a big stride forward for the army. Until the operation's relative success became apparent, most Pakistanis were skeptical of the military's intentions. Assumptions about the nexus between the militants and the military were so deep-rooted that nobody believed the army would ever seriously take on the terrorists. The arrest of dozens of militant leaders, including Muslim Khan and Maulvi Omar, the dreaded spokespeople for the TTP, and the killing of over 1,600 rebels, removed at least some doubts.

Following up on its Swat strategy, the military decided to conduct a similar operation in the parts of South Waziristan that the TTP had turned into its operational base. Sararogha became the South Waziristan headquarters after they seized the town in a surprise raid on a paramilitary fort on January 25, 2008, instantly executing half of the two dozen Frontier Corps soldiers, a move that filled the roughly eight thousand inhabitants with fear and forced them into silence. Stones and debris still litter the ground of the fort—the result of heavy artillery fire the army used while entering the town. "It all started from here, the challenge to the state of Pakistan," Brigadier Muhammad Shafiq, the commanding officer, told me during a recent visit. "Sararogha has turned into a symbol of the TTP terror in the region."

Three divisions began their advance on South Waziristan on October 17, 2009. By early November, the army had managed to reoccupy the mountainous valleys of Sararogha, Laddah, and Makeen. The military campaign forced the leaders of the TTP to abandon their strongholds and disperse. This operation created another humanitarian crisis, with half a million people fleeing for safety, most taking refuge in camps in and around Dera Ismail Khan or joining friends and family.

The mass exodus allowed the army to move into what General Kayani had called a "black hole" with relative ease. The TTP put up resistance in places, laid booby traps on major arteries, and ambushed the security forces, but since most of the population had moved out, the army had little hesitation in bombing out militants holed up in compounds and tunnels that provided them shelter and escape routes.

When the soldiers recaptured key strongholds, they found dozens of Arabic books, magazines, and teachers' manuals on warfare and bomb building. These documents and others left at seminaries in Sararogha and Laddah suggest not just the presence of Arab fighters, but the convergence of Al Qaeda and local militant groups. Several handwritten notebooks explain how Al Qaeda's ideology binds followers of various shades of Islam together. They explain the configuration of suicide vests and improvised explosive devices and underscore how Al Qaeda's techniques of insurgency have traveled from Saudi Arabia through Iraq to Afghanistan and Pakistan.

Since October 2009, as a result of the army's push into South Waziristan, militants have fled to other remote valleys in the forested border regions of North Waziristan, Orakzai, and Kurram, where they have leaned heavily on their local allies to engage the army and to train local fighters for terror missions in Pakistan and Afghanistan.

In the opening months of 2010, the Pakistan army remained busy hunting down militants in all seven tribal regions. Two infantry divisions were deployed in the Malakand region around Swat. A division from the XIth Corps (7th Infantry Division) was in North Waziristan and the 9th infantry division of the same corps was pounding militant strongholds in South Waziristan. The Zarrar Battalion of the Special Services Group, an elite commando force, was also helping out in sting operations wherever needed. Supporting the army in all seven tribal regions were the paramilitary Frontier Corps. Additionally, over twenty-two thousand tribal militia members were out to back up the military campaign. This meant that in total, Pakistan had deployed over two hundred thousand men in the tribal regions.

Since the offensives in Malakand and Swat in May 2009 and in South Waziristan in October, many remote towns and villages in the tribal areas are back under government control. In some instances, they are under government control effectively for the first time.

The army succeeded in reestablishing a precarious peace, but by now it was clear that the terror born in FATA was fast on the move.

"Pakistan needs to change its threat perception, which is right now focused on India and needs to be refocused on the western border where the Taliban and Al Qaeda activists operate," General David Petraeus, commander of U.S. Central Command, told a Senate hearing in early April 2009. "This starts, frankly—all of this in Pakistan begins with them embracing the idea that the biggest threat to their country's very existence is the internal extremist threat rather than the threat to their east."

America's advice did not evoke much enthusiasm among the interested parties in Islamabad. And yet recapturing the tribal areas from the clutches of extremist militants, and preventing more land and towns from drifting under their control, should be a top priority for the security establishment. General Kayani, who seems to have developed a good personal rapport with General Petraeus and Admiral Mike Mullen, keeps telling his U.S. visitors that the army will neutralize all of the militant groups in due course. He warns them that "this requires extreme caution and consideration for the future." Foreign troops will soon be gone, he says, and we shall have to coexist with the very tribes that will be hurt when we move against the militants nestled among them. The sense one gets from those leading the general headquarters is that they are not ready to compromise Pakistan's own immediate and long-term interests for the sake of American concerns.

General Petraeus and Admiral Mullen visited Islamabad again in December 2009, showering praise on the Pakistan army for its operations in Swat and South Waziristan. In their interviews with local private TV channels, both men expressed their satisfaction with the work of the ISI and the Pakistan military. The two generals were in Islamabad to lobby for President Obama's new plan for Afghanistan, announced on December 1 in a speech at the United States Military Academy at West Point. "We are in Afghanistan to prevent a cancer from once again spreading through that country. But this same cancer has also taken root in the border region of Pakistan," Obama said. "We cannot tolerate a safe haven for terrorists whose location is known and whose intentions are clear." He then committed an additional thirty thousand troops, at a staggering annual cost of $30 billion. Obama also promised a sustained, long-term strategic partnership with Pakistan.

Richard Holbrooke, Obama's tough-talking special representative to Afghanistan and Pakistan, was quick to explain what the administration had in store for Pakistan. On December 6, 2009, he told CNN that "safe havens in Pakistan" were a bigger problem than corruption and chaos in Afghanistan. "I have to say that corruption is critical to our success, but it's not the governing issue in this war," he said. "To me, the most important issue for our success is dealing with the sanctuary in Pakistan."

Holbrooke, Petraeus, and Mullen—even President Obama—have all essentially been telling the American people and the world that the real problem lies in Pakistan and not in Afghanistan, where over three decades of war and turmoil have rendered the country dysfunctional, entirely dependent on corrupt government officials, notorious war- lords, and foreign handouts.

Holbrooke's statement was rooted in what are now entrenched pre- conceptions about Pakistan, namely that:

1. Al Qaeda and the Taliban leadership are hiding in Pakistan (in Balochistan and FATA)
2. Terror groups attacking India, Afghanistan, and coalition troops in Afghanistan are using Pakistani territory as their base
3. Sections of the Pakistani military establishment continue to maintain contacts with, and support, some of these groups (Lashkar-e-Taiba, the Afghan Taliban, and the Haqqani network)
4. Pakistan's nuclear weapons could fall into the hands of one of these groups
5. The military establishment continues to dominate the civilian government, thereby blocking its own reform

But are these assumptions in fact all true? They underscore a fun- damental lack of trust in Pakistan's security establishment, which in the end could undermine the accomplishment of Obama's goals.

Perceptions, right or wrong, drive people's fears. The most com- mon misperception in the region revolves around the causes of their current troubles, which are widely believed to have been created by the United States to justify direct action inside FATA and the NWFP against suspected terror centers. Scores of intelligentsia, including professors, bureaucrats, and technocrats, as well as bazaaris and day laborers, somehow believe that the United States wants to establish itself in Pakistan the way it did in Saudi Arabia, Qatar, and Iraq, and is therefore creating conditions for such a role.

Another perception that currently dominates public discussion in the Frontier Province and elsewhere is that of a U.S. administration that is bent upon denuclearizing Pakistan, discrediting Islam, and cutting Pakistan down to size—dividing its four provinces into smaller units for easier management.

Despite the public appreciation voiced for the Pakistan army's operations in Swat and FATA, there is little doubt that Pakistan's military is exposed to continual pressure and opprobrium from the United States. This raises questions as to the limits of effective cooperation. The Pakistan army remains wary of the large influx of Americans into Pakistan and the string of official leaks questioning its will to fight certain militant groups.

Misgivings about U.S. intentions erupted into a standoff in December 2009, when Islamabad announced that all visas for Americans and other nationals would henceforth require clearance by the ISI. This decision triggered a row between the two establishments, and thereby brought visa processing to a grinding halt. As a retaliatory move, the United States withheld the release of almost a billion dollars promised to Pakistan in coalition support funds (CSF), which the army has been receiving every year since December 2001.

Between 2002 and 2008, Pakistan received $6.6 billion in military aid to help fight militants. Under the bilateral arrangement, Pakistan has been providing logistic and intelligence support to the coalition forces in Afghanistan and has deployed more than 120,000 troops on the border to Afghanistan. Until 2008, these operations cost the United States as much as $80 million a month, but allegations of over-invoicing led to a halt in payments, with the result that, as of February 2010, the United States owed Pakistan almost $2 billion in coalition support funds. According to the *Boston Globe*, from 2004 to 2007, 76 percent of U.S. reimbursements to the Pakistani army—a total of $2.2 billion—were paid without adequate documentation of how the costs were arrived at.

Military-to-military cooperation, however, continues. A number of U.S. military and intelligence advisers regularly visit the Waziristan regions, primarily Wana and Miranshah. Some one hundred U.S. Marines are busy training the Frontier Corps in FATA. The FC has received new combat equipment and vehicles worth millions of dollars as part of an attempt to gear it up for counterinsurgency operations. The United States has donated some twenty-six used helicopters for counterinsurgency operations and committed eighteen new F-16 aircraft. In February 2010, President Obama asked Congress for an additional $500 million to take U.S. counterinsurgency support for Pakistan to $1.2 billion annually. The decision was made partly in recognition of the Pakistani army's actions against militants in Swat and South Waziristan.

In early October 2009, Congress passed a bill, sponsored by senators John F. Kerry of Massachusetts and Richard G. Lugar of Indiana, to send $7.5 billion in nonmilitary aid to Pakistan over the next five years. Kerry described Pakistan as the world's greatest security risk and argued that stabilizing the country and stopping Al Qaeda were the United States's main security concerns. The senator called the bill a "landmark achievement," and said that U.S. assistance for roads, schools, courts, and hospitals would help build trust and foster good relations between the United States and Pakistan. House Speaker Nancy Pelosi said the new funding gave Pakistan "the tools, support, and capability it needs to defeat Al Qaeda and other terrorist groups."

By the end of 2009, the United States had spent $270 billion on operations in Afghanistan in support of 70,000 troops. Compared with that, the $7 billion paid to Pakistan for a deployment of 120,000 troops on the border with Afghanistan would seem to be a good deal. Another $5 billion—averaging about $450 million per year—went into social sector funding. President George W. Bush also helped Pakistan with a $3 billion budgetary support package, including a loan write-off worth about $1.5 billion in 2003.

This expenditure has recently come under scrutiny in the United States and elsewhere as journalists have questioned the oversight of "tens of billions of dollars" pouring into Pakistan, a country of more than 170 million inhabitants. It matters little to most outsiders that suicide bombings—more than 210 since March 2002—have not only scared off foreign investors but also drained the national economy. One terror incident alone—a suicide bombing on a Shiite procession on December 29, 2009, in the southern city of Karachi—resulted in losses of $200 million; the bombing itself killed about one hundred people but the rampage by the outraged crowd within a couple of hours of the strike saw thousands of shops plundered and burned to ashes.

And yet there do seem to be clear violations of laid-down procedures for the spending of U.S. funds, and the issue of inappropriate application of funding, overinvoicing, and corruption is alarming. "The Pentagon ended up paying for a radar system in an area of Pakistan even though terrorists in that area had no air attack capability," the *Globe* reported. "U.S. taxpayers also paid the Pakistani army for road and bunker construction that may or may not have occurred. Even when the Pentagon got tough with Pakistan, questioning $22.3 million for helicopter repairs, that scrutiny came only after $55 million was already gone for helicopter 'maintenance' that barely happened, if at all."

Former president Pervez Musharraf admitted in interviews he gave in London that the army had used some of these funds to counter threats from India. This did little to help bilateral military relations. Kayani told a group of Pakistani journalists in early February 2010 that the army was trying to improve its accounting systems to make financial transactions more transparent. He underlined, however, that the issue of U.S. military assistance had been blown out of proportion.

For years, Pakistani military and intelligence agencies helped indoctrinate, motivate, and train jihadi cadres for export in the neighborhood—to Jammu and Kashmir and Afghanistan. Since 2001 many of their former wards have gone their own way, some, inspired by Al Qaeda, co-opting suicide bombing into their jihad. These human bombs, originally designed to destroy the enemies of Islam and Pakistan, have begun to explode themselves inside their own country, killing their fellow Muslims, civilian and military alike. The terror that was planned and nurtured in the tribal regions is now knocking much closer to home. They are now threatening the very existence of the country that midwived their creation. This book tells the story of how that happened, and what can be done to bring the situation back under control.

# Contents

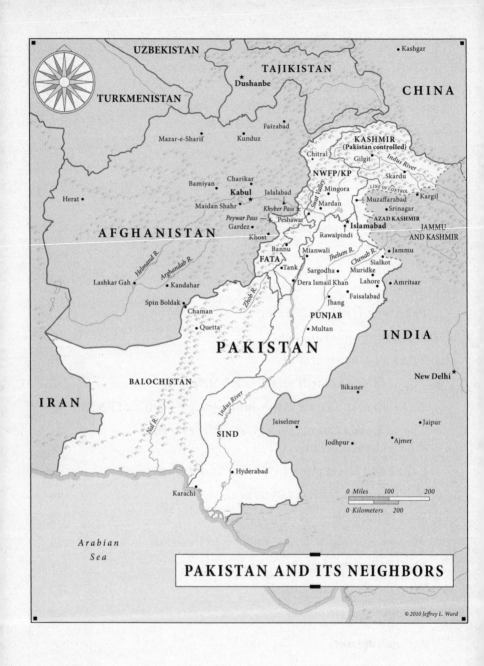

UZBEKISTAN

TAJIKISTAN

Dushanbe

CHINA

• Kashgar

TURKMENISTAN

Faizabad •

Mazar-e-Sharif •        Kunduz •

KASHMIR
(Pakistan controlled)

Chitral •        Gilgit •        *Indus River*

Bamiyan •        Charikar •

NWFP/KP        Skardu •

Herat •        **Kabul** ★        Jalalabad        Mingora •        LINE OF CONTROL        • Kargil

Maidan Shahr •        *Swat Valley*        Mardan •        Muzaffarabad •        • Srinagar

**AFGHANISTAN**        *Khyber Pass*

Peywar Pass        Peshawar        ★ **Islamabad**        **AZAD KASHMIR**        JAMMU

Gardez •        Rawalpindi •        **AND KASHMIR**

Khost •        • Jammu

Bannu •        Mianwali •        *Jhelum R.*        Sialkot •

**FATA**        • Tank        Sargodha •        Muridke •        • Amritsar

Lashkar Gah •        • Kandahar        Dera Ismail Khan •        Lahore •

Spin Boldak •        Jhang •        Faisalabad •

Chaman •        **PUNJAB**

• Quetta        • Multan        **INDIA**

**PAKISTAN**        New Delhi ★

**BALOCHISTAN**        Bikaner •

**IRAN**        *Indus River*

Jaiselmer •        • Jaipur

**SIND**        Jodhpur •        • Ajmer

• Hyderabad

0 Miles        100        200

Karachi •        0 Kilometers        200

*Arabian
Sea*

## PAKISTAN AND ITS NEIGHBORS

© 2010 Jeffrey L. Ward

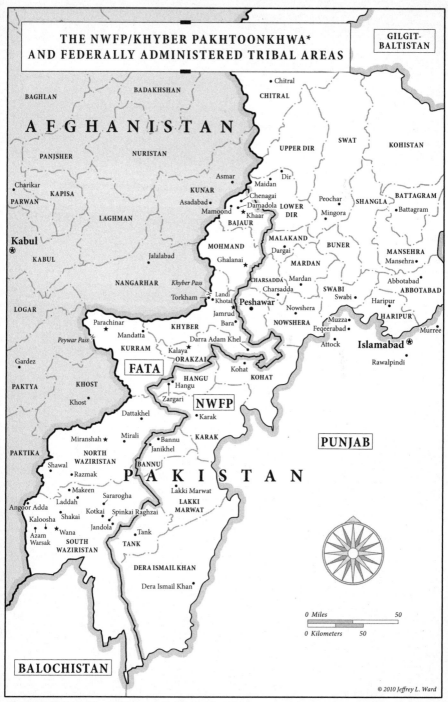

THE NWFP/KHYBER PAKHTOONKHWA*
AND FEDERALLY ADMINISTERED TRIBAL AREAS

GILGIT-
BALTISTAN

BAGHLAN

BADAKHSHAN

Chitral

CHITRAL

AFGHANISTAN

SWAT

KOHISTAN

PANJSHER

NURISTAN

UPPER DIR

Charikar

KAPISA

Asma

Dir

BATTAGRAM

PARWAN

KUNAR

Maidan

Peochar

SHANGLA

Battagram

Asadabad

Chenagai

LOWER

LAGHMAN

Mamoond

Damadola

Khaar

DIR

Mingora

Kabul

Jalalabad

BAJAUR

MALAKAND

MANSEHRA

KABUL

MOHMAND

Dargai

BUNER

Mansehra

Ghalanai

MARDAN

Abbotabad

LOGAR

NANGARHAR

Khyber Pass

CHARSADDA

Mardan

SWABI

ABBOTABAD

Torkham

Landi
Khotal

Charsadda

Swabi

Haripur

Murree

Peshawar

Jamrud

NOWSHERA

Muzza

HARIPUR

Parachinar

Bara

Nowshera

Feqeerabad

Islamabad

Peywar Pass

Mandatta

KHYBER

Attock

Gardez

KURRAM

Darra Adam Khel

Rawalpindi

Kalaya

FATA

ORAKZAI

Kohat

PAKTYA

KHOST

HANGU

KOHAT

Hangu

Khost

Zargari

NWFP

Dattakhel

Karak

PUNJAB

Miranshah

Mirali

Bannu

KARAK

PAKTIKA

Janikhel

NORTH
WAZIRISTAN

BANNU

Shawal

PAKISTAN

Razmak

BANNU

Makeen

Lakki Marwat

Angoor Adda

Laddah

Sararogha

LAKKI
MARWAT

Kaloosha

Shakai

Kotkai

Spinkai Raghzai

Azam
Warsak

Wana

Jandola

Tank

SOUTH
WAZIRISTAN

TANK

TANK

DERA ISMAIL KHAN

Dera Ismail Khan

0 Miles        50

0 Kilometers    50

BALOCHISTAN

© 2010 Jeffrey L. Ward

*The North West Frontier Province was renamed Khyber Pakhtoonkhwa on April 8, 2010.

# THE
# MOST
# DANGEROUS
# PLACE

# 1

# Pakistan's Dangerous Game

Pakistan's history since its formation in 1947 has not been a happy one, but I do not believe that extremism and terrorism are part of our DNA. When I look back over the years, I believe the turning point was in the mid-1970s, when the civilian government of Zulfiqar Ali Bhutto decided to recruit dissident Afghans as assets to deploy against a new government in Kabul that was leaning alarmingly toward the godless Soviet Union. It was then that Pakistan's semiautonomous tribal areas became the springboard and the training ground for Afghan dissidents.

A quarter century later, in 2001, the 9/11 terror attacks in the United States were followed by Operation Enduring Freedom in Afghanistan. The subsequent vicious and bloody military campaign in Pakistan's tribal border regions, known as the Federally Administered Tribal Areas (FATA), brought the region, particularly the Waziristan, Mohmand, and Bajaur agencies, to international attention.

Until the launch in the early 1980s of the anti-Soviet jihad, sponsored by America's Central Intelligence Agency and the Saudi Arabian General Intelligence Directorate (GID) and executed by Pakistan's powerful Inter-Services Intelligence agency (ISI), most of the tribal lands—governed by the Frontier Crimes Regulation, a legacy of British colonial rule—had largely been ignored, underfunded and devoid of basic infrastructure. The writ of the government in Islamabad was both minimal and rather compromised. This combination of factors offered a fertile environment for many illegal activities: drugs, gun-running, smuggling goods imported under the Afghan Transit Trade

Agreement via Karachi port on the Arabian Sea, as well as space for criminal gangs to shelter fugitives from Pakistani law. The majority of local government functionaries *benefited* from this environment, receiving direct bribes from smugglers, drug peddlers, and kidnappers, and sharing in illegal cross-border transactions, and therefore did little or nothing to stop them. The federal government turned a blind eye to these activities in return for loyalty from the tribesmen, whom the military establishment considered the first line of defense on the western border.

Major General Naseerullah Babar, the inspector general of the Frontier Corps (FC) in the North West Frontier Province capital of Peshawar (he was later Pakistan's interior minister under Benazir Bhutto from 1993 to 1996), initiated a process that was to influence more than two decades of the country's Afghan policy. The Frontier Corps is stationed in the North West Frontier Province (NWFP) and Balochistan and is under the interior ministry, not the army. Its primary task is to help local law enforcement agencies maintain law and order when called upon to do so. Border patrol and antismuggling operations are also delegated to the FC.

Babar tasked Brigadier Aslam Bodla and Aftab Sherpao (the latter was then a captain in the Pakistan army—he subsequently became NWFP chief minister twice and was Pakistan's home minister between October 2002 and November 2007) and a few Pashtoon police officers, including Syed Fida Younus, to enlist Afghans to aid Pakistan's push into Afghanistan.

By October 1973, chosen Afghans started visiting Pakistan regularly for briefings. Most were put on the payroll of the Frontier Constabulary, the police force deployed in the Frontier Regions, between FATA and the southern districts of the NWFP. In early 1974, Pakistan's embassy in Kabul received a list of 1,331 Afghan nationals and their families from a colonel with the ISI, with instructions for monthly payments to be made to the Afghans. The document was coded for fear of interception. I was given this information by a former official who had served at the embassy for several years.

Younger Afghans in the group, including Gulbuddin Hekmetyar,

Burhanuddin Rabbani, Younus Khalis, and Rasool Sayyaf, were then selected for commando training at Cherat, a mountainous area some eighty kilometers southeast of Peshawar where the Pakistan army's Special Services Group commandos train. These Afghans later formed their own mujahideen groups. They not only received training in guerrilla warfare but also ample funds to mold public opinion in favor of Pakistan and against the pro-Moscow parties. Through the FC, Pakistan began earmarking small arms and modest funds for its proxies in Afghanistan—less than $200,000. Everything went through the FC, where Babar created an inspection team to look after its "boys." Typewriters, Xerox machines, and stationery were provided to develop, print, and distribute propaganda material inside Afghanistan.

At that time, almost the entire Afghan group formed the Hezb-e-Islami, but from 1977 onward, the Pakistan army chief, General Zia ul-Haq, divided them. During one of our meetings, Babar told me he never fathomed why Zia did this.

Well before the Russians moved into Afghanistan in December 1979, Babar claimed he became the bridge between Pakistan's "boys" and the Americans. The first contact came about in May 1978 when Babar sent Rabbani and Hekmetyar to American diplomats in Islamabad for an evaluation. "They (the Americans) asked for my assessment of these people, whom I would refer to in my phone conversations with the American diplomats [by the code names of] 'mason' or 'carpenter' being on his way to Islamabad."

General Zia seized power in July 1977, in a midnight coup, deposing embattled prime minister Zulfiqar Ali Bhutto. A year earlier, Bhutto had, of all the potential candidates for the top military post, picked Zia, considering him to be a nonambitious loyalist. But the loyalist would soon turn on his master, taking advantage of the turmoil that had resulted from a controversial national election in March that year. Tainted by widespread rigging in favor of Bhutto's liberal Pakistan People's Party (PPP), the election results were rejected by the opposition, an alliance comprising several right-wing parties. Initially Bhutto, who had a decade earlier charmed Pakistan's poor with his promise of "bread, clothing, and housing," refused to budge and attempted to save his disputed victory by giving in to some of the demands of the opposition. These included a ban on alcohol, gambling, and horse racing as well as the adoption of Friday, the Muslim holy day, as a weekly holiday.

In July, following weeks of tough and tense negotiations, Bhutto's PPP reached an agreement with the opposition: fresh elections would be held for about one-third of the National Assembly seats. But as the two sides were about to seal their understanding, Zia moved his troops in the wee hours of July 5, put Bhutto and his opponents under arrest, and declared martial law. Bhutto's contempt for Zia, which he displayed during their meeting a week later at Murree, a hill station some fifty kilometers north of the capital, Islamabad, and his antiarmy belligerence during his brief freedom in 1978, sealed his fate. Zia saw no way but to put Bhutto under house arrest again, opening an old and controversial murder case against the former prime minister. (The family of a former PPP leader had accused Bhutto of his murder.) The Lahore High Court, stuffed with anti-Bhutto judges, found him guilty and sentenced him to death. Bhutto petitioned the Supreme Court, but it upheld the verdict, even though three of the seven judges seriously questioned the prosecution and rejected the case. By then, fearing the populist leader's return, Zia had made up his mind. He turned a deaf ear to international appeals for clemency and sent Bhutto to the gallows on April 5, 1979.

As Pakistan's new military dictator, General Zia ul-Haq was initially lukewarm to the idea of using Afghan protégés. The ISI was not yet involved in the anti-Soviet operation and Pakistani financing, which had begun with Bhutto, was on the wane. General Zia finally woke up when, following the Saur Revolution of April 1978, the Soviets installed a pro-Moscow government in Kabul in December 1979.

Soon after the Soviet army invaded and occupied Afghanistan, the United States enthusiastically adopted the idea that the Russian presence could be thwarted with the help of Afghan opposition forces, which the Pakistani establishment had groomed as proxies since the mid-1970s. They included Gulbuddin Hekmetyar, Maulvi Younus

Khalis, Professor Burhanuddin Rabbani, Professor Abdurrab Rasool Sayyaf, Nabi Mohammedi, Sibghatullah Mujadeddi, and scores of others. General Zia eventually agreed to turn Pakistan into a conduit for funds and arms from the CIA and GID.

## The Zia Years: The Rise of the Religious Right

During General Zia's repressive rule, in the first three years in particular, he introduced a rash of new measures to turn Pakistan into a more overtly Islamic state. Shortly before his ouster, Bhutto had banned alcohol and declared Friday a public holiday, but General Zia, who combined religious zeal with political shrewdness, took the Islamization drive to new levels, with military officers and civilian bureaucrats falling over one another to prove their Islamic credentials.

The noted U.S. author Stephen Cohen wrote in his comprehensive study of the Pakistan army, *The Idea of Pakistan:*[1] "For Zia, a more truly Islamic Pakistan would have the moral qualities necessary to stand up to India, since its scientists, generals, and politicians would be strengthened, not weakened, by their faith. Zia also cynically used Islamic groups internally against leftist opponents, especially the PPP, though he was not above betraying them when he felt the alliance had outlived its usefulness."

One of Zia's most lasting transformations of Pakistan was in the area of education. His wide-scale project of curricular reform found an unexpected ally in the University of Nebraska, which had had an association with Afghanistan ever since 1975, when its Afghan Center linked up with Kabul University. In the early 1980s, the university was tasked by the CIA with producing new textbooks that would help inspire the Afghans to "jihad" against "infidel Soviets." This message made its way into the pages of primary school textbooks in forms like this alphabet song:

*A [is for] Allah. Allah is one*
*B is for Father (baba). Father goes to the mosque . . .*

> *D [is for] Religion (din). Our religion is Islam. The Russians*
>     *are the enemies of the religion of Islam . . .*
> *J [is for] Jihad. Jihad is an obligation. My mom went on*
>     *jihad. My brother gave water to the Mujahidin . . .*
> *P [is for] Five (panj). Islam has five pillars . . .*
> *V [is for] Nation (vatn). Our nation is Afghanistan . . . The*
>     *Mujahidin made our country famous . . . Our Muslim*
>     *people are defeating the communists. The Mujahidin*
>     *are making our dear country free.*
> *Z [is for] Good news (muzhdih). The Mujahidin missiles*
>     *rain down like dew on the Russians. My brother gave*
>     *me the good news that the Russians in our country will*
>     *taste defeat.*

The lessons for older students were more explicit: one fourth-grade mathematics question asks students to use a bullet's speed and its total distance traveled to calculate the elapsed time before it strikes its Russian target in the forehead.

This ambitious reform of the Afghan curriculum took place at printing houses in Peshawar, which was by then home to half a million Afghan refugees. General Zia also ordered a drastic review of the curriculum at home, with a special emphasis on the virtues of the Islamic way of living that would, he hoped, throw up a new Islamized generation.

It was under General Zia that Pakistan became the battleground for the Saudi-Iranian proxy war—both countries poured in millions of dollars to sponsor parties that propagated their respective religious ideologies. An unchecked growth in seminaries of various schools of thought, future "nurseries of jihadists," became common under General Zia, who hoped to pitch the religious parties and their affiliated seminaries against liberal political forces that had until then largely governed the political process in Pakistan. The funding of religious seminaries thrived during the Zia years, to the detriment of the state educational system, which began its decline, a slide that continues to this day.

In a curious coda to this story, in early 2002, the Afghan Center at the University of Nebraska was approved to begin a fourteen-month, $6.4 million cooperative agreement with USAID, designed to assist in the opening of primary and secondary schools in Afghanistan by printing and distributing textbooks in both Dari and Pashtu to all Afghan schools from grades one through twelve. The project included in-service teacher training and the production of instructional kits for teachers. When it was completed, more than fifteen million textbooks and thirty thousand teacher kits had been produced and distributed to Afghan schools.

This time around, the earlier changes in the curriculum were reversed. In accordance with the review's stated objective—"removing objectionable content" that "promoted violence, hatred, and war"—*Kalashnikov, mujahid, jihad,* and other loaded terms were replaced with Pashto and Dari words, such as *book, mother,* and *world.*

A cameraman, a resident of Peshawar, told me that almost all the big printers in the city were consumed with the task of publishing the revised books, with a lot of Afghan teachers working day and night to "correct" past mistakes, expunging traces of the pedagogy now implicated in the "jihadization" of both Afghanistan and Pakistan. An elderly Afghan teacher was one of the dozens of academics tasked with revising the curriculum. Squatting in a corner of the USAID hangout inside the camp, surrounded by Pashto and Dari textbooks, he scribbled on a big register. "We are now removing what we inserted into these books twenty years ago," he said.

## The ISI and the Afghan Jihad

Pakistan's border regions became the staging posts for the new anti-Soviet jihad because of their proximity to the eastern and southeastern Afghan provinces of Paktika, Paktia, Nangarhar, Kunar, Zabul, and Kandahar. These lawless regions served as transit posts for both weapons and Islamist zealots pouring in from all over the world. They also provided training grounds and storage compounds for the ammunition the CIA had begun to funnel to the "mujahideen," a term that

became synonymous with the U.S.-led challenge to the Russian invasion. Besides dozens of training camps located in FATA and Balochistan, where ISI instructors trained Afghan mujahideen, hundreds
of new seminaries catered to the tens of thousands of Afghan refugees
and also served as indoctrination centers for recruits in the war against
the godless communist forces next door.

This new role offered Pakistan an opportunity to realize its long-
cherished dream of "securing strategic depth in Afghanistan through
a friendly and pliant government in Kabul." This at least was the prem-
ise when General Zia decided to co-opt his security and intelligence
apparatus into covertly fighting the CIA-funded war. Once victorious,
it was hoped these proxies would look after the interests of Pakistan
and provide a safe and secure western border, thereby allowing the
military to concentrate on the border with India.

Paul Todd and Jonathan Bloch, writing in *Global Intelligence: The
World's Secret Services Today*, noted that the CIA funneled almost $6
billion, while Saudi Arabia matched the United States in arms funding
for the Afghan jihad, providing some $5 billion by 1992.[2] "A network
of ISI-run training camps in both Pakistan and in Afghanistan itself
had instructed over 35,000 foreign Mujahidin from throughout the
Islamic world by the early 1990s, a significant proportion from Saudi
Arabia. They were to continue their activities, often taking would-be
jihadis directly from Pakistan's 20,000 Saudi-financed madrassas. In
1989 the Makhtab al-Khidmat or services centre, the Peshawar-based
Saudi-ISI headquarters coordinating the Afghan Jihad, was supplanted
by a more clandestine body, the military base of Al Qaida. In some
estimates, over 100,000 Islamist radicals were to emerge out of the
Afghan conflict to form a loose, globally connected network."

After 1992, Todd and Bloch said, the CIA left the scene but the ISI,
which had grown tenfold to almost 20,000 operatives in the interven-
ing years, continued to expand, "rising to an estimated 40,000 and a
$1 billion annual budget by the mid-1990s." Viewed against Pakistan's
financial resources and its gross national product (GNP), this figure is
probably extremely inflated, yet it is undeniable that the anti-Soviet
jihad helped the ISI grow into a monolithic organization. Working

relations between the ISI and the Saudi GID continue to date, but Afghan-specific funding dried up after the United States disengaged from the region following the Soviet withdrawal in February 1989.

The engagement brought substantial material resources—ammunition and arms appropriate for guerrilla warfare—to the ISI and by extension to the army. The involvement in the Afghan jihad had in fact bestowed a double duty on the ISI: intelligence and operations. This was bound to have consequences for domestic politics. Even after General Zia's death in an air crash in August 1988, the army continued to use the ISI infrastructure to influence and nudge government policies in the direction the army high command deemed best. It pitched right-wing politicians and religio-political parties as a counterweight to mainstream parties such as the Pakistan People's Party (PPP) of Zulfiqar Ali Bhutto to pursue its India and Afghan policies.

This was not the first time the army had relied on Islamic groups for its narrow political purposes. During the Bengali separatist movement in then East Pakistan (now Bangladesh) in 1970–71, the Pakistan army co-opted Jamaate Islami (JI) cadres in its crackdown against Bengali intellectuals, politicians, and other supporters of the Bangladesh movement. With this began the sad and ill-fated trend of using Islamist parties to neutralize or eliminate political opponents, ethnic separatist leaders, and those groups and persons considered to be against the army's scheme of things.

When General Zia ul-Haq ousted Zulfiqar Ali Bhutto in a coup, he took the policy even further. He not only openly praised groups like the JI but sought their help in running the government. He also made sure that the JI and its Afghan associates, Hekmetyar's Hezb-e-Islami in particular, received adequate supplies of arms and money for their jihad against the Soviet forces. In Peshawar, the ISI set up cells to cultivate Arab and African volunteers for the jihad.

These ties deepened in the late 1980s, when the ISI began training Kashmiri dissidents, many of whom had fled to Pakistan after the controversial Kashmir election of 1989, first under the flag of the Jammu and Kashmir Liberation Front (JKLF) and then under the Hezbul Mujahideen (who subscribed to the JI school of thought). The ISI went on to support smaller emerging groups and even helped various Pakistani-based groups, such as Lashkar-e-Taiba (LeT) and Harkatul Ansar (later Harkatul Mujahideen), to operate in Kashmir.

The ISI-led military establishment pursued a path that turned out to be fraught with danger. Public opinion on the consequences has been divided, but in recent months this division has narrowed because of the sharp deterioration in the security situation. A consensus has emerged within Pakistan that the establishment's attempt to extend its influence deep into Afghanistan backfired.

General Ashfaq Pervez Kayani, who became the chief of army staff after General Musharraf gave up the post in late November 2008, insists the issue of strategic depth in Afghanistan has been universally misunderstood. During a long discussion on FATA militancy at his Rawalpindi residence on January 16, 2009, General Kayani claimed that the goal was a "peaceful, stable and friendly Afghanistan—nothing less, nothing more. We cannot wish for Afghanistan what we don't for Pakistan." Kayani said this in an attempt to reject allegations, largely coming from Washington, London, and Kabul, that Pakistan had always dreamed of colonizing Afghanistan. "That is not possible, nor are we oblivious to Afghan history, which tells us that this nation has never accepted foreign rule," said Kayani, recalling the bloody nose the Russians got in Afghanistan and the resistance the U.S.-NATO-led coalition is currently facing there.

Back in the 1980s, Osama bin Laden had also found sanctuary on the fringes of Miranshah in North Waziristan, the tribal agency that borders the eastern Afghan province of Khost. When the Soviets pulled out of Afghanistan in February 1989, the Americans turned their back on the region. The tribal lands fell off their radar, but religious groups, business cartels, and the drugs mafia continued their business as usual. Little government attention was focused on the legacy of jihad, and this indifference has come to haunt Pakistan as an Al Qaeda–inspired insurgency sweeps through the rugged tribal territories and areas adjacent to them.

# 2

# A Cauldron of Militancy

The spotlight fell on Pakistan's tribal areas again in late 2001 when, in the aftermath of the deadly 9/11 attacks on the World Trade Center, the United States cobbled together an international coalition and unleashed the questionable "Global War on Terror." Operation Enduring Freedom began on October 7, 2001, and within weeks swept Al Qaeda's hosts, the Taliban, from power, leaving thousands of Al Qaeda fighters, mostly Arabs, Africans, Uzbeks, and Chinese Uighurs, no choice but to retreat into Pakistan's tribal areas.

By December of that year, Pakistan had begun deploying army units in the remote mountainous region of Tirah, which overlooks Afghanistan's Tora Bora mountains, as well as in the Waziristan and Mohmand region. Lieutenant General Ali Jan Orakzai, the corps commander then responsible for the entire FATA region, told us during a briefing at his Peshawar headquarters in June 2003 that most of the border had been secured through the deployment of thousands of troops, even in areas that were hitherto considered virtual no-go pockets due to their remoteness and inhospitable nature. General Orakzai played down reports from American military and intelligence officials and allegations from the Kabul administration that thousands of foreign fighters were holed up in Waziristan—he was essentially in a state of denial.

After their retreat from Afghanistan, the majority of foreigners settled down in the North and South Waziristan and Bajaur regions, where networks operated by Afghan war veterans Jalaluddin Haqqani and Gulbuddin Hekmetyar became instrumental in securing shelter for Bin Laden's surviving fighters. Haqqani and Hekmetyar acted as the umbrella group for the reorganization of Al Qaeda, which co-opted local leaders like Baitullah Mehsud and Abdullah Mehsud, who was captured during Operation Enduring Freedom in Afghanistan, kept at the notorious Guantánamo Bay Camp X-Ray, and released after a couple of years.

Once safely ensconced, Al Qaeda began reorganizing its cadres with the help of the Haqqani clan and Hekmetyar's Hezb-e-Islami, playing on the sympathies the coalition's onslaught had created for the Afghan Taliban and their one-eyed leader Mulla Omar. The presence of Al Qaeda's top brass, including Dr. Ayman al-Zawahiri, Bin Laden's deputy, provided the requisite inspiration to the ultraconservative and religious tribesmen of Waziristan to join the ranks of the Pakistani Taliban, which came to be known locally as Al Qaeda. The Arabs brought with them two gifts for FATA residents: money, which they showered on people they trusted to host them despite warnings by officials, and ideas of Muslim fraternity and Islamic ideology, which appealed to the emotional tribesmen. Al Qaeda also introduced the tribesmen to its version of jihad—including suicide attacks, a technique it had mastered in Iraq.

Since the launch of the antiterror war in October 2001, Al Qaeda has gone from being a discrete organization to an ideology that transcends borders. Already in 2005, Rolf Tophoven, director of the German Institute for Terrorism Research and Security Policy, had concluded that "the US-led onslaught had forced Al Qaeda and its affiliates to form decentralized small units that were spread across the world and threatened the States more than the group did when it attacked the US on Sept 11, 2001."[1]

According to Tophoven's assessment, there are more than thirty thousand Muslim extremists in Germany and about ten thousand active supporters and affiliates of Al Qaeda in the United Kingdom. Most of these people have had a direct or indirect connection with Pakistan or Afghanistan.

Jason Burke, a British journalist and one of the best sources on Al Qaeda, says that "Al Qaeda has metamorphosed from an organization to a movement that can be called 'Al Qaedaism.'" The term denotes Al Qaeda's transformation from a discrete group with specific linkages to affiliates into a movement that more loosely inspires radicals into attacking in its name. This transformation has allowed Al Qaeda to transcend the physical limits imposed by its isolation in the remote border areas of an obscure part of the world to an organization of global infamy. Al Qaeda may no longer provide operational leadership, but its "central command" offers inspirational leadership, encouraging others to attack.

Al Qaeda's ranks soared in the green Wana valley in South Waziristan, in the high, rugged mountains and partially forested ranges in Shawal that separate South from North Waziristan, and in small towns like Miranshah and Mirali. Pakistan's military and civilian authorities did not focus on these dangerous developments: their repeated attempts to prevent influential elders from sheltering militants and their demand that they turn over wanted people—both local and foreign—simply fell on deaf ears. Al Qaeda rewarded this defiance with money and motivation. Nor did the authorities make a serious effort to dislodge Al Qaeda and its local affiliates from the region. Old ties with the likes of Haqqani and Hekmetyar and an overwhelming empathy for "anti-American mujahideen" worked against efforts to flush out Al Qaeda leaders and those inspired by them.

Sympathetic officials and operatives within the intelligence agencies—the ISI, the Military Intelligence (MI), and the civilian Intelligence Bureau (IB)—as well as those within the armed forces, would look the other way when confronted with the challenge of arresting Al Qaeda and Taliban, or stopping their movement to or from Afghanistan.

During several visits to both North and South Waziristan, I saw foreigners openly walk or drive by in central towns and hamlets like Wana, Azam Warsak, Miranshah, and Mirali. Clad in salwar kameez, the traditional local attire, and usually sporting turbans or traditional caps, these foreigners would frequently visit Internet cafés and local restaurants. The civilian and military authorities—through their intelligence networks—were fully aware of this foreign presence, but they either lacked the will to lay hands on them or did not want to touch them at all. This phenomenon was rooted in history: the ISI's long involvement with militant outfits who patronized scores of Pakistani groups, including those led by Baitullah Mehsud, Hafiz Saeed, and Maulana Masood Azhar.

For a long time, Pakistani officials denied the alleged nexus between the intelligence agencies and the militants. "Al Qaeda might have its bases in the tribal areas of Pakistan but no state organ is supporting it," President Musharraf said in an interview with the private television channel Geo News on October 6, 2007. He claimed terrorist elements were on the run or confined to their hideouts because of the stern action being taken against them.

Once Musharraf resigned in August 2008, his successors, President Asif Ali Zardari and Prime Minister Yousuf Raza Gilani, took a more candid position. Within days of the deadly bombing of the Marriott Hotel, on September 20, 2008, one of their most trusted aides, Rehman Malik, suggested that the investigation into the Marriott bombing would end up pointing to Al Qaeda and Taliban militants based in the Federally Administered Tribal Areas. Earlier, the *News* of July 21, 2008, reported that Malik had tabled a report ahead of Gilani's first visit to the United States that spoke of the presence of more than eight thousand foreign fighters in the tribal areas.

Long before high-ranking Pakistani officials admitted to the new reality, the U.S. intelligence network and NATO-led military and intelligence officials based in Afghanistan had all arrived at a consensus: FATA is "Al Qaeda Central." "The next 9/11 will come from FATA," said General David Petraeus, while he was the commanding general in Iraq. The congressional Commission on the Prevention of Weapons of Mass Destruction Proliferation and Terrorism issued a report titled *World at Risk* on December 2, 2008. It featured a scary pronouncement on Pakistan, calling it "the geographical crossroads for terrorism and weapons of mass destruction."

In its introduction, the commission members noted: "The border provinces of Pakistan today are a safe haven, if not the safe haven, for Al Qaeda." The commission quoted from the February 2008 testimony to the House Intelligence Committee by Mike McConnell, director of National Intelligence, which said: "The FATA serves as a staging area for Al Qaeda's attacks in support of the Taliban in Afghanistan as well as a location for training new terrorist operatives for attacks in Pakistan, the Middle East, Africa, Europe, and the United States." The report also noted that "another senior intelligence official responsible for dealing with terrorism recently affirmed that Al Qaeda has strengthened its ties with Pakistani militants in the past year, replenished its mid-level lieutenants, enjoys in the FATA many of the benefits it enjoyed in Afghanistan before September 11, and remains the most serious terrorist threat to the United States."

U.S. intelligence outfits were incensed that despite the Pakistan army's much-touted 120,000-strong deployment, about four peace deals in South and North Waziristan between April 2004 and February 2008, and countless rounds of talks with tribal elders, Pakistan had been unable to plug the border to Al Qaeda and the Taliban, who had been piling up misery on Afghan and coalition troops inside Afghanistan, making every year bloodier than the previous one. Nor could Pakistani forces regain real control over these troubled lands. This stoked frustration and gave rise to doubts about the sincerity of the ISI and the Pakistan army in hunting down Al Qaeda and Taliban militants.

Many believed the ISI was still playing favorites among the militant groups; while the army was busy going after terror networks inside FATA, U.S. officials suspected the ISI was still maintaining contacts with Haqqani, Hekmetyar, and Mulla Omar. U.S., Afghan, and Indian intelligence openly accused the ISI of direct complicity with the Haqqani network, which carried out a deadly suicide bombing outside the Indian embassy in Kabul in July 2008.

Pakistani officials peddled another conspiracy theory: Baitullah Mehsud, the violent leader of the TTP, they said, is a U.S. proxy, backed and funded by the United States and other interested countries to keep the Pakistan army busy in FATA. They also accused India of funding "miscreants" based in FATA and Balochistan, a province that shares a 1,360-kilometer border with Afghanistan, for terrorist activities.

Rehman Malik, who was then internal security adviser to the prime minister, touched on the issue again on January 21, 2009, when he spoke of the role of external factors in FATA. "Foreign hands are patronizing terrorists in Swat and the Federally Administered Tribal Areas but we are determined to flush out terrorists from Swat and FATA," Malik told the media after addressing a seminar in Islamabad. Pakistan's Military Intelligence and civilian Intelligence Bureau officials often allude to the "Invisible Indian hand" in Balochistan's unrest, which cost 433 lives in 2008, accompanied by damages to gas power infrastructure worth several billion rupees.

Joe Biden, Barak Obama's vice president, warned in his address to the Democratic Party Convention in Denver on August 28, 2008, "The resurgence of fundamentalism in Afghanistan and Pakistan [is] the real central front against terrorism. The fact is Al Qaeda and the Taliban—the people who actually attacked us on 9/11—have regrouped in those mountains between Afghanistan and Pakistan and are plotting new attacks."

## Musharraf's Ban

As Pakistan and the United States exchanged mutual vows of cooperation in the antiterror war, senior American civilian and military officials—through media leaks and in private meetings—kept conveying their reservations, casting doubts over Pakistan's sincerity in taking on insurgents. At first these doubts were amply justified.

Under intense pressure from the United States and India, Musharraf banned most sectarian organizations, including the Jaish-e-Mohammad (JeM), Sipahe Sahaba Pakistan (SSP), Lashkar-e-Jhangvi (LeJ), Sipahe Mohammad (SM), Lashkar-e-Taiba (LeT), and Harkatul Mujahideen (HM) in a nationally televised speech on January 12, 2002. Soon after that, their leadership either went underground or was apprehended. More than two thousand zealots associated with these outfits were arrested, only to be released a few months later. Most of their workers melted into the population for the time being. Gradually they sought sanctuary in FATA, where they created new alliances under new names with various pro–Al Qaeda Taliban outfits.

Musharraf's move was precipitated by the attack on the Indian parliament in New Delhi on December 13, 2001, but at best, it was more tactical than strategic. Realities on the ground hardly changed: the top tier of leadership renamed their outfits and either went underground or moved their training facilities to the Waziristan, Bajaur, and Mohmand agencies. The tribal areas soon began buzzing with religious zealots from various parts of Pakistan, providing them a common base for new anti-American alliances. The state of Pakistan gradually lost all authority over these militant groups in most of FATA territory. If the ban's objective was to eliminate radical militant groups, it fell far short of that. Instead, it nudged disparate groups closer to one another for a larger objective: the jihad against the Americans in Afghanistan.

Muhammad Amir Rana, a Pakistani terrorism and militancy expert, says that the January 2002 ban forced the targeted militant organizations to restructure for the sake of survival. The logic behind the restructuring was that jihadi groups would no longer use the words *jihad, lashkar, jaish* or *mujahideen* (all connoting war), so as to appear more political than militant.[2] Rana and other analysts agree that the continuous hunt by the Americans, together with the ban by the Pakistani government, prompted them to join Al Qaeda's underground groups and start operations on Pakistani soil. This instilled fear into the government machinery as well as people at large.

In the new structure, movers and shakers of the Muttahida Jihad Council (established in 1991 and used as an umbrella organization for the anti-India jihad in Kashmir) co-opted five Pakistan-based organizations: Lashkar-e-Taiba, Jaish-e-Mohammad, Brigade 313, Al-Badr Mujahideen, and Jamaatul Furqan. Their leaders agreed that no organization would issue any press statements or disclose their activities and operations. These five outfits—all headquartered in Pakistan's most populous province of Punjab—drew inspiration from Gulbuddin Hekmetyar, Jalaluddin Haqqani, Mulla Omar, and Maulvi Nabi Mohammedi.[3]

Markaz-al-Daawatul Ershad, essentially Lashkar-e-Taiba's parent organization, which is ideologically close to the pro-Saudi Arab-Afghan war veteran Professor Abdurrab Rasool Sayyaf, was an exception. It realized the gravity of the situation just after the shift in Pakistan's projihad policy in January 2002, renamed itself Jamatud Dawa, dissolved LeT's Pakistan chapter, and shifted its offices to Pakistan-administered Kashmir.

Jaish-e-Mohammad converted into Tehreek-e-Khudamul Islam (Movement of the Servants of Islam), Harkatul Mujahideen into Jamiatul Ansar (Party of Hosts), and Sipahe Sahaba became Millat-e-Islamia (Islamic Fraternity). From December 2001 to August 2002, these organizations remained silent, but in time they resumed their activities. They also worked through certain affiliated charity organizations; Jaish-e-Mohammad, for instance, carries out its charity work through Al-Rehmat Trust, which represents the nonmilitant face of the JeM and also raises funds for the organization. Al-Ershad Trust performs similar functions for the Harkatul Jihad-e-Islami and Al-Asar Trust works more or less the same way for the Harkatul Mujahideen in Pakistan.

## The Punjabi Taliban

The ideological nexus between groups based in and outside FATA is underscored by the presence of what was rapidly becoming a new Punjabi Taliban—activists of the Punjab-based organizations mentioned above—scattered all over FATA, attached either to Baitullah Mehsud (South Waziristan), Mulla Nazir (South Waziristan), Mulla Faqir (Bajaur), or Tehreek-e-Nifaze Shariate Mohammadi, which operates in Swat.

A number of these organizations had their roots in the anti-Soviet jihad and had moved to Kashmir after the Russian pullout from Afghanistan. But their contacts with the mujahideen-turned-Taliban remained, with Jaish-e-Mohammad, Lashkar-e-Taiba, and Harktul Mujahideen running several training camps in Afghanistan in the 1990s. They helped out the Taliban in their fight against the Afghan Northern Alliance as they trained their men for the jihad in Kashmir.

According to Muhammad Amir Rana and Mubasher Bukhari's *A to Z of Jihadi Organizations in Pakistan* and Amir Mir's *The True Face of Jehadis*, among the more than 450 terrorists captured by Pakistan until late 2003, more than 200 were Yemenis and Saudis. At that time, as many as two-thirds of the prisoners at Guantánamo Bay were from Pakistan, all of them captured inside Afghanistan. About fourteen Harkatul Mujahideen, seven Jaish-e-Mohammad, and eleven Harkatul jihad militants of Pakistani origin were among the Guantánamo Bay inmates.[4] This underscored the presence of hard-core Punjabi jihadis within the militant ranks—both Taliban and Al Qaeda. Punjabi militants also filled and supplemented the ranks of Kashmiri militants, who have been battling the Indian government since 1989 for what they call "independence from India."

When a dispute arose in a village in the Mohmand agency in August 2007 over control of the shrine of the Pashtoon freedom fighter Haji Sahib Turangzai and the mosque adjacent to it, it came to light that some 300 masked Urdu-speaking Taliban members were among the 3,500 militants who had occupied the site. Most of these were ethnic Punjabis and members of the SSP, Lashkar-e-Jhangvi, and Harkatul Mujahideen. "No one recognizes the Punjabi/Urdu speakers guarding the shrine. I talked to an Urdu-speaking Talib who belonged to Punjab and could not speak Pushto," a local who asked not to be named told the *Daily Times*.[5]

"Some Taliban have a good command over English, Urdu, Arabic and Pashto and are issuing statements in several languages to the national and international media," the paper quoted the source as saying.

Commander Maulvi Iqbal and several of his fighters who fell during skirmishes with U.S.-led coalition forces in Afghanistan's Paktika province, which borders South Waziristan, in March 2008, were later identified as close Punjabi associates of Mulla Nazir, the Taliban chieftain in Wana. A dozen or so bodies of his fallen men were transported from Paktika and buried in Wana.[6]

Most of the Punjabi Taliban are associated with groups like Harkatul Mujahideen, Jaish-e-Mohammad, Lashkar-e-Jhangvi, Sipahe Sahaba Pakistan, and Al-Badr. One of their leaders is Owais Qadri, who comes from Jhang, a big town in central Punjab, riven with Shia-Sunni acrimony. Sipahe Sahaba Pakistan's Qari Hussain Mehsud is blamed for stirring anti-Shia sentiment in the Kurram agency and is accused of killing a former political agent of the Khyber agency along with thirteen other members of his family and guests—in a telling demonstration of the weakness of the government's writ in the region, he has not been apprehended. Hussain, who was born in South Waziristan to a religious family, studied and grew up in the central Pakistani towns of Faisalabad and Jhang before returning to Waziristan, where he hooked up with Abdullah Mehsud, an ex–Guantánamo Bay detainee, and became one of the Taliban's most important leaders.[7]

According to sources in Kabul, most trainers of recruits from the Middle East, Africa, and Central Asia are predominantly Pakistani Punjabis.[8] An elderly Punjabi called Chacha Akhtar used to be in charge of the Pakistani Taliban contingent at the Rishkore camp south of Kabul. Wanted on criminal charges in Pakistan, Akhtar had shifted his family to this camp in early 2001.

Scores of activists and fighters from these Pakistani jihadi organizations were based in Afghanistan when the antiterror war began on October 7, 2001. The first wave of aerial strikes inflicted heavy losses on militant outfits, most of whom had settled down in the southwest district of Kabul. Pakistani militant outfits lost important commanders and hundreds of warriors to the U.S. bombings. Harkatul Jihad-e-Islami lost as many as 340, Harkatul Mujahideen lost 79, Jaish-e-Mohammad 36, and Lashkar-e-Jhangvi 27 militants in the coalition attacks.

# 3

# The Kaloosha Operation

"Tahir Jan is dead."

In the early hours of March 16, 2004, this news reached the village of Kaloosha, some ten kilometers west of Wana, in South Waziristan. The men of the Zillikhel tribe were outraged. They poured out of their homes and by the afternoon they had surrounded the few hundred South Waziristan Scouts, members of Pakistan's Frontier Corps, who were laying siege to the house of Noorul Islam—a wanted Al Qaeda sympathizer. The Scouts believed that Tahir Yuldashev, or Tahir Jan, as he was known locally, the charismatic leader of the Islamic Movement of Uzbekistan (IMU), was hiding there along with at least twenty-five of his followers.

This area was under the control of five Islamist militants—Nek Mohammad, Noorul Islam, Mohammad Sharif, Maulvi Abbas, and Maulvi Abdul Aziz. The Scouts suspected that these men were allowing foreign terrorists from the Afghan Taliban, as well as Arab, Chechen, and Uzbek militants, to shelter in the region. The Uzbeks had opened their first training camp near Mazar-e-Sharif in northern Afghanistan in the late 1990s. Following their escape from Operation Anaconda in March 2002, most were now making their last stand in the Pakistani tribal lands. Welcomed wholeheartedly and greeted with open arms in December 2001, they faced few problems in finding support and shelter among the Ahmadzai Wazir tribesmen of Wana. Yuldashev became a star speaker at local mosques. Now, the IMU leader and his army responded to the call for surrender by unleashing a massive barrage of gunfire.

One month later, locals in Wana and the nearby village of Sheen Warsak told me that rumors of Yuldashev's death provoked a strong local reaction. Hundreds of armed tribesmen had surrounded the Scouts: Tahir Jan was a well-known figure in the region, held in high esteem for his chivalry and love for Islam. Though wounded, he managed to escape in the ensuing frenzy.

What followed was bloody and messy. Cross fire brought down at least eighty Scouts and other soldiers; the army claims it lost forty-six people but others put the numbers much higher. Scores of vehicles belonging to the Scouts and to the army were rocketed and torched by the angry tribesmen. Because of the constant state of war, rusting hulks of many vehicles still lie on the road between Azam Warsak and Kaloosha, and the walls of the neighboring apple orchards are riddled with bullet marks.

When the army regrouped and moved back in full force, in what came to be known as the Kaloosha operation, it bulldozed about eighty houses, overrunning decades-old irrigation channels; leveled wells and tube wells; arrested more than two hundred locals; and according to one of them, killed scores of people as well. Dozens of Scouts who had been hiding in mosques and houses were rescued by soldiers from Wana disguised in civilian clothes. Colonel Khattak, the Scouts' commander, could come out of a shelter alive only after a few tribal maliks (leaders) and reporters who had relatives in the area managed to escort him to safety.

This series of dramatic events left a trail of grievances. During the extended operation, the locals alleged, the army and the Scouts plundered not only the demolished houses but also those hastily evacuated by their owners. "Several families have lost jewelry, antique utensils and whatnot," said Abdullah Khan Wazir, a resident of Kaloosha. He questioned claims by Major General Shaukat Sultan, head of the Pakistani army's public relations department, the Inter-Services Public Relations (ISPR), that several foreigners had been arrested during the operation. "[Since] they did not spare even local young students," Abdullah Wazir argued, "if they had killed or captured a foreigner, why didn't they parade him?" A teacher from a local private school described the fate of one of his students—a boy of ten. "They shot him in the head, breaking the skull in two while looking for Al Qaeda people; they even humiliated our women," he said, his voice shaking. Unleashing a new cat-and-mouse game, the authorities and the military began forcefully asking for the eviction of foreign militants. The locals—caught between personal gains and denial of the presence of foreigners—largely remained intransigent. Scores of meetings between officials and tribesmen and intratribal consultations—jirga—yielded little result.

"Those were really terrible days," recalled Noor Mohammad, the elder brother of my friend Allah Noor (Noor is a common name in this area—it means enlightenment or spirituality). It was April and we were having dinner in the courtyard of their fortresslike house, and he described how foreigners, mostly Arabs and Uzbeks, were frantically moving from one shelter to another to escape arrest. As he spoke, we heard several thuds, constant reminders of artillery fire coming from inside the military camp near the airfield. Allah Noor explained that this had become routine ever since March 2004. He recalled a chilling encounter during the operation when a tall stranger, clearly an Arab, knocked at their door in the middle of the night. "It must have been about two o'clock when we heard the knock," he said. Alarmed, his brothers and he picked up their guns, drew near the door, and asked who it was.

"A Muslim brother, a friend of your brother Noor Ahmed," the stranger replied in broken Pashto. "I need to spend the night here."

The Noor family, following a brief consultation, let the stranger in and offered him some food and a bed, without asking any questions. Everybody went to sleep and when they got up, the stranger was gone.

"We didn't ask him what he was up to because it is not in our tradition," Noor Mohammad said.

Two days later, the stranger returned in the middle of the night, again looking for shelter.

He got shelter. I was not told whether he paid or not.

The Kaloosha operation, undertaken jointly by the Scouts and the army to flush out foreign militants from a fifty-square-kilometer area near Wana, sowed the seeds of dissent among many locals, created a feeling of hatred for the army, and laid the groundwork for a new concentration of militants in Waziristan under the leadership of the Taliban and Al Qaeda. Kaloosha marked a turning point in the security establishment's approach to the militants it had once fostered and trained: the losses made many high-ranking officers realize that the problem was far more serious than they had thought, and the bloody standoff between the Uzbeks, their local supporters, and the security forces definitively exposed the presence of foreigners in the area, and their hold on the tribes. After Kaloosha, the authorities began asking the local tribes to hand over foreigners, particularly the Uzbeks, because they had taken the lead in gunning down Pakistani security personnel. Locals viewed the operation as a betrayal because even while the political administration was negotiating with their leaders on the fate of foreigners, the army deployed troops in Angoor Adda, Azam Warsak, Kaloosha, and Shakai, which foreign militants were known to use as transit points to cross into or out of Afghanistan.

"We were stabbed in the back," said an Ahmadzai Wazir tribal elder. "We were promised dialogue and development funds, but all the time plans for military operations against our tribes were well under way."

## Waziristan Sinks into Terror

Soon after the defeat of the Taliban and the retreat of Al Qaeda to Pakistani tribal areas in December 2001, the Waziristan region was flush with money. This newfound affluence was very obvious.[1] The new Afghan government, led by President Hamid Karzai, resumed the payment of stipends to ethnic tribal elders. These stipends, which had for many years been paid by Afghan rulers to select local tribal elders as "goodwill" gestures, effectively prevented them from making trouble in Afghanistan. However, after the April 1978 Saur Revolution by Afghan socialists, Kabul stopped paying them. The resumption of stipends was intended to prevent the Taliban and Al Qaeda from establishing sanctuaries in the tribal areas. But many of the recipients (and this is confirmed by locals) managed to collect money from Kabul as well as from the Taliban and Al Qaeda.

Khan Malik Bakhan, an influential local leader, was known to be one of Al Qaeda's hosts. When I met him at his home in Wana in April 2004, he firmly refuted my suggestion that he might be sheltering foreigners. "I have given my commitment to the government not to allow any foreigners here and will honor it," Bakhan told me, clearly taking offense that I should question his loyalty.

But equally clearly, many sometimes did succumb to the temptation of making money off foreign guests. Close friends who accompanied me into Bakhan's compound in Wana told me afterward that even while the elderly malik bragged about his "uprightness and loyalty to the authorities," a ten-foot-high wall separated us from about a dozen Uzbek and Arab militants who had put their trust in him for their stay in Wana.

One of my friends, Malik Inayat Abdullah, a tribal elder and resident of Wana, was in fact upset that his area was hosting Uzbeks and not the Arabs. "Uzbeks are short of funds but Arabs have plenty of money and they are generous too," he told me. Initially he would not acknowledge the presence of foreign guests at his second home nearby, but later he reluctantly admitted, "We have just one Uzbek as a guest and we are not demanding much [money] of him." He promised to show me the compound but later backed out.

These were times when all the big families in and around Wana were hosting at least one foreigner, some of whom had even brought their families along.

A follow-up trip to Wana and its outskirts in June 2004 confirmed that despite government claims of "damage control," the region was gradually turning into a battlefield between the security forces and the militants. Al Qaeda had injected new spirit into its cadres, who became increasingly determined to go down fighting.

A Waziri friend recalled that on June 9, a Pakistan army captain posted at the Torwaam check post in the Shakai hills, some forty-five kilometers north of Wana, grew suspicious when he spotted a bearded man carrying a shovel walk up to the post. When the captain demanded to know what he was doing, the man replied he was a farmer looking for rotting wood and bush (used locally as fuel for cooking stoves). The captain told his men to stay alert and spread out around the post. A few hours later, a dozen people clad in Scouts' and army commando fatigues conducted a swift surprise attack on the post, killing five and injuring another six.

The man with the shovel was actually an Al Qaeda fighter disguised as a farmer on a reconnaissance mission. The Torwaam check post was not the only one attacked; several hours later, in the early hours of June 10, the militants struck at the Narai Ubba militia post some ten kilometers north of Wana, killing nine army personnel.[2]

The incident triggered a massive response from the Pakistani army and the militia, which embarked on retaliatory action that left over seventy militants dead, and destroyed at least three hideouts in different parts of the mountainous valleys.

"We saw the bodies of three foreigners brought to the Frontier Constabulary camp in Wana," said a Waziri friend who gave up a steady job with the Tochi militia, a local police force, because of his ideological differences over the army's hunt for militants. "They were wearing commando and Scouts' uniforms. One local, also among the dead, was wearing the same uniform," he said.

This was a new tactic that the militants adopted from early June onward—to approach the security posts dressed in militia uniform or military fatigues; another was to lob rockets from a distance at the forces. This impelled the Pakistan army and the paramilitary forces to move into the Shakai area in large numbers, pounding suspected hideouts with helicopter gunships and fighter aircraft.

On June 10, 2004, the army captured the village of Mandatta, fifty-five kilometers from Wana, in a blitzkrieg operation. To their surprise, they discovered a massive cave under the tree-covered mountains. It was a big living complex inhabited by Arabs, Europeans, Uzbeks, and Chechens "speaking all languages . . . from different countries," a local, Abdullah Wazir, a former member of Al Qaeda, told me while sipping tea in a mud fort in Kaloosha. He had trained with them for about a week and said some Indian and British Muslims were among the trainees. His commander, an Arab militant, had sent him home to his dismay when he came down with a severe intestinal disorder.

The cave complex, high in the mountains, exemplified the engineering skills of Al Qaeda operatives. They had used empty rocket shells as ventilation pipes, piercing the thick rock of the cave to allow fresh air in. The army recovered small mobile welding machines, apparently used for joining the rocket hulls together into long ventilation pipes. The stocky Waziri added that to treat their wounded, they used an ointment that instantly numbed the affected body part to help the person reach the sanctuary in time for treatment. An Al Qaeda fighter who was wounded in the Mandatta military operation told him that the area served as a training camp for Al Qaeda fighters.

Abdullah recalled that his injured friend was admitted to the Wana hospital only after he had introduced him as a Waziri tribesman. "The paramilitary doctors on duty there were not sure whether to attend to my friend. They asked how and where he had received the bullet wounds. I told them my friend was caught in the cross fire between the military and the militants during the Mandatta operation. Once they heard this, the doctors immediately treated his wounds," Adbullah Wazir told me during an extended chat over dinner. During the course of the discussion, Abdullah had promised to take me to his home in the Sheen Warsak hamlet some day. Though I persisted for several days, he dithered.

"You have a guest at home, I presume," I eventually said pointblank.

Surprised by the direct question, Abdullah denied it.

"But your reluctance to take me home indicates something fishy," I said, smiling to take the sting away from my words.

Abdullah was clearly uncomfortable. "There is no one at my place," he assured me. "Your suspicion is misplaced." Sensing his discomfort, I changed the subject as we ate our raisin rice and yogurt, but my conviction that several Ahmadzai Waziris were hosting "nice paying guests" at that time remained unshaken. Not surprisingly, another friend who had made a similar promise also backed out at the last minute, citing "family reasons."

During those months of April and May, Wana residents treated the government claim to have killed dozens of foreigners with derision. "In Saudi Arabia, the government killed one terrorist and paraded his body before the media, but here all we have seen are just a few dead bodies," an influential local malik, Abdul Jalil, said scornfully. "Where are those arrested foreigners that the government is chest-thumping about?"

## Turning South Waziristan into Kashmir

"Pakistan created the Kashmir insurgency for India; we will turn South Waziristan into Kashmir for Pakistan," said a local Al Qaeda militant. He was staying in Ghwakha, a small village on the periphery of Wana. "We will avenge Nek Mohammad's brutal murder," said another. They had all congregated to condole the death of Nek Mohammad, the leader of the local militants who had been sheltering Al Qaeda and Taliban insurgents in the area between Wana and Azam Warzak. Nek Mohammad had been killed on June 9, 2004, in one of the very first drone attacks. It was a somber occasion. The moment the condolence prayers for Nek Mohammad's departed soul were over, his uncle said firmly, "Thank you, gentlemen, you may leave now." We found out later that the gathering was meant to nominate Haji Mohammad Omar to succeed Nek Mohammad, and they did not want strangers around. As we drove out of the isolated walled compounds and filmed the demolished houses of many alleged Al Qaeda supporters we came across several gun-toting Pakistani Taliban. They warned us threateningly to shut down the camera and told us that it was still a no-go area for nonlocals. This was the very place where the Uzbek leader Tahir Yuldashev had been cornered in mid-March.

Under existing laws, the political agent, who exercises extraordinary authority under Pakistan's draconian Frontier Crimes Regulation, can order the demolition or confiscation of a person's property or banish that person from the area if found guilty of a crime (see Chapter 5 for a discussion of the administrative structures governing FATA). The authorities invoked that law after a series of meetings with elders of the Ahmadzai Wazir tribes, to punish Noorul Islam, Mohammad Sharif, Maulvi Abdul Aziz, and Maulvi Abbas for sheltering Yuldashev and killing scores of paramilitary soldiers. In Azam Warsak and on the way to Bagar, where the army had recently conducted operations against terrorists, antiarmy sentiment was quite strong, and again we were asked to leave as soon as possible.

In various encounters with locals and purported Al Qaeda activists, almost everyone denied having any links whatsoever with the radicals. Surprisingly, most were open in their defense of Al Qaeda and the Taliban. "If the rulers bring upon their own Muslim people the misery that the Israelis and Americans have imposed on innocent Palestinians and Iraqis, no God-fearing Muslim would hesitate in picking up the gun," Abdullah Wazir told me over dinner. Another man, who introduced himself as Commander Zarar Khan, did not mince his words: "Al Qaeda and Taliban are one—their mission is common and that is to put down the Americans and their allies, be it Musharraf or anybody else." Khan claimed he had been part of the Shakai operation against the army in early June.

Ameer Rehman, an educated lower-middle-class political activist and member of the Pashtoon nationalist Awami National Party (ANP), had this to say: "I have never seen foreigners here, some may be there. But how can you connect them with every act of violence without any proof?" He blamed the wave of militant Islamization of the region on what he called the Mulla, Military and Malik Alliance. This clique, an alliance of the clergy, the army, and landowners, is determined to maintain the status quo, the century-old administration system for the tribal areas that was devised by the British. And Rehman believes it strongly endorses the support given to the Afghan mujahideen and subsequently to the Taliban.

Effectively, almost everybody in Waziristan lived in a state of denial until it dawned on them, a couple of years after the Kaloosha operation, that the short-term gains from hosting "foreign guests" had brought upon them prolonged misery. Their hospitality, tolerance, and protection had permitted Al Qaeda to organize itself and consolidate its hold. Because of this, the entire region fell under the unprecedented electronic surveillance of American satellites and a network of FBI informers.

The economic blockade that the authorities imposed in Wana on May 2, 2004, to punish its residents for helping militants was crippling but of little consequence. Only nonlocals—people from surrounding areas—could bring in or take out agricultural produce and daily commodities. This meant that most vegetables and fruit were rotting as the Wana bazaar, comprising at least 5,600 shops and kiosks, remained shuttered through to the turbulent summer of 2005. Ripe and rotting apples and apricots hung from the trees in orchards. Farmers did not bother to pluck them because they knew there were no buyers.

Many residents had found alternative sources of livelihood. So despite the outcry over the blockade, a good number of locals were undeterred from allowing foreigners to live in their homes and under their protection. The ethic of the tribe held that come what may, Waziris surrender their guests only over their dead bodies. Though of course nobody actually admitted to hosting foreign "guests."

Based on what I saw and heard during my visits to the region, it was not difficult to draw certain conclusions: although the majority of Ahmadzai Wazir and Mehsud tribesmen (as well as others in Bajaur and Mohmand) denied the presence of foreign Al Qaeda cadres, privately they relished the resistance that the Arab, Chechen, Uzbek, and Uighur Muslims and Americans of foreign origin were putting up. Radical Muslims, both local and foreign, were simply oblivious to threats and persuasion.

Until 2006, the year the militants came out in the open, ambushing army convoys, rocketing military and government installations, and abducting as well as executing government civilian and army personnel, most people in the Federally Administered Tribal Areas were convinced that the Pakistani government was a partner in their oppression, which was aimed at forcing them to betray the Al Qaeda and Taliban militants in their region. Standing up to army oppression seemed to be the only option to them. Even if they only bluffed about turning "Waziristan into Kashmir," Al Qaeda fighters appeared ready to lay down their lives for the cause.

Social norms, religious dogmas, and financial benefits had all combined to nudge FATA tribesmen into taking a position against the state's authority. Equally significant was the climate of fear created by the militants, who spared no one they considered close to the government or to the United States. Betrayal was rewarded with physical elimination. Government servants—both civilian and military—were scoffed at and considered American agents, while political opponents were looked upon as infidels. This attitude resulted in thousands of target killings.

### Target Killings: The Al Qaeda Way?

A flying visit in May 2005 to the sprawling Shakai valley, north of Wana, confirmed the conclusions I had drawn during earlier visits to Waziristan. Less than a year earlier, the area had been infested with foreign and local militants, engaging the army and paramilitary troops in fierce battles from their hideouts in the hills and from inside village houses. Now it was open and buzzing with life, a couple of schools had reopened, and several road-construction and water-well projects were under way. The army was running medical camps to save people an arduous journey through rough, mountainous terrain to the Wana hospital.

All this looked impressive if weighed against the fact that until March 2004 the army's presence, even in Wana, South Waziristan's main city, was minimal. By June, the military and the Scouts had extended their reach to strategic landmarks and hilltops.

As it turned out, all was not quite as it seemed. People at large *sounded* happy that school enrollment had gone up, that water supply schemes were materializing, and that roads were being built. The locals were also apparently pleased that the situation was peaceful—the army had incurred more than 250 casualties in fifty-one minor and major operations that had resulted in the killing of 306 militants, including over a hundred alleged foreigners. But many of those dubbed foreign militants were actually local tribesmen.

"We have eliminated the miscreants [the Pakistan army's term for Al Qaeda and Taliban militants] from the area," Major General Niaz Mohammad Khattak said triumphantly while addressing elders drawn from areas around Shakai. "Ask the people; they will tell you how they lived in fear until our arrival here."

Away from gatherings where officials were bragging about their successes, the atmosphere was altogether different. I interviewed several people in two different locations to elicit their views on the situation. "It is very good now; we are very happy," they assured me, echoing what the army officials and political leaders had just told us.

"But why and how was it bad before?" I asked.

"We didn't know it was bad," responded an elderly Waziri tribesman.

"We are told there were Al Qaeda people here," I insisted.

"We don't know who Al Qaeda is; we only know Afghan refugees whom the government had itself allowed into these areas," one of them said defiantly.

"By the way, how would you tell someone from Al Qaeda or the Taliban apart from a local? They all look like us; they are all refugees," said an orange-turbanned elderly Wazir. Another was equally voluble in refuting my suggestion that the militants had held them hostage.

"No, we have been free, and moving around. All we need is peace, medical facilities, water, and roads," said Bazim Khan Wazir.

Weren't there any mujahideen and Taliban here? "No we don't know, we never heard of these people, nor did we see them," came the response from a well-built young man with long hair, a big mustache, and a white cap.

The gruesome murder the next day of the former legislator and tribal chief Malik Faridullah Khan, near Jandola, between South Waziristan and the town of Tank, appeared to be a direct reaction to his chest thumping and to that of General Khattak. During a meeting with elders, both had boasted of their "strength which enabled them to break the militant hold over Shakai." In the presence of visiting journalists, his speech in the national language, Urdu, sounded odd, because he was a Pashtoon from the area, who would have more naturally spoken to his fellow tribesmen in their common tongue. General Khattak acted more intelligently and delivered his speech in his native Pashto language.

"Everything is fine," Khan told me after his speech. "We hope things will improve further," he said, unaware that this would be his last hurrah in the long-drawn-out battle against militants, who do not forgive those who betray them or hurt their interests. Khan had been instrumental in facilitating the army's entry into Shakai. Khan had just crossed through the Jandola check post into South Waziristan when unknown armed assailants rained Kalashnikov fire on him, killing him on the spot. It was several hours before his blood-soaked body was discovered.

A day later, locals stumbled upon two bodies in the Sheenpond mountain range around twenty kilometers north of the town of Mirali in North Waziristan. A note in Urdu was placed beside the bodies of Jalat Khan and Fazal Noor, saying that the two had been killed for spying for the United States and warning other U.S. agents that they could expect the same fate. Jalat Khan was said to be the leader of a criminal gang.

If locals are to be believed, more than three hundred alleged informers have been eliminated in this way since March 2004, when the army and the militia met with unexpectedly strong resistance in Kaloosha. (When I met with General Kayani in 2009, he said that Military Intelligence alone had lost around seventy-five operatives in Waziristan since Baitullah Mehsud had formed the TTP in late 2006.)

Locals believe that these people were killed by Al Qaeda and the Taliban in retaliation for the fast depleting safe havens afforded them in North and South Waziristan. For security reasons, the militants became extremely careful about selecting shelter, but local tribesmen also became increasingly cautious in offering them accommodation, for fear of inviting missiles fired from CIA-operated drones.

These cold-blooded murders help explain the feigned ignorance expressed about Al Qaeda and the Taliban. People fear revenge killings and are not prepared to risk their lives by admitting to the presence of militants in their ranks, let alone acknowledging publicly their harassment and fear.

Journalists who visited Hakimullah Mehsud, a leader of the Pakistani Taliban, in late November 2008 in the mountains of the Orakzai agency brought back several tales of such harassment and high-handedness. "We were put up with various local people for the night. They served us plain bread and tea in the morning, with helplessness writ large on their faces," one based in Peshawar told me. "People in these areas stuff you with food, but in our case the treatment was shabby. This made it quite clear that people out there were living both in fear as well as poverty, and hence the cold shoulder they gave us," the journalist said, requesting that his name not be published.

The government would like the world to believe that all that the people of FATA require are peace and basic amenities: water, roads, and medical facilities. It did not fully appreciate that it was dealing with ultraconservative and secretive tribesmen with an overwhelmingly strong sense of pride and honor. Therefore, the authorities and the army were self-congratulatory when they should have been self-effacing in a culture where even a single word can cause lifelong offense.

Against this backdrop, the authorities resorted to putting their point across through pamphlets dropped from military helicopters in different parts of South Waziristan in June 2006. These pamphlets contained critical questions about the "designs of the foreign militants" hiding in South Waziristan. Titled *Is This the Reward for Hospitality?*, the pamphlets provided details of an incident on October 1, 2005, in which four schoolboys—Shah Hussain, Ahmad, and two brothers, Nizamuddin and Khan Mohammad—from the Shamankhel Mahsud tribe were killed by a toy bomb planted by foreign militants at Bangashwala on the Jandola-Wana road.

The pamphlet, in Urdu and Pashto, pointed out that after the boys' funerals the Shamankhel tribesmen killed one of the suspected militants, an Uzbek, arrested his Tajik accomplice, Khalid, and chased away a third. It said this was proof of the presence of foreign terrorists in South Waziristan. "Is it jihad or a return for your hospitality?" asked the pamphlet, published by "a well-wisher of the Pakistan Army." The pamphlet praised the tribesmen for taking on the foreign terrorists, expressed support for the military operations in the area, and declared that terrorists who target children should be denied sanctuary and forced to leave the area.

But such sporadic nonviolent endeavors to contain the cancer from spreading to other areas proved futile.

The following chapters are an endeavor to explain why and how each tribal agency turned into a hotbed of radicalism, and how Al Qaeda ideology found a foothold in the region. The current turmoil in FATA stems from decades of neglect, political expedience, and the connivance and complacency of successive Pakistani governments. Each in turn failed to foresee the grave consequences that would spill over from the cauldron of religious radicalism that had begun to simmer immediately after the anti-Russian jihad, and that, by 2009, had erupted into a full-fledged and vicious insurgency.

FATA has become an arena for the competing interests of Russia, Iran, India, and China as well as the United States—fueling speculation that all five countries might have their fingers, through their proxies, in the pie that is now unglamorously called Af-Pak, once again tethering together Afghanistan and Pakistan.

Ironically, it was the United States and its Western and Muslim allies that originally sowed the seeds of militant Islam in the region by throwing their weight and resources behind the Afghan resistance cobbled together by General Babar and eventually embraced by General Zia. Pakistan was used then to raise the jihad. And in the aftermath of 9/11, the United States and its allies again fell back on Pakistan, this time to undo the jihad—taking down the very forces they had jointly raised and groomed.

# 4

# The Taliban in North and South Waziristan

FATA is divided into seven agencies and six small pockets of tribal areas known as Frontier Regions (FR). The agencies are North Waziristan, South Waziristan, Khyber, Kurram, Bajaur, Mohmand, and Orakzai. The Frontier Regions are Peshawar, Kohat, Bannu, Lakki, Tank, and Dera Ismail Khan. The FRs are essentially transition areas between FATA and the adjoining settled districts of the North West Frontier Province. They are jointly administered by the NWFP and the tribal agencies.[1]

The Waziristan region was a chronic headache for the British; even after the creation of Pakistan, Waziris continued to support Pakhtoonistan/Pashtunistan (the joining of all Pashtun areas to create a new state) and hence maintained good relations with Afghanistan. Since the 1970s, Waziris have joined the ranks of the Pakistani armed forces in considerable numbers as compared to members of other tribes. The transport business in the region is their monopoly. It is the kidnapping-for-ransom business, however, that they are most notorious for. Waziris are fond of music and dancing, and despite the Taliban's influence they continue to cherish these activities.

As Al Qaeda militants fleeing from Afghanistan sought shelter in North and South Waziristan, the region increasingly became a target of missile strikes undertaken by U.S. and coalition forces based in Afghanistan. The presence of these foreign militants has led to divisions within the Taliban ranks, particularly in South Waziristan. Pakistani military operations in North Waziristan began in 2002 and have led to a full-fledged military confrontation with Waziris.

Many important Al Qaeda leaders, including Abu Zubayda and Khalid Sheikh Mohammad, transited through North Waziristan on their way to the Punjabi cities of Faisalabad and Rawalpindi, where they were captured in 2002 and 2003, respectively. Several militant tribal leaders have become legendary figures. Turning in their comrades to government authorities, as demanded by the army, amounted to treachery, which explains why none of the tribesmen ever handed over any significant Taliban or Al Qaeda operatives to the authorities.

South Waziristan, the largest agency in the tribal areas, is home to around 425,000 tribesmen from the Mehsud and Wazir tribes. The Ahmadzai Wazirs boast dozens of subtribes and clans; the Zillikhel Wazirs, for instance, are divided into three clans: the Yargulkhel, Kakakhel, and Ishmankhel.

The Mehsud and Wazir tribes are proud of their formidable reputation as warriors and are known for their frequent blood feuds. Almost half a century ago the historian Sir Olaf Caroe wrote that the Mehsuds, the majority tribe, would never consider submitting to a foreign power that has entered their land. They are reputed to be good marksmen and the most independent of all the tribes. Mehsuds are as valiant as they are ferocious, and believe in protecting a refugee even at the cost of their lives. The tribe has been notorious for murders, for abductions for ransom, and, of late, for waylaying Pakistan army and government officials. Mehsuds have also produced many senior civil and military officers.

As the Taliban moved into South and North Waziristan, it split along tribal lines. Baitullah Mehsud formed the Tehreek-e-Taliban Pakistan (TTP), with its stronghold in the Mehsud Wazir area, while his former associate Mulla Nazir continued his activities under Tehreek-e-Taliban (TT) in the Ahmadzai Wazir region. Among the reasons for the split were differences over the activities of foreign militants, particularly the Uzbeks who opposed the Pakistan army, attacking it wherever possible. Both Mehsud and Nazir were committed to the jihad against foreign troops in Afghanistan, and the Afghan war veteran Jalaluddin Haqqani served as the patriarch for both factions. Haji Gul Bahadur in North Waziristan also enjoyed Haqqani's patronage. All of them provided shelter and sanctuary not only to Arab and Uzbek militants but also to several Pakistani radical groups who fled to Waziristan after Pervez Musharraf's January 2002 ban on religio-political groups.

## Tehreek-e-Taliban Pakistan (The TTP)

Tehreek-e-Taliban Pakistan, or the Pakistan Taliban Movement, emerged as a powerful new entity in 2007 in the context of a series of military operations—U.S.-led missile strikes on the one hand and an incursion by the Pakistan army into the Mehsud area of South Waziristan on the other. Until then, most of its component groups were loosely organized, with ties to the Afghan Taliban.

The TTP came into being when Abdullah Mehsud, who had fought with the Taliban in Afghanistan, returned to Waziristan from the Guantánamo Bay camp. He briefly led the Taliban in Waziristan before blowing himself up in Pishin, Balochistan, during a siege by Pakistani security forces in 2006. After Abdullah Mehsud's death, Baitullah Mehsud, a leading member of the Afghan Taliban, who was no relation but from the same tribe, organized all the groups operating in the FATA region that professed similar ideologies and successfully knit them into what is now known as the TTP. The surrender of as many as 250 Pakistani troops to the militants during their incursion into South Waziristan in August and September 2007 shocked the country and was widely regarded as the worst humiliation suffered by the Pakistan army on its own national territory since it became an active ally in the U.S.-led antiterror war. Most of the captured soldiers were released in the first week of November in exchange for 25 Taliban prisoners.

Qari Hussain Mehsud, one of Baitullah Mehsud's close associates, a member of the rabidly anti-Shia outfit Sipahe Sahaba Pakistan (SSP) who had moved into Waziristan after Musharraf's January 2002 ban, called some of his friends in the media on Friday, December 14, 2007, to announce the formation of the TTP. The new organization would be guided by a forty-member central shura (assembly), comprising representatives from all seven FATA agencies. Even today TTP leaders from these regions meet regularly, but they avoid large meetings for reasons of security.

The new TTP was in fact a revival of an older organization of the same name founded in 1998 in the Orakzai agency by Mohammad Rahim, a veteran of the Afghan war. The organization banned television, videocassette recorders, and music in Orakzai. Rahim denied he had any contacts with the Afghan Taliban and claimed he was setting up the group "to cleanse the society of crime"—an idea common to many smaller Taliban factions in Pakistani territory.[2]

The new TTP employs modern, more lethal techniques, operates across all seven tribal agencies, and has the allegiance of a very large number of Taliban groups, most of them wedded to anti-Americanism and determined to enforce sharia. Its creation marked a new and more threatening development, arising out of a realization among most local and foreign militants that they needed a central command figure who could transcend tribal differences. In Baitullah Mehsud they found a unifying force. Individual Taliban groups in areas other than Waziristan looked to him for guidance, but such is the secrecy in which they operate that few acknowledged the links openly. Thus when Haji Gul Bahadur, the Taliban supremo in North Waziristan, told the BBC in May 2008 that his group had nothing to do with the TTP of Baitullah Mehsud, most observers felt it was a tactic meant to confuse the authorities, rather than the truth. Inspired by Osama bin Laden's Al Qaeda, most militant groups in FATA share a common ideology and are opposed to the international coalition against terrorism. They have come together under the umbrella of the TTP because they share the same goal—to drive foreign forces out of Afghanistan and enforce sharia wherever possible.[3]

In May 2008 Mehsud gave an interview with Pakistani journalists in which he reaffirmed his resolve to fight on until the eviction of foreign troops from Afghanistan. Other TTP leaders, including Maulvi Faqir of Bajaur, Maulvi Fazlullah of Swat (who is the Taliban chief administrator), Mulla Nazir of South Waziristan, and Mangal Bagh Afridi of the Khyber agency, share more or less the same objectives: foreign troops must leave Afghanistan, Pakistan must end its cooperation with the U.S. and NATO forces based in Afghanistan, and sharia must replace the existing legal system, which these militants condemn as "corrupt and repressive."

Footprints of the TTP can be found throughout the tribal areas; from the Khyber agency to North Waziristan, almost all incidents of abductions, killings of officials, attacks on military convoys, or on government infrastructure bear the hallmarks of the TTP. "Baitullah is the prime suspect for links with foreign instigators. His people have been all around—killing government and nongovernment officials as well as abducting and executing innocent people and also fighting battles inside Afghanistan," a senior intelligence official told me in Peshawar in early February 2009.

Proof of the TTP's involvement in Afghanistan—and of the close association between the Afghan Taliban and the TTP—came in early June 2008, when about eighteen militants belonging to the TTP fell to air strikes by coalition forces on militant positions in Afghanistan's Helmand province. All eighteen were from Makeen village in the Waziristan agency. One of Baitullah Mehsud's senior commanders informed a newspaper that after hectic efforts, four bodies were brought back to Makeen in South Waziristan through unfrequented routes. He said dozens of Mehsud's tribal militants, led by Commander Khan Ghafoor, had gone to Afghanistan to fight against the U.S.-led forces there. Around two dozen militants had been sent to retrieve the remaining bodies.

A journalist belonging to one of the FATA tribes whom TTP activists regularly call upon to disseminate their views says the organization is growing in influence among jobless youth in Waziristan, and money seems to be no problem with them.[4] He said the TTP is using a strict interpretation of Islamic sharia (as espoused by Mulla Omar of the Afghan Taliban) to promote its political agenda. "The TTP successfully converted their defensive war into an offensive and proactive campaign by taking on the Pakistani military and the government through rocket and suicide attacks on army housing colonies, cantonments and installations such as the Pakistan Ordnance Factories near Islamabad in June 2008," he said. "They have a strong political agenda and conviction backed by their own interpretation of religious beliefs that justifies killing for the sake of God and Islam, regardless of whether the target is a Muslim or non-Muslim." Ruthless attacks on Pakistani military and government targets offer ample evidence that while publicly the TTP wants to counter U.S. hegemony, it also wants to keep Pakistani forces on tenterhooks.[5]

That as many as three hundred high-profile Pakistanis, including Pervez Musharraf and several of his ministers and army commanders, were on Baitullah Mehsud's hit list underscores the transborder agenda of the TTP. Intelligence officials believe the leadership of the Pakistan People's Party (PPP), Muttahida Qaumi Movement (MQM), a politico-ethnic party based in Karachi, the Awami National Party, which stands for ethnic Pashtoons' rights, along with several anti-Taliban Shias and senior officials of intelligence and law enforcement agencies could be TTP targets. The TTP's aim is to wipe out rival political outfits in the area. With dozens of commanders in its fold and thousands of common fighters, the TTP has become a major force in the Waziristan, Bajaur, and Mohmand agencies, and its numbers are multiplying in the Khyber, Kurram, and Orakzai agencies.[6]

The TTP is essentially a conglomerate of about two dozen commanders from various FATA areas; its central consultative forum is a large shura comprised of representatives from all seven tribal regions, with the chief commander from respective regions designated as deputy emir. Maulvi Omar, who belongs to the Bajaur agency, acted as the organization's spokesman until his arrest on August 18, 2009. Today, TTP sources claim, the shura has forty-two members, though no independent confirmation is available. Members in each of the seven FATA agencies draw inspiration from the emir, but operate independently.

TTP activists and media managers usually maintain a one-way contact with certain journalists based in Peshawar or in southern districts of the Frontier Regions, such as Dera Ismail Khan, Tank, Karak, Kohat, and Bannu. The militants mostly use cellular phones and switch them off within minutes of their conversation. TTP activists seem to possess hundreds of mobile phones, something that became crucial after the authorities cut off most of the fixed phone network ahead of the October 17, 2009, operation in South Waziristan. They spend substantial sums on vehicles, fuel, and communications equipment, and are well equipped for casualties; injured militants are provided quick and effective treatment in the mountains.

What Pakistan faces today is not a ragtag army comprised of just a few thousand religious zealots and criminal thugs. Beyond a doubt, the TTP is out to destroy the entire Pakistani security establishment. This will be possible only if the security forces face a continuous and sustained challenge all over the border regions, where one-fourth of the Pakistan army is now deployed. One thing is clear: a long, bloody struggle lies ahead.

# 5

# A Question of Justice:
# An Administrative Profile of FATA

I n September 2005 during a visit to Miranshah, the administrative headquarters of North Waziristan, I came across the news of a bomb blast near an electricity distribution facility owned by Pakistan's state-owned electricity and water resource development organization in Mirali. The impact of the blast disabled the transformer, plunging Mirali into darkness. A day later, the villagers received an order from the political agent (PA), the administrative head of the area, to hand over the person responsible for the blast or face a penalty of approximately $65,000 (PKR 5 million).

"No need to panic," said my host, Mehfoozullah. "We will negotiate it downwards with the authorities," he said, explaining that every tribe maintains a so-called "national fund" to meet such contingencies. All members of the tribe—businessmen, farmers, transporters, and shopkeepers—contribute a certain fraction of their income to the national fund to take care of such "crises." Mefoozullah later told me the tribe paid just about a fifth of what the PA had demanded.

In a similar incident a couple of years ago, a day before the North West Frontier Province's governor was to inaugurate a new telephone exchange in Mirali, unknown attackers blew up the main phone line distribution boxes, thereby sabotaging the program. Outraged, the PA called for the elders of the tribe, demanding that the perpetrators be produced, or the tribe would face a fine of about $178,000 (PKR 15 million). After several rounds of negotiations, the PA agreed to bring the penalty down to about $12,000 (PKR 1 million).

Mirali has been a hotbed of militancy since early 2002, when the retreating Taliban and Al Qaeda began to take refuge there. Dozens of U.S. missile attacks and scores of Pakistan army operations have borne out the view that radical Islamists had gathered in this small town. But the situation in FATA today is in part a result of its unique history, administrative structure, and culture.

The Federally Administered Tribal Areas are spread over 27,220 kilometers and run in a narrow belt along the 2,430-kilometer border with Afghanistan, popularly known as the Durand Line, named after Sir Mortimer Durand, who surveyed and established it during 1890–94.[1] Although part of Pakistan, FATA functions as a semiautonomous region, run under special laws designed and implemented by the British in 1901. It served as the buffer between the British Empire and Russian-influenced Afghanistan. The system of governance established by the British in the early twentieth century continues to operate in tandem with jirgas (assemblies of tribal elders) that determine the law and its execution when necessary.

The 1998 national census put FATA's population at 3.2 million (the current estimate is 3.5 million), that is, less than 2.5 percent of Pakistan's total population. Official statistics notwithstanding, the literacy rate is known to be dismally low because of the region's conservative culture and poor educational facilities. The socioeconomic infrastructure is also extremely deficient with inadequate medical care, insufficient access to clean water, and few roads. Less than 10 percent of the land area is cultivable.[2] Most people live off smuggling "custom-free" goods from Afghanistan into Pakistan, car theft rackets, drug trafficking from Afghanistan, and the illegal sale of locally made weapons.

Geographically, FATA runs north to south, forming a wedge between Afghanistan and the settled areas of the NWFP. As many as sixty Pashtoon tribes inhabit FATA lands. The numbers rise above four hundred if all subclans are counted. The largest and most influential tribes are the Afridis, Bangash, Daurs, Mehsuds, Mohmands, Orakzais, Safis, Shinwaris, Tarklanis, Turis, Utman Khels, Ahmadzai Wazirs (South Waziristan), and Utmanzai Wazirs (North Waziristan).

The Durand Line, which divided Pashtoon tribes between British

India and Afghanistan in 1893, has always been viewed with resentment by the Pashtoons. After Pakistan's emergence in 1947, this line became a major source of tension between Pakistan and Afghanistan.[3]

Despite being a legal-geographical part of Pakistan under Article 247 of the Constitution, the FATA region remains in the clutches of an entrenched political administration, which, in association with approximately thirty-five thousand tribal elders called maliks, perpetuates a system that sometimes requires Pakistani nationals to seek permission to visit these areas. The rules for the media and non-Pakistanis are even more stringent.

The alliance of bureaucrats and the maliks opposes any attempt to reform the legal-administrative structure. The existing set of laws, called the Frontier Crimes Regulation (FCR), gives the office of the political agent not only great power, but also funds that are not auditable or are extremely difficult to audit. The maliks, too, enjoy a privileged status within the tribal society that they are loath to relinquish.

## Laws

The Frontier Crimes Regulation is a complex body of laws that comprises six chapters, sixty-four sections, and three schedules, FCR 40 being the most notorious. This addresses the topic of collective responsibility and allows the PA to punish any tribe or subtribe if he deems fit. This means if someone damages government property in Area A, the PA can punish people from Area B on mere suspicion and impose heavy penalties. If a crime takes place in Area C, the tribe living in the area is responsible for redemption, even though rivals might be responsible for the act.[4]

FCR 40 empowers the political administration to jail anyone for three years without assigning a reason. The PA and his subordinates can arrest members of any tribe who are "accused of the breach of peace or for the purpose of maintaining good behaviour to execute a bond" (sections 40, 41), failing which the accused or male members of his tribe can be imprisoned for up to three years (sections 43, 44) without any right of appeal in any civil or criminal court (section 48). The term of imprisonment can be extended if the magistrate (who is the PA) is of the opinion that it should be extended further (section 45).

Frequently this section is invoked when the PAs arrest people who raise their voice against their authority. The PA conducts business with the border tribes on behalf of the central government of Pakistan. However, under the FCR, the PA, usually a civil servant, acts as a prosecutor, investigator, and judge in dealing with crimes. He nominates members of a council of elders, locally known as a jirga, to inquire into a dispute. The findings of the council of elders are not binding and the PA can reject the jirga's recommendations. Nobody can question him nor can his acts be challenged in any civil or criminal court (sections 10, 60).

Sections 20 and 21 allow an entire tribe that is considered hostile or unfriendly to be jailed, their property seized or confiscated or both, and even allows their houses to be demolished (sections 33, 34). Fines can be imposed and recovered from the whole tribe that an accused person belongs to (section 22); if a tribe is held to be guilty of conniving at crimes, the money that its members earn from government schemes or jobs can be forfeited under section 26. These sections are called Territorial Responsibility, implying that every person of a tribe is responsible for any crime that takes place in the territory of the tribe.

Additionally, tribesmen living within eight kilometers of the border of the district cannot undertake any construction without permission; if on military grounds a village or habitation is found dangerous, it has to be removed. An infamous clause directs that no *hujra* can be constructed or used as such without the approval of the PA. The *hujra* is central to Pashtoon culture—it is a social meeting place, usually in front of the house, with an opening to the main street. Residents of the area usually get together in *hujras* to watch TV, listen to the radio, help resolve conflicts, and discuss the issues of the day.

Under clause 40, the PA can ask any member of the tribe to provide security if he determines this would prevent murder or sedition. If a person fails to do so or the PA finds the securities inadequate, the person may be imprisoned for three years. Such a period of impri-

sonment can be extended to a total of six years. The PA also decides if
the imprisonment is to be simple or rigorous. These provisions continue even though they are in violation of the Constitution of Pakistan
(articles 8–28) and the Universal Declaration of Human Rights.

The PA is thus the "pivot of the entire administrative setup of the
tribal areas," says Khalid Aziz, an analyst who held the position in the
early years of his career. "The PA controls, governs and rules the areas
with the help of the FCR. The PA administers justice in accordance
with local and tribal customs. He avoids interfering with domestic
affairs of the tribes who are regulated by an unwritten 'code of honour'
which the tribesmen guard fiercely."

Rule 40 of the FCR empowers the PA or the assistant political agent
to force a person to execute a three-year bond, with or without sure-
ties, for good behavior. The objective of such bonds, which can be revived after three years, is said to be to maintain peace and to prevent
warring parties from violence. Offenders can be arrested any time,
either on suspicion or on the basis of information provided to the
authorities by paid informers, usually from within the community.
Granting bail against personal or third-party bonds and awarding
punishment, including up to three years of jail, without assigning a
reason is within the purview of the PA or his deputy. The informers
are paid handsome amounts from the PA's secret funds, depending
upon the nature and circumstances of the case. The bail bond is confiscated by the state and the bail amount is realized from the culprit in
case the terms of bond are violated.

The jirgas of local elders and maliks can intervene to the extent
that they can plead for the convict to be forgiven. Sometimes the
jirga also invokes the tribal tradition of Nanewati to preempt the
conviction of an individual wanted by the authorities. Nanewati is
the practice where, in the presence of the tribal elders, the wanted
person simply appears before the PA, pleads guilty, and also asks for
forgiveness.

There is no appeal against any decision, order, decree, or sentence
passed by the PA or the assistant political agent. Though the final review
of such orders and sentences rests with an FCR Appellate Tribunal,

few cases make it to the tribunals. Appeals against decisions by the PA or his deputies can take years before coming to a verdict.

The Law and Order Department for FATA was created in 2006. According to the FATA Web site (www.fata.gov.pk) its functions include "[to] establish the writ of the government, ensure security and protection of tribesmen, readdress grievances of the people, frame rules for Khassadars/Levies, ensure a poppy-free FATA, administrate justice through courts, ensure the availability and control of essential commodities, livestock, etc., to the tribesmen, deal with emergencies/ natural calamities . . ."

FATA elects members to the federal legislature through adult franchise. The system of devolution introduced elsewhere in the country in 2001 by means of provincial Local Government Ordinances (LGOs) has not been extended to the tribal areas. A separate LGO for FATA has been drafted and is awaiting promulgation. A system of partial local-level governance does, however, operate through councils in the tribal agencies and the six Frontier Regions (FRs). Elected councillors are involved in various aspects of development planning and decision making.

## Security Apparatus

A number of law enforcement agencies currently operate in the tribal areas. Led by the officers of the Pakistan army, the Frontier Corps (FC) is the principal force responsible for law and order in FATA and is required to man the border between Afghanistan and Pakistan. Every tribal agency has at least one FC comprising a minimum of five wings known either as Scouts or Rifles—for example, the Bajaur Scouts or Mohmand Rifles. The FC chief, usually a major general from the Pakistan army, is called the inspector general. Another law enforcement agency in FATA is the Frontier Constabulary; its officers are from the police and the ranks are filled by tribesmen or personnel from the settled districts of the NWFP. The Frontier Constabulary is required to man the border between FATA and the settled districts of the NWFP— the Frontier Regions.

Along with the military-led Frontier Corps and the police-led

Frontier Constabulary, various militias, usually known as Khassadars, drawn from local tribes, are responsible for the administrative control in the region. In fact, the Khassadars form the first tier of security inside the tribal areas. The institution of Khassadari, introduced by the British imperial government of India in 1921, ensures the good conduct of the tribes and imposes on them the obligation of allowing the safe passage of ordinary travelers and government officials through their tribal lands. The British strengthened this system when they came into the tribal areas in 1893. Now this system operates all over FATA.

The distribution of the Khassadar jobs is the hereditary prerogative of the tribal chief. Members of the Khassadar force draw salaries from the tribal chief, who gets the money from the federal government in proportion to the area his tribe controls. The Khassadars must provide their own weapons.

The Levies Force is another law enforcement agency in FATA. Levies are essentially government jobs with pensions, and the policing of their respective area is their primary responsibility. The government provides salaries and service rifles to the Levies and they can be replaced by selection.

Basically, Khassadars are militiamen drawn from tribes for policing their respective areas and are employed by a local elder called the malik. The Khassadar and Levies forces ensure good conduct of the tribes for safe passage through their areas. Levies, Scouts, and Rifles are essentially government institutions, although they, too, are mostly drawn from local tribal populations; these militias are paid by the government, normally through the political agent.

## Origins of the Security Forces Specific to FATA

The first militia in the Indian subcontinent was the Turi Militia, which was raised out of the Turi tribe of the Kurram agency in 1892 by Captain C. M. Dallas. The Turi Militia eventually became the Kurram Militia in later years. Subsequently, many militias were raised in different areas and the local tribes enrolled as soldiers.[5] The main objective of raising local militias was to remove the army from these regions, where maintaining control was becoming increasingly difficult for the British. The militia and Scouts system, which functioned with the help of local officials and elders, was devised by the British to deal with the continuing resistance to their presence while maintaining law and order and providing employment to local youth. These militias were also established to ensure effective central control over these unruly areas with their rugged, inhospitable terrain. The officers were from the central armed forces, while the sepoys and the noncommissioned ranks were mainly drawn from local tribesmen. Some of the famous militia corps created by the British exist even today. This system formed the basis of the modern-day Frontier Corps, Levies, and Frontier Constabulary.

## Social System

Because FATA is predominantly Pashtoon, the social system is based on the Pashtoon code of conduct, which has a unique character based on long-standing Pashtoon tribal traditions or principles.

### Nikat

One of the main pillars of the tribal system, nikat essentially denotes the resources that the government pays to a tribe. This payment depends on the area that is controlled by that particular tribe. These shares were originally determined by British rulers in the early 1900s and remained unchanged, making the current rates of nikats for certain tribes unrealistic or even absurd. Until 2005 even government development funds were distributed in proportion to benchmarks set nearly a century earlier.

### Moajib

Subsidies and goodwill allowances payable to certain privileged people within tribes are known as *Moajib*. Usually, heads of tribes receive the moajib but the sums involved are negligible as these rates have not been revised for many decades. Moajib are conceived to guarantee the continuous allegiance of the tribe to the state. During the Mughal and Durrani periods these subsidies were paid in lieu of right of way through various passes. The British followed this tradition in every new area brought under their control.

## Maliki/Lungi Allowance

Maliki allowance is hereditary, that is, transferable to the next generation. It can range from $25 to $433 (or PKR 2,000 to PKR 34,600) a year. Maliks are usually nominated by the governor of the North West Frontier Province. Malik Faridullah, a former MP from the Shakai valley in South Waziristan, who was gunned down by unknown militants in June 2005 for alleged collaboration with the government, was the highest paid malik, with an annual government allowance of PKR 34,600. Second to him was General Jamaldar Khan of the Orakzai agency, who until his death had received $425 (PKR 34,000) a year. His son, former minister G. G. Jamal, now receives this money.

This allowance keeps the holders of this title on the right side of the political administration and in the loop regarding important decisions about their communities or their areas.

Next to the maliks are the lungi holders, usually nominated by the governor. They can be called the second-tier tribal leadership, drawing small amounts, sometimes as low as a few cents (PKR 5 ). The maximum payment for a lungi holder would not be more than a couple of thousand rupees, and is handed over by the political agent. The latter terminates the lungi title upon the death of its holder, and can pass this on to any of the deceased's relatives he chooses. Like the maliks, lungi holders are essentially the bridge between their tribe and the government.

## Collective Tribal Responsibility

The principle of collective tribal territorial responsibility is enshrined in the customs and usages prevailing in the tribal areas. Under this system, even if a crime originates elsewhere, the section of the tribe on whose soil the crime is committed is held accountable and answerable to the government. Political agents use (and very often abuse) this system to impose heavy penalties on tribes for "failing to guard government assets and installations in their areas."

*Easement Rights*

Under the Durand Agreement, the same tribes living on either side of the Pakistan-Afghanistan border are allowed free ingress into one another's areas. No immigration restrictions can be imposed on the long and porous border. This gives an added complexity to the problem of policing or securing the border because militants take cover of these easement rights and cross the border using fake permits that show them to be members of the divided tribes.

At least forty thousand Afghans, Pakistanis, and tribesmen cross the border daily from Torkham, some fifty kilometers west of Peshawar. Torkham is located in the Khyber agency, connecting with Afghanistan's Nangarhar province. The other important international border crossing is Chaman in Qilla Abdullah in the northwest of Balochistan, which connects with Kandahar province in Afghanistan. The crossing at Chaman was in the news when Pakistani officials attempted to impose restrictions on the cross-border movement through a new biometrics system. The Afghans rejected it, as did the tribes living across the Durand Line. In fact, combatant groups and individuals have exploited the Easement Rights Regulation to sneak in and out of the tribal areas to plan raids and for training or shelter from the time of the anti–Soviet jihad in the 1980s.

## A Push for Reform

Against the backdrop of widespread resentment, demands by tribesmen to have the FCR replaced or amended are growing. Fifteen years ago, in January 1995, I attended several meetings that the political agent of the Khyber agency, Amjad Ali Khan, held with tribesmen from the agency at his office in Peshawar. The demand that resonated the most was the tribesmen's desire to be rid of the FCR. The PA tried to deflect the demands by playing on the conservatism of those present. "Would you like to see the corrupt Pakistani police desecrate your homes; would you like them to intrude into your private homes the way they do all over Pakistan?"

The meetings were held to counter the influence of Maulana Sufi

Mohammad's Tehreek-e-Nifaze Shariate Mohammadi, which at the time had galvanized tens of thousands of people across the Malakand division of the NWFP. Their most disturbing demand revolved around the desire to replace Pakistani secular law with Islamic sharia. Interestingly, the specific demand for sharia has not featured very high in tribal jirgas of FATA elders. In the vacuum caused by the absence of a legal justice system and the tribals' powerlessness to challenge decisions by the PA or his subordinates, nonstate actors—the likes of Sufi Mohammad, Mangal Bagh Afridi, and Baitullah Mehsud—have stirred public emotion and exploited the yearning for justice for their own objectives.

The main reason for the popularity of successive Islamist movements in the tribal areas stems from the draconian system of the FCR. If the hundreds of conversations I have had with friends and common people in the region are any indicator, the search for a fair justice system and the craving for equal citizenship has come to be synonymous with sharia.

A grand tribal jirga held in Peshawar on June 14, 2007, representing various tribes drawn from all the seven agencies demanded a separate legislature for FATA to enable the people to sketch out policies that are more in sync with their culture and traditions rather than an import from Islamabad.

Other demands made at the conclusion of the jirga were for good governance, education and employment opportunities, the introduction of a system of local governance, the extension of Islamic financial assistance (the Zakat Act), setting up utility stores, the resolution of border disputes through peaceful means, and the inclusion of tribal elders, intellectuals, and parliamentarians in the proposed Pak-Afghan peace jirga that was held for the first time in August 2007. Several such meetings organized by the government and political parties separately voiced more or less similar demands.

Perhaps because of this, Prime Minister Yousuf Gilani, in his maiden address to the nation in March 2008, announced the good news that the FCR would be abolished. While this pleased and surprised many, countless others were shocked because Gilani offered no alternative. Gilani's detractors, including several bureaucrats and maliks, believed that abolishing the FCR overnight might create a vacuum and result in chaos.

As the year 2009 came to a close, residents of FATA were still waiting for the prime minister's promise to become a reality. Since then, all that has happened is that the federal law ministry has attempted to prepare draft proposals that amend rather than repeal the FCR. The amendments, if made, are likely to give tribesmen a right to appeal the decisions of the PA. They may not do away with the collective responsibility clause but might restrict its scope. The government is finding it hard to completely replace the FCR with the normal laws of Pakistan in FATA because of stiff opposition from strong pressure groups like the civil bureaucracy and the maliks. Under the current system, bureaucrats and maliks constitute a privileged class. That is why most of them want to retain much of the FCR and tailor amendments to restrict their scope. Little do they realize that the emergence of the militants has introduced a new element into the century-old power structure and that this explosive new development requires the introduction of new and ingenious ways to reassert the state's authority.

On Pakistan's sixty-second Independence Day, August 14, 2009, President Zardari at last announced long-awaited political reforms in FATA, including freedom of activity for political parties. These promises have yet to be implemented, leaving the field open for religious groups to promote their narrow worldview. At the moment, the military has helped restore the balance of power and reestablished the writ of the state in Pakistan's tribal areas, but a long-term solution clearly lies in inclusive political reforms that could empower the tribesmen and turn them into equal citizens of the Islamic Republic of Pakistan. The army, applying brute power, can hold on to the areas that once belonged to terrorists and militants only for a limited period of time. If we have learned anything in the eight long years of the war on terror, it should be that military means alone will not snuff out the threat of militant extremists, who draw sustenance from armed confrontations.

# 6

## The Al Qaeda Connection: Arabs, Uzbeks, and the Haqqani Network

Mulla Nazir Ahmed split with the loosely knit Taliban movement led by Baitullah Mehsud in early 2007, largely over the role of Uzbek militants hiding in the region. After escaping from the Kaloosha operation of March 2004 and surviving the injuries he sustained during the cross fire with the Pakistan army, Yuldashev hardened his opposition to the government of Pakistan and grew closer to Al Qaeda. He set up a private jail to try to punish people he thought were a problem. Yuldashev's status in Waziristan took a hit when his vigilantes began targeting Pakistan army and government officials. These strikes turned the Uzbeks, in some people's eyes, from revered heroes to villains.

Mulla Nazir turned against the Uzbeks once they began taking army and government officials hostage, torturing them brutally, and even killing them. (The Uzbeks viewed Pakistan and its military as active combatants in the U.S.-led war on terror and therefore considered targeting them legitimate; they had also not forgiven the army for its role in the Kaloosha operation.) Whenever the Uzbeks carried out an antiarmy attack, the military would turn its guns on the suspected areas. This situation caused widespread resentment among the locals, who thought they were being unnecessarily sandwiched between the militants and the military, turning them into targets of reprisal by both parties.

Beyond this, it was widely felt in South Waziristan that the Uzbeks ignored and undermined one of the strongest traditions of the region, which is to show respect to tribal elders. Alien to the land and culture, they relied solely on the power of their guns and wallets. In the complex sociology of the tribal culture, where questions of honor and respect are deeply ingrained and observed, this behavior was unacceptable.

Thousands of Punjabi Taliban began pouring into Wana in the last quarter of 2006 from central and southern Pakistan. Eventually, they all vowed allegiance to Mulla Nazir at the house of a local spiritual leader, Peer Adil, in the Musa Qilla hamlet of South Waziristan. Following the oath of allegiance, all those present vowed to continue their jihad against foreign troops in Afghanistan. "They also undertook not to harm Pakistani interests," recalled a local journalist, who monitored developments from his base in Wana. Mulla Nazir entrusted the Punjabi Taliban with the task of looking after Arab Al Qaeda militants—those "comrades" who were retreating from Afghanistan into Waziristan for shelter. There was no mention of IMU (Uzbek) militants in that meeting, which annoyed Tahir Yuldashev.

The Musa Qilla meeting brought Mulla Nazir closer to the local Pakistan army commanders, which Yuldashev construed as an alliance being mounted against him, in conjunction with those Arabs who were still sympathetic toward Pakistan. This inevitably deepened the existing animosity between Nazir's forces and the Central Asian dissidents. With the new battle lines drawn, the IMU embarked on a lethal offensive, carrying out target killings and ambushing Pakistan army convoys and installations, a move that triggered clashes with Nazir in November 2006.

A senior intelligence official recalled that Nazir did make several attempts to patch things up with Yuldashev, telling him their prime target was the foreign troops in Afghanistan and he should refrain from targeting Pakistani tribal elders, government officials, and military personnel as well as strategic installations.[1] But these attempts did little, and the differences between the two groups grew. Pakistan's military and intelligence agencies leaped to exploit the growing breach between locals and foreign militants, and got Mulla Nazir on board for a crackdown against the Uzbek fighters.

In March 2007, Nazir, who reportedly holds dual Afghan and

Pakistani nationality, put together a tribal lashkar—an army of local tribesmen—and mounted a vicious campaign against the Uzbeks living in the hamlets of Sheen Warsak, Azam Warsak, and Kaloosha, west of Wana, the administrative headquarters of South Waziristan. The Ahmadzai Wazir tribe dominates the western parts of South Waziristan, and as such controls the economically lucrative border trade routes between Afghanistan and Pakistan. Mulla Nazir, an Ahmadzai Wazir himself, found little difficulty in forging alliances with influential local leaders and commanders who, along with the embedded army commandos, became the mainstay for his anti-Uzbek campaign.

The Pakistan army supported Mulla Nazir and his militants by embedding sharpshooters and tacticians in the tribal forces. In early March 2008, Pakistan army officials began to insist the tribesmen had turned the tables on foreign militants; the commander of Pakistani troops in the tribal areas, Major General Gul Muhammad, claimed the tribal army had eliminated up to two hundred foreign militants.[2] He would not admit to army involvement in the operations. In fact, the army provided vital intelligence about the movement of the Uzbeks, cut down their supply routes, deployed heavy artillery, shelled their positions, and embedded well-trained and seasoned army personnel from the local area in Nazir's militant outfit, all of which contributed significantly to Mulla Nazir's success. Military officials played up Mulla Nazir's achievements but conceded later (in private conversations with the author) that logistic support was provided to the tribal chief because "he had asked for it."

"We did provide support to Mulla Nazir, there was no way around it," said Major General Shaukat Sultan, the then head of the Inter-Services Public Relations (ISPR) department.[3] Sultan admitted that army sharpshooters and strategists were part of the lashkar that swept across the tribal areas and forced the Uzbek militants to flee the region. Officials claimed as many as 250 Uzbeks were eliminated during the operation. Under the tribal tradition, locals can always call in the army or paramilitary for support. To preempt suspicion, Mulla Nazir invoked this tradition and told his people that all the elders had asked the army for "logistic support." Local journalists recall that a Pakistan army officer—disguised as Taliban—supervised the entire operation against Uzbek fighters. Even the media management was in the hands of the army.

Although the army officially denied any involvement in Mulla Nazir's campaign against the Uzbeks, local and foreign media kept confronting the military authorities with questions on the issue. Musharraf finally opted to break his silence, and in his typical indiscreet way went public with an admission. "Troops were involved in the offensive," he said.[4] This statement instantly turned the armed forces and their institutions into prime targets of both the Uzbek and hardcore Al Qaeda elements.

Officials dealing with the tribal areas at the general headquarters of the Pakistan army (GHQ) in Rawalpindi, just south of Islamabad, said the operation was part of a new strategy comprising three elements: coercive deployment, political engagement, and socioeconomic development, to "win over the hearts and minds of the people."[5] This new strategy appeared to be a result of the intense pressure that the United States and NATO members had been exerting on Pakistan for a stronger and more sincere effort to contain the spreading lawlessness of its tribal areas, from which Pakistani, Afghan, and foreign militants were now waging an expanding insurgency across the border in Afghanistan.

Mulla Nazir's alliance with the authorities, and the active support of disguised Pakistan army commandos, mostly from the province of Punjab, drove a wedge between him and the brothers Haji Sharif, Noorul Islam, and Haji Omar, who had been staunch supporters of Yuldashev. The brothers sided with Yuldashev. Eventually they had to abandon their ancestral homes in Azam Warsak, Kaloosha, and Sheen Warsak, and they reportedly took refuge inside North Waziristan.

Yuldashev and his thousand or so Uzbek fighters took refuge in the area of South Waziristan then dominated by Baitullah Mehsud and moved to North Waziristan, under the protection of the Haqqani network. Despite the new physical limits put on IMU's domain, the organization grew in influence and morphed into a lethal non-Arab Al

Qaeda entity. Several drone attacks in August and September 2009 triggered new rumors of Yuldashev's death, though none could be confirmed.

It was in fact the Uzbeks' activities that prompted the October 2009 military operation in South Waziristan. Senior military officials, including General Kayani, admitted that the wild and inhospitable region bordering Afghanistan's eastern Paktika province—the mountainous and rugged area populated by the Mehsud clan—had turned into Al Qaeda's den. "It is a do-or-die situation for them [the Uzbeks] so they are scrambling for protection and would do anything for survival," General Kayani told me and a few other analysts days before the army charged the Mehsud areas from three directions. Military officials believe that dismantling the Uzbek terror network is critical to changing the dynamics of Waziristan. They are Al Qaeda's most dedicated ally in Waziristan, they reckon, and among the deadliest enemies of the Pakistani security forces.

## The Arab Question

Foreign journalists have questioned why Nazir's operation was directed at Uzbeks only. "There is no sign the offensive has targeted Arabs associated with Al Qaeda, still thought to shelter in South Waziristan," observed an Associated Press report after Pakistan's army ferried journalists by helicopter to show them how they had regained control of the region. "The government says that foreigners are being hunted by local tribesmen, but reports from Wana suggested that only the Uzbeks were the target of Mulla Nazir's fighters. The real Al Qaeda—the Arabs—found no mention in either official or unofficial reports from Wana."[6] And yet underlying all such condemnations was the fact that the Central Asians were not the only foreigners Nazir wanted to fight. "We will continue our jihad [in Afghanistan] if that is against America, the Russians, British, or India, as long as we have souls in our bodies," one of Nazir's aides told Pakistani reporters in Wana.[7]

Pakistani officials helped foster this alliance between Mulla Nazir and the Arab fighters, hoping the Arabs could be helpful in gathering information on Afghanistan from their comrades, particularly those who retreated into Waziristan after accomplishing missions against the U.S. and NATO forces.

Nazir reportedly received millions of rupees from the authorities as reward for his assault on the Uzbeks—mostly in the form of stipends and funds for development schemes in his area. Two assassination attempts against him therefore came as no surprise. One of the would-be assassins, a youngster from Bajaur armed with an explosive-laden belt, was intercepted just a few yards from Mulla Nazir in June 2007. The boy told his interrogators that the Uzbek militant Saiful Asad had given him the task of "blowing up Mulla Nazir." He is an agent of the infidels, the boy said. That the boy had traveled all the way from the Bajaur agency to carry out the mission underscored another fact—militants of different schools of Islamic thought were spread out over most of the tribal areas.

During 2008, Wana and the surrounding hamlets remained firmly in Mulla Nazir's control, and an unwritten understanding with the authorities enabled the army and government officials to move in and out of the area easily. Local residents say that after the mop-up operations were concluded in some parts of South Waziristan, more Arabs returned to the area and were moving around freely. A journalist with good access to Taliban ranks said that hundreds of Arabs were also hiding in Mirali, a small town a few kilometers away from Miranshah, where they had occupied the houses left behind by Mehsud tribesmen who fled the area during the December 2007–January 2008 military operation. Unlike the Uzbeks, who are now despised by the local tribesmen, the Arabs have good relations with them.[8]

The thirty missile strikes on targets in the Waziristan region in the last four months of 2008 were all directed against Arab Al Qaeda operatives. After almost every attack, the U.S. military authorities or CIA sources announce the names of wanted Arabs they claim were killed in the missile strikes. But not once was a single body paraded to back up these claims. This not only invited the militants' mockery but also raised doubts about the veracity of such claims. It also led to public outcry as the air strikes claimed the lives of countless noncombatants, largely women and children.

"Unfortunately, the leaders live among families and whenever we hit them, many women and children also fall victim," a U.S. intelligence official based in Islamabad told me in December 2008. "We track them [the militants] from point A to B very precisely and therefore are able to take them out the moment they get together with other operatives after carrying out missions in Afghanistan," he said.

A January 16, 2009, report in the *Washington Times* said the Al Qaeda stalwarts who had found refuge in Waziristan areas included Khalid Habib (a deputy to Al Qaeda's third in command Shaikh Said al-Masri), Abu Khabab al-Masri, Abu al-Hassan al-Rimi (a leader of cross-border operations against U.S.-led forces in Afghanistan), Abu Sulaiman al-Jaziri (a senior external operations planner and facilitator for Al Qaeda), Abu Jihad al-Masri (Al Qaeda's senior operational planner and propagandist), and Usama al-Kini (who was accused of planning the Marriott Hotel bombing in September 2008 and was killed on January 1, 2009, by a drone-fired missile strike).

During the Taliban's rule, two categories of Arabs entered Afghanistan: those who, filled with the jihadi zeal, kept pouring in from different parts of the Arab world until the war on the Taliban and Bin Laden began in October 2001, and those who had moved in from Pakistan after their visas had expired and settled in the eastern parts of Afghanistan, mostly Jalalabad. Many had stayed on after the Soviets pulled out of Afghanistan in 1989.[9]

Almost all of them—several thousand—either perished in the American attacks on Kandahar and the vicinity of Jalalabad and the Tora Bora mountains, or landed in jails. Most were among the seven thousand prisoners the Western coalition said it held by the end of December 2001. More than two hundred were caught by Pakistan's border security forces after they gave up their fight in the Tora Bora mountains.

The Arabs today are subdivided into two groups: the Egyptians and the Libyans. Dr. Ayman al-Zawahiri led the Egyptians while Abu Lait el Libi led the Libyans until his death in a drone-fired missile attack in early 2008. Yahya Libbi, who escaped from the Bagram jail outside Kabul in 2005, reportedly now leads this group. U.S. and Afghan intelligence sources corroborate the increased presence of Arabs, mostly from Iraq, in Waziristan. Tribal sources, who feed satellite networks like CNN and Al Jazeera from the region, also privately confirm that Arabs are using the Waziristan region as their sanctuary.

## A Peace Deal in North Waziristan

On September 5, 2006, Musharraf's government brokered a peace deal in North Waziristan, which it claimed was with local tribesmen and elders, to stop the cross-border movement of Pakistani and Afghan militants. Under the three-page agreement signed by seven militants and three hundred tribal locals, all signatories pledged to halt attacks on government installations and security forces, stop cross-border movement of their fighters for combat missions against American and NATO troops inside Afghanistan, and not shelter foreign Al Qaeda-linked fighters. They also undertook to offer up any foreign fighters who renounced violence before the authorities for registration. On its part, the government pledged not to undertake any ground or air operation against the militants and to resolve issues through local customs and traditions. Though there was no direct mention of local or Afghan Taliban, the agreement came into being with the full support of the Afghan war veteran Jalaluddin Haqqani, his son, Sirajuddin, and Haji Gul Bahadur, who holds considerable sway over militant forces in North Waziristan and coordinates closely with the Haqqani clan on operations inside Afghanistan. All these forces were represented by people of their choice when the peace deal was brokered, but none were mentioned by name.

Local Taliban—the TTP as well as others—suspended the deal in May 2007, alleging violations by the authorities. But the deal came to life again on February 17, 2008, weeks after the new governor, Owais Ahmed Ghani, took charge, and both sides agreed to respect each other's existence. "After eight and a half years, the governor, that is me, was able to spend the night in Miranshah, meet with the people, talk to the tribal elders . . . that is a huge advantage [of negotiating with the locals]," Ghani told me at the Governor's House in Peshawar in late September 2008. Ghani shed some light on intriguing developments in North Waziristan: despite relentless U.S. pressure to hunt down Al Qaeda and their supporters, the Pakistani intelligence apparatus apparently maintained contacts with members of the Afghan Taliban (the Haqqani clan) and the Pakistani militants led by Haji Gul Bahadur in North Waziristan. The latter, after a long silence, resurfaced in the media in early July 2008 after a meeting with Mulla Nazir from South Waziristan. This led to the creation of a new alliance called the Shura Ittehad ul Mujahideen, or Taliban Alliance.

The ostensible purpose of the alliance was to isolate Baitullah Mehsud, to unite all the Taliban, including possibly those led by the TTP, and to keep up the anti-U.S. campaign. Bahadur and one of Haqqani's sons met Mehsud once, but Bahadur skipped the next two meetings, triggering speculation that he and his allies might have acted to facilitate the government's goal of isolating Mehsud. This was of course a trade-off; the Taliban would not harm government interests in North Waziristan and in return the authorities would not go after them. "We understand Bahadur and Haqqani plan to raise a parallel organization from Waziristan to Bajaur to contain Baitullah Mehsud's influence," said a senior intelligence official dealing with FATA affairs.[10] This explains why tribal sources close to the militants played down some of the intimidating statements by Bahadur and his allies as "insignificant," or a "fixed match," as a FATA friend dubbed it. Both the Taliban forces and the government keep trading charges to dispel the impression of collaboration. For instance, on August 6, 2008, Bahadur's alliance claimed responsibility for the missile attacks and bomb blasts in South Waziristan the previous day. Rival Taliban suspected of links with Uzbek militants and with Baitullah Mehsud appeared to be the targets. The Taliban Ittehad spokesman, Ahmadullah Ahmadi, vowed the group would retaliate against any attack by the government.[11] One of Bahadur's allies, Abdul Khaliq Haqqani, issued a statement the same day claiming he had prepared a group of suicide bombers to be used against the government.

Tribal sources—officials and journalists—interpreted these statements as fake posturing because, they argued, the Taliban Ittehad had a good rapport with the authorities, based on the understanding that it would refrain from targeting the Pakistan army or government interests. Under the peace deal, it had pledged not to shelter foreigners. Yet the ground reality betrayed this undertaking; the Haqqanis in particular continued to serve as the patrons of all foreign Taliban/Al Qaeda forces in the region. Although the Haqqanis are friends with Mulla Nazir, they reportedly continued to provide shelter to the Central Asian IMU fighters after the latter were forced to leave South Waziristan in March 2007.

## Al-Masri and the Politics of Drone Strikes

In the early hours of July 28, 2008, several missiles launched from low-flying drones killed six people, including Abu Khabab al-Masri, an Egyptian chemist regarded as one of Al Qaeda's top bomb makers. The target was a small madrassa and a mosque run by a local cleric, Maulana Jalilur Rahman, at Zyara Leeta village in the border town of Birmal. The missiles destroyed two buildings and caused damage to a few others in the vicinity of the madrassa. A large number of Wazir tribesmen immediately thronged the village and helped retrieve the bodies of the slain and the injured from the rubble. Some of those who took part in the rescue operation told me that all the bodies were mutilated beyond recognition.

"Nobody could recognize whether they were locals or Arabs as their bodies were split into pieces," said Mohammad Nawab. He said five of the dead were Arabs who had just returned from Afghanistan's Paktika province and were resting at the madrassa. Pakistani security officials refused to confirm or deny this, but said Abu Khabab al-Masri might have been killed in the strike.

The fifty-five-year-old al-Masri carried a $5 million bounty on his head, but there have been reports before of his being killed. Spokesmen for NATO and U.S.-led coalition forces in Afghanistan denied involvement in any cross-border strikes, but could not speak for the CIA, which also operates drones. If the intelligence-fed reports were true, then al-Masri joined the list of about ten Al Qaeda operatives killed in such attacks.

The targeting of al-Masri gave rise to the suspicion that an intelligence agent from among the Arabs living in Wana might have spied on him and reported on him to the U.S. forces.

"Probably that is why Al Qaeda activists and sympathizers in North Waziristan, including Bahadur and Haqqani, felt betrayed and lobbed rockets at possible suspects," one official conjectured. They suspected that U.S. and Afghan informers had infiltrated the ranks of Mulla Nazir and his Arab guests. These suspicions grew as U.S. drones kept raining missiles on suspected hideouts. Between July 28 and late October 2008, MQ-9 Reaper aircraft carried out almost twenty missile strikes in the entire Waziristan region. The CIA operates these medium-to-high altitude, long-endurance unmanned aircraft in Afghanistan. The MQ-9, primarily a hunter-killer, acts as an intelligence, surveillance, and reconnaissance asset, employing sensors to provide real-time data to commanders and intelligence specialists at all levels.

Coinciding with the attack in South Waziristan were reports flying in from intelligence officials in Washington, as well as from within Pakistan, about the "influx of foreigners into Waziristan." In July 2008, only days before Prime Minister Yousuf Raza Gilani was to embark on his crucial maiden visit to the United States, he was informed by the security establishment that as many as eight thousand foreigners could be hiding in FATA, predominantly in Waziristan. Although the government of Pakistan accepts the fact that foreign fighters are present, the unusually large number quoted in an official report set off alarm bells in Islamabad.[12]

Interior adviser Rehman Malik did not want to reveal the source of the staggering figure and told the *News* that the actual number of foreign fighters was probably closer to a thousand. Interestingly, the beefed-up figure began emerging in late 2007, and its main source lay in Washington. American diplomats and U.S. media representatives began dropping hints that foreigners in FATA might be multiplying. This was in sync with the claims of the U.S. defense secretary, Robert Gates, and other officials that following the "squeeze in Iraq," Al Qaeda was now pouring its resources into Afghanistan and Pakistan's border areas. An unidentified source, quoted by a knowledgeable Pakistani journalist, Hamid Mir, in the *News* in July 2008, claimed that "experienced and hardened Al Qaeda fighters were coming from Iraq to Afghanistan via Iran by road."[13]

Until late 2007, most accounts by locals in North and South Waziristan put the number in the hundreds and not the thousands. During visits to both agencies in 2004 and 2005, I saw several Arabs and Chechens moving around in Wana, Miranshah, and Mirali. But continued search and surveillance by the Pakistan army, guided by U.S. and NATO forces based across the border, pushed foreigners into hiding or into keeping a low profile. Eventually they assumed the role of planners and trainers, thus going off the scene.

The biggest attraction for these young militant guests from the Middle East, Central Asia, and Europe was the steady surge in the number of U.S. troops in Afghanistan. Many young Muslims are going to Pakistan and Afghanistan to fight the U.S. troops who, they believe, have come to Afghanistan not to fight terrorism but to occupy more Muslim lands, including Pakistan.

At a meeting of the Shura Ittehad ul Mujahideen in late July 2008, Bahadur accused Prime Minister Yousuf Raza Gilani and the government of killing innocent tribesmen to please the Americans. He condemned the U.S. missile attack on Zyara Leeta village of South Waziristan that killed Masri and called it "a gift of the Pakistani prime minister for the Americans during his visit to the United States." That Bahadur took on the premier underscored a certain realpolitik: the interlocutors of most militant groups are the military or its intelligence outfits and not the civilian government, so Taliban leaders can afford to hurl taunts at civilian leaders, which raises their esteem in the eyes of their followers. They can also capitalize on political blunders and turn botched military operations into a powerful recruitment tool.

## The Siege of the Red Mosque and Its Fallout

The Lal Masjid, or Red Mosque, situated in the heart of Islamabad, and its affiliated madrassa, Jamia Hafsa, built illegally on state land, shot into world headlines when female students of the Hafsa seminary occupied a public library adjacent to the seminary in January 2007 and began demanding the enforcement of sharia law. Fully supported by their male comrades, many of whom were trained militants, these students—wrapped in black head-to-toe veils—consistently challenged the writ of the state by kidnapping alleged sex workers, taking policemen hostage, raiding massage parlors, and pressing shopkeepers to burn CDs and DVDs. Despite warnings from the authorities to vacate the public library and several rounds of talks, the students stood their ground under the guidance of their mentors—Maulana Abdul Aziz and his younger brother, Abdur Rasheed Ghazi. The standoff made headlines and eventually culminated in a military operation on the complex in July 2007 called "Operation Silence," during which Ghazi, his mother, and dozens of others were killed. More than a dozen Pakistan army soldiers and officers also fell to bullets fired from inside the complex. For several weeks, this blatant challenge to state authority played out in the heart of Islamabad, revealing the confidence with which the zealots felt they could enforce their brand of sharia in the capital.

The government later discovered interconnected corridors in the basement of the Jamia Hafsa, from which the militants would fire on the law enforcement officers and then run away. The militants also used the female students and children as safety shields.

Most of the jihadist and Islamist outfits—Haqqani's network, the TTP, and other like-minded organizations—saw Operation Silence as an assault on an "Islamic institution being run by two revered brothers Aziz and Ghazi." For them, this assault reflected the American desire to crush Islamist forces in Pakistan, and was an attack on their soul. The reaction cut across the sectarian divide, fueled by Al Qaeda's

Ayman al-Zawahiri, who called on all Islamic forces to "avenge the martyrdom of hundreds of innocent boys and girls."

Calls to act on solidarity with the victims of the Red Mosque resulted in a dramatic wave of suicide bombings and ambushes across Pakistan; out of the fifty-six suicide attacks in 2007, at least thirty-six came after the operation. Security forces in the tribal areas also suffered unusual losses in the months after the raid. It was as if the Islamists had found a new cause and rallying cry, and decided to notch up the violence inside Pakistan.

The raid on the Red Mosque stoked antiarmy sentiment to such an extent that military personnel refrained from appearing in public without adequate security arrangements. Several friends in the army told me they had been advised not to visit markets in uniform. The assassination of former Prime Minister Benazir Bhutto on December 27, 2007, was probably the climax of the reaction to the raid on the Lal Masjid, which most Islamists condemned as "a desecration of a holy place."

## The Haqqani Factor in North Waziristan

Khalifa Sirajuddin Haqqani, Jalaluddin Haqqani's son, and Maulana Bakhta Jan—both Afghans—loom large over North Waziristan, which borders Afghanistan's Khost province. They call themselves Taliban. Both were part of the talks that led to the September 2006 peace deal in the area, and they continue to dominate the political landscape in the Waziristan region, providing spiritual and tactical guidance to the Afghan and Pakistani Taliban movement in North Waziristan as well as across the Durand Line, largely in the eastern Afghan provinces of Kunar, Paktia, and Paktika.

On June 21, 2006, as peace talks were still under way, Sirajuddin Haqqani issued a decree that it was no longer the Taliban policy to fight the Pakistan army. This marked the end of significant fighting in South Waziristan. The Taliban intentionally did not circulate the decree in North Waziristan, thereby keeping up pressure on the government as the terms for a comprehensive accord were being worked out. Paradoxically, despite their commitment not to target Pakistani government and military, Haqqani and his colleagues continued to shelter IMU fugitives and their supporters from South Waziristan because of their ideological affinity.

The truce between the Haqqani network and government forces would not last long. In mid-July 2007, Maulvi Abdul Khaliq Haqqani, another son of Jalaluddin Haqqani, issued a press statement saying that the deaths of the students at the Red Mosque and its adjoining seminary Jamia Hafsa in Islamabad would be avenged. "The target of our suicide attacks are and will be security officials. Those who don't understand our viewpoint will also be targeted," he said.[14]

The Haqqani network, which is officially known as the Amaraat-e-Islami Afghanistan (AIA), is closely linked with Al Qaeda leadership on both sides of the border. Dozens of Pakistani militants belonging to the Jamiatul Mujahideen, Jaish-e-Mohammad, and Lashkar-e-Jhangvi live in the area under their protection, and all have been playing host to fleeing Al Qaeda leaders and operatives. Both Khalid Sheikh Mohammad, arrested in March 2003, and Abu Zubayda, arrested in Faisalabad a few months earlier, transited through North Waziristan, and enjoyed Haqqani's hospitality. "The combination of sanctuary in Pakistan, deep links on both sides of the border and steady support from Arab and other jihadist networks has made Maulvi [Jalaluddin Haqqani] a formidable threat to the stability of Afghanistan," observed the *New York Times*.[15]

The Haqqani network is suspected of being behind four large-vehicle suicide bombings in eastern Afghanistan in 2008, including the attack mounted on the Indian embassy in Kabul in July 2008. The *New York Times* wrote that according to Afghan security officials, one of Haqqani's senior lieutenants masterminded a multipronged attack on the Serena Hotel in Kabul that killed seven people in January 2008, as well as the assassination attempt on President Karzai in April of the same year.

A raid on the Mumba-e-Uloom seminary in North Waziristan on July 29, 2008, was triggered by information that the Haqqani network was working overtime to prepare to send insurgents into Afghanistan. The seminary belongs to Jalaluddin Haqqani and has been almost deserted following several similar raids by Pakistani and U.S. forces. It is located in Dande Darpa Khel, half a kilometer north of Miranshah.

Local residents attribute the election of Kamran Wazir from North Waziristan to Pakistan's national legislature in February 2008 to Haqqani's influence and Kamran's close relations with Al Qaeda figures. Kamran's father runs a hospital, Zakeem, in Miranshah, which reportedly provides treatment to Al Qaeda and Taliban fighters. A black American Al Qaeda operative was treated here during the January 2008 operation before being arrested in the town of Bannu.

In recent years, Haqqani has brought Afghan Taliban–style restriction to the areas under his control. In May 2007, a Haqqani-led Taliban shura imposed a stringent ban on the sale of CDs and cassettes, and the playing of music in buses and passenger coaches in North Waziristan. The shura also ordered owners of music and video shops in Miranshah to wind up their businesses immediately.[16] Armed volunteers raided music centers and CD shops in the town and asked people to stop playing music in shops, buses, and homes. The shura threatened violators with "consequences." This decree is only one small indication of the Taliban's strength and influence in Waziristan.

A former ISI operative, Khalid Khwaja, was executed somewhere in North Waziristan in the summer of 2010 several weeks after an obscure group calling itself the Asian Tigers had abducted him along with British journalist Asad Qureshi and Colonel Sultan Ameer Imam, a former ISI official who had mentored the mujahideen and the Taliban since the first Afghan jihad. Qureshi was released after several months but Colonel Imam remained traceless until his body was found in North Waziristan in late January 2011.

# 7

# Crime and Corruption in
# Khyber and Bajaur

The Khyber Pass is an extremely important artery that connects Peshawar with Kabul and is crucial for U.S.-NATO food and fuel supplies. The Khyber and Bajaur agencies that flank the pass have experienced a surge in Talibanization and an increase in criminal activities in recent years—attacks on U.S. or NATO supply trucks and the plundering of their goods are now common, as are kidnappings for ransom. The Bajaur agency is a hotbed of militancy, a tradition that dates back to the anti-Soviet jihad in the 1980s. It borders the eastern Afghan province of Kunar and is thus ideal for groups with cross-border linkages.

Adjacent to Malakand and Swat, Bajaur was virtually the birthplace of the Pakistani Taliban movement founded by Maulana Sufi Mohammad, most of which has now morphed into Tehreek-e-Taliban Pakistan. The TTP is led in the region by Maulvi Faqir Mohammad and Mulla Fazlullah (Sufi Mohammad's estranged son-in-law and the TTP representative for the Swat region). Both Khyber and Bajaur have witnessed numerous military operations targeting both militants and criminals. Bajaur in particular has been a tough test case for the Pakistani government. As of February 2009, the military and paramilitary forces remained locked in fierce battles all over Bajaur, resulting in the displacement of close to three hundred thousand people. Nearly two years after moving into Bajaur, the military declared victory in the mountainous region on March 1, 2010, claiming most areas had been cleared of militants and the government writ established. A good number of the displaced also went back to resume their lives, but the majority of Bajaur residents continue to stay in camps in Mardan and Peshawar. Schools officially reopened on March 15 in an aura of fear and apprehension that militants, forced to disappear into the mountains, might return to destroy them.

The Khyber agency derives its name from the world-famous Khyber Pass, which provides the most vital link between Pakistan and Afghanistan. With a population of around half a million, it is inhabited by two important tribes: the Afridi and Shinwari. Afridis are widely known for being courageous, although British historians remember them as a rebellious and treacherous tribe. While often short-tempered, they are known to be good fighters, pragmatic in choosing their battles and making alliances. They respect Sufis (mystics) and their shrines, which intellectually aligns them with Barelvi Sunnis, the antithesis of conservative and pro-Taliban Deobandi groups. Interestingly, the Afridi tribe has also produced great works of literature.

Shinwaris, the second largest tribe, are also influential, but its members mostly inhabit the Nangarhar province of Afghanistan. They are largely involved in business activities. In recent years, particularly after 9/11, the Khyber agency has turned into a troubled area, known for hosting criminal gangs, warring religious factions, and dozens of illegal radio stations. These groups are promoting their brand of Islam, playing up the prevailing socioeconomic injustices and exploiting the absence of a legal justice system in the tribal areas. Individual groups run their own parallel systems of governance and dispense justice through Islamic sharia courts.

The Talibanization of the Khyber agency is relatively recent and differs from that of other agencies. Three groups loom large over Khyber: Lashkar-e-Islam, founded by Mufti Munir Shakir and currently led by Mangal Bagh Afridi; Ansarul Islam, founded by Pir Saifurrehman and headed by Mehbubul Haq; and Amar bil Maroof wa Nahi Analmunkir—which translates as the Promotion of Virtue and Prevention of Vice (PVPV)—founded by Haji Naamdar, who was assassinated in August 2008, and now led (in a diminished form) by Haji Niaz.

Most groups in the area are Sunni outfits with minor ideological deviations affiliated to the Deoband school of theology. Deoband is a city in India where, in the nineteenth century, the revival and purifi-cation movement of Islam on the subcontinent began. Calling for a "return to the basics," the concept underlying the movement was the belief that Muslims were drifting from the tenets of the Sunnah and Quran into the realm of Sufism, which the Deobandis perceived as being a Hindu conspiracy to introduce Hindu rituals into Islam. Some observers believe that Deobandis, instead of focusing on the message of the Quran and Sunnah, fixate on the literal meaning of certain Quranic verses.

Lashkar-e-Islam represents the hard-line Deobandi school of thought, akin to Lashkar-e-Taiba and Jamiatul Mujahideen, which justifies the use of force for religious ends. They are quite puritanical and believe in following the Quran in letter and spirit, as practiced in ultraconservative Saudi Arabia. They reject visits to shrines and tombs of saints as un-Islamic.

Ansarul Islam follows the Quran and Sunnah in a way that most in Pakistan describe as adhering to the Barelvi school of thought. Barelvis take a relatively liberal view of the religion, including Sufism, and see no problem in praying at tombs and shrines of saints who are seen as intermediaries between man and God. This branch of Sunni Islam, founded in the north Indian city of Bareilly, is implacably op-posed by the Deobandis as being unfaithful to the basic tenets of Islam. Peace, tolerance, harmony, and acceptance of other faiths and sects have remained at the core of the Barelvi interpretation of the Sunni faith.

The PVPV identifies closely with the Afghan Taliban, and repre-sents a fairly rigid version of Islam in which women practically do not have any role. They also believe in direct contact between God and man and can be categorized as followers of the Salafi school of theol-ogy. Since Haji Naamdar's death, the PVPV has lost its relevance; its followers today are modest and its activities are restricted to peaceful endeavors in its mosques and seminaries. Officials claim most of its followers are involved in criminal activities such as abduction for ran-som and extorting protection money from transporters for safe pas-sage through the Khyber Pass.

The Khyber agency is a conduit for the huge volume of smuggled goods that cross both sides of the Durand Line along with drugs and weapons. Political power, territorial authority, protection money made off transporters and goods combined with various versions of militant Islam are all at play in the strategically important Khyber agency. Most of the area hosts markets for foreign smuggled goods and has a thriving industry in fake products manufactured or packaged in small industrial units. Historically, several armies transited through the Khyber Pass, fighting and bribing the Afridi tribes while at the same time entering into deals of convenience with them. The bulk of Afghans forced out by the Soviet occupation of Afghanistan in 1979 used the Khyber Pass to find shelter elsewhere in Pakistan.

Khyber is also a hotbed for criminal gangs that operate under the cover of the Taliban. Pilferage or hijacking of food trucks is quite frequent. Border officials told me at Torkham that at least ten thousand cargo trucks transit every month through this international crossing point. An official of a private freight company in Kabul spoke of more or less the same number of trucks crossing through Torkham, the last Pakistani post on the Peshawar-Jalalabad route. The gangs usually target containers and trucks carrying fuel and food supplies for the U.S. and coalition troops based in Afghanistan. In late March 2008, for instance, these gangs torched about a hundred oil tankers parked near Torkham. The extent of the ensuing flames suggested the tankers were set on fire after much of the oil had been stolen. Approximately 75 percent of the U.S. supplies in Afghanistan, including 40 percent of the vehicle fuel, passes through Pakistan, either on land or through the country's airspace, and Pentagon officials say they are working on contingency plans to send the supplies through other countries for security reasons.[1]

On November 10, 2008, criminals waylaid as many as thirteen trucks carrying fuel and foodstuff for the U.S. and NATO forces near Jamrud, about half an hour after they had entered the Khyber agency. Officials said eleven trucks contained wheat and two were carrying military vehicles. They were intercepted at four places in the Khyber Pass on the way to the Afghan border by a group of sixty masked gunmen. "They popped up on the road suddenly and took away the trucks. Not a single shot was fired," Reuters quoted officials as saying. A military offensive followed the hijacking, with two helicopter gunships targeting the Godar, Saurkamar, and Varmado Mela areas of Jamrud; finally the security forces managed to recover all the trucks after a brief gun battle. Soon after the clashes, Mustafa Kamal, a key figure of the Khyber agency's branch of the TTP, warned that the group would attack the Peshawar airport if the military operation was not stopped. He said his group would not "forgive" the political agents of the Khyber agency and Jamrud for ordering "the killings of innocent people." Just before the attempted truck hijackings, seven rockets had landed at the Peshawar airport. Kamal's statement could be regarded as indirect proof that the TTP actually fired those rockets.

A civilian intelligence official told me that many incidents of hijackings go unreported. "If the incident involves [just] one or two trucks, the coalition forces prefer to keep quiet," the official said in Peshawar in early November 2008. Most of the clothing and foodstuff stolen from these containers—flak jackets, daggers, first-aid kits, canned food, blankets, cooking oil, sleeping bags—end up in the markets on the outskirts of Peshawar, called Karkhano Market. In March 2007, several containers went missing en route from Karachi to Afghanistan via Torkham. They were, in fact, hijacked in the Karak frontier region some seventy kilometers south of Peshawar, after which the American security apparatus adopted a different security and surveillance system, which tracks the cargo electronically all the way from Karachi to Kabul, making it easily traceable. Despite the satellite-based surveillance, pilferages or the abduction of containers remains a hazard. Security officials believe that the vehicles are burned because that is the easiest way of eliminating evidence of thefts. After looting the trucks and silencing the drivers at gunpoint or taking the drivers onboard, the gangs ignite the vehicles.[2]

Although attacks on vehicles carrying cargo for U.S. and NATO troops in Afghanistan became more sporadic in the latter part of 2009, they never ceased. In a strike on November 24, 2009, a group of ten armed men ambushed a tanker carrying fuel on a major road in Peshawar shortly before it was to enter the Khyber Pass. The attackers, armed with Kalashnikov rifles, ordered the driver and his assistant off the vehicle and fired several rockets at the tanker, triggering a massive fire. Such attacks usually coincide with army actions against militants and criminals. This time the militants were retaliating only a day after Pakistani ground troops and attack helicopters launched a new operation against militants in some troubled spots of the Khyber agency.

Local traders and residents say that the combination of criminal gangs and the Taliban disrupts regular trade but provides a source of income for security and government officials. Zia ul-Haq Sarhadi, who heads an association of Pakistani customs agents helping traders move goods through the customs post at Torkham, claimed the average number of trucks has dropped to 250 a day from 500 in early 2007, before violence escalated.[3] "Political authorities depend on the Frontier Constabulary to provide law and order in the area but FC officers receive bribes from Haji Amal Gul of the Malaka Dinkhel tribe to allow smuggling of goods through the Soorghar area," a Khyber agency trader said.[4]

Pakistan's ambassador to Afghanistan, Tariq Azizuddin, was abducted from the Khyber agency on February 11, 2008. He was on his way to Kabul when he was waylaid by unknown armed men and handed over to the TTP. Azizuddin (now Pakistan's ambassador to Turkey) was freed on May 16 under circumstances still shrouded in mystery; in the days preceding his release, the government had struck some deals with the Taliban in South Waziristan, resulting in a swap involving the release of about forty Taliban militants and about seventeen security forces personnel who had been in the custody primarily of Baitullah Mehsud's fighters.

## A Parallel Government: Vigilante Justice and Sharia

March 2006 saw some bloody feuds between rival Taliban factions in the Khyber agency, resulting in more than two dozen deaths in two days just a dozen kilometers from Peshawar, where the governor, the Frontier Corps inspector general, the political agent, and the army corps commander's headquarters are located. Both Lashkar-e-Islam and Ansarul Islam defied the writ of the government. In February 2006 a tribal jirga ordered Pir Saifurrehman, the head of Ansarul Islam, to leave the area to ease tensions, and he reportedly retreated to Punjab for shelter. The expulsion, however, helped little; rival FM stations continued to spit venom against one another. Radical clerics held their ground, making a mockery of the administration as well as of the tribal jirga, which had been asking them to shut down their radio stations.[5]

Mufti Shakir had meanwhile set up his own sharia court, which adjudicated all crimes according to his understanding and interpretation of sharia law—mostly the Taliban way. In some areas of the Khyber agency, Lashkar-e-Islam practically established a parallel government, launching an illegal FM radio station while its armed vigilantes punished anybody they considered to be in conflict with their agenda. In May 2007 Lashkar-e-Islam activists demolished ten houses after picking up all their valuables. Local militia acted as silent spectators. "Armed LI activists patrol government roads and have set up illegal check posts as well. They forced private and public girls' schools to close down and occasionally also forcibly shut down boys' schools and colleges," according to the *Daily Times*.[6]

Residents of Bara district have alleged that when political authorities ordered the Frontier Corps to take action against Lashkar-e-Islam in 2006, the paramilitary Scouts initially refused to comply. Local civilians as well as scores of government officials saw Lashkar-e-Islam's actions as doing a service to God by keeping the area under order and purifying it from all vices. The inaction of security forces rendered the authorities helpless. Residents also alleged that some members of the Khassadar force—local police—were aligned with Lashkar-e-Islam. They voiced their apprehensions to several Peshawar-based newspapers, saying Peshawar was not immune to what was happening in Bara and that repercussions would affect the city if Islamabad did not put an end to this parallel government.

Finally, following external pressures, the authorities cracked down. In late 2007 the political agent in charge of the Khyber agency invoked the Frontier Crimes Regulation 40 and consigned Mufti Shakir to indefinite detention. But he was quietly set free in the latter half of 2008, and he now lives an obscure life somewhere outside Khyber. Mangal Bagh Afridi, who replaced Mufti Shakir as head of Lashkar-e-Islam, continues to command authority and respect in the region. Concentrated in several pockets of the Khyber agency, Lashkar-e-Islam continues to oppose "un-Islamic" practices: no films, no video, no music CDs are allowed for open sale in the markets. Criminals, if held, are punished, as they were by the Afghan Taliban under Mulla Omar.

The surge in religious fundamentalism on the one hand and crime on the other prompted Haji Naamdar to revive his PVPV, which he had founded in late 2003 and lost interest in the following year. In fact, the creation of Tehreek-e-Taliban Pakistan in late 2007 provided him with a reason for becoming active again.[7] Haji Naamdar reportedly sheltered several TTP militants—both local and foreign—who had fled the military operation in South Waziristan in January 2008. This continued until a suicide attack, in early May 2008, orchestrated by the TTP at Naamdar's headquarters in Takya, in the town of Bara, left around twenty people injured. With the abduction of the Pakistani ambassador and execution of several officials, a turning point occurred for the Khyber Taliban. A small group led by Baitullah Mehsud's deputy, Hakimullah Mehsud, started interfering in local matters, beginning with the detention and execution of about a dozen government and security officials.[8] They indulged in target killings of government functionaries besides dispensing vigilante justice.

A day after the attack on his compound, Naamdar ordered the TTP to leave the Khyber agency.[9] "All militants belonging to Baitullah Mehsud's group have been ordered to leave the Khyber agency following the confirmation that this [strike] was ordered by Baitullah," a close aide to Naamdar told reporters on May 3, 2008.[10] Hakimullah defended the attack by telling Naamdar that he had "documentary evidence that [Naamdar] was a government puppet posing as a mujahid."[11] To justify his act, Hakimullah presented a photograph of Naamdar published in a Peshawar-based Urdu-language daily, showing him seated next to the Frontier Corps colonel Mujahid Hussain.

"We have ordered the attack to kill you because the picture leaves no doubt about your credibility," Hakimullah reportedly told Naamdar on the phone while requesting the remains of the suicide bomber.[12] Several security and intelligence officials admitted their contacts with Naamdar, saying he listens to them and does not condone crime or killing in the name of Islam. The situation in Khyber, therefore, remains tense, and the jihadis continue to be at loggerheads.

Crime, corruption, and religious conviction keep the agency on the boil. According to an intelligence official, the authorities reached out to Haji Naamdar and his group so that they could counter the influence of Hakimullah Mehsud and the TTP. Although the government's overtures to Naamdar made him suspect, according to people based in the Khyber agency Naamdar had only reached a verbal understanding with the authorities and undertook not to attack government interests. He agreed not to interfere in government matters, while officials kept quiet on the activities of his vigilantes, who traveled all the way to Peshawar to prosecute criminals. He was used as a shield against the TTP threat that looms large all over FATA.

The absence of any justice system and the abuse of the Frontier Crimes Regulation have combined to turn the Khyber agency into an explosive powder keg. Intertribal rifts and personal rivalries further strain a society where the rule of revenge reigns supreme. An aversion to foreign troops and commitment to the cause of the Afghan Taliban, as well as an ideological affinity with Al Qaeda, serve as common denominators to the militant organizations, but these are insufficient to keep them from fighting one another.

In June and July 2008, Lashkar-e-Islam and Ansarul Islam fought fierce battles not only in the Jamrud and Bara regions of the Khyber agency but also in the remote and mountainous Tirah valley. These skirmishes left more than a hundred dead. The Pakistan army took out several of their camps and facilities when it launched the Sirat-e-Mustaqeem (literally, the Straight Path that Allah shows) operation in late June, prompted by rumors that Mangal Bagh Afridi was getting ready to seize strategic locations in Peshawar.

## The Lure of Taliban Justice

The nexus between the smuggling mafia and the administration is too often ignored or understated under the pretext of respecting local tribal customs and traditions. In the last few years, members of the community have been raising alarms, but the administration has refused to counter the increasing influence of Taliban elements led initially by Haji Naamdar and, after his assassination in 2008, by his successor, Niaz Gul. These men provide protection in the area of their influence—regardless of who pays them. Smugglers, murderers, government and nongovernmental organizations usually use the Taliban cover for passage through the region, thus ensuring a good source of income. Naamdar was not himself a smuggler but he reportedly provided protection to them.

For the sake of the short-sighted objective of maintaining peace in the area, authorities have not dared to touch these militants. As long as they fought one another without disturbing the other areas of Pakistan, they merely watched as a silent spectator. The government did, however, jump into action when Lashkar-e-Islam zealots started kidnapping and punishing people around Peshawar for their "un-Islamic practices."

Taking advantage of the administration's indifference and corruption, the vigilante groups blatantly attempted to deliver their version of justice even in Peshawar, the provincial capital, picking up criminals and awarding them Islamic punishments. That is why, despite the heavy presence of the army and a huge police force—backed by the ISI, Military Intelligence, the Intelligence Bureau, and several other outfits—a wave of speculation that the Taliban was getting ready to march on the city gripped Peshawar in June and early July 2008. To quash rumors and to reestablish its writ in the Khyber agency, the government mounted the Sirat-e-Mustaqeem operation that summer, causing Mangal Bagh Afridi and others to flee into the mountains. But this victory was temporary.

"When the inspector general of police told a high-level meeting in May that Taliban are knocking at the doors of the provincial metropolis and its periphery, everybody, including intelligence officials, appeared alarmed," said an intelligence officer.[13] "It seemed," recalled another more senior officer, "as if a revelation had struck them all, although every informed person in the town knew how the Taliban had been preying on common people and targeting them with psychological propaganda tactics."[14]

In November 2009, the security forces demolished compounds that allegedly belonged to criminal gangs or their leaders. The military used gunship helicopters and heavy artillery to take out suspected crime dens, mostly disguised as Taliban shelters. These operations and the wave of suicide bombings that followed directly affected business, with traders in Peshawar reporting sales drops as large as 80 percent. Yet despite this, many residents were sympathetic to the militants.

Dr. Mazhar Durrani, a Peshawar resident, said that people like Mangal Bagh and Haji Naamdar had created an aura about themselves, and came to be seen as the deliverers of justice. Durrani recalled how his widowed aunt had approached Mangal Bagh for justice after her in-laws refused to surrender her share of property left behind by her husband. "Mangal Bagh summoned the brothers, rebuked them and asked them to be fair to her." The terrified brothers agreed on the spot to do what was needed to fulfill their obligations.

An intelligence official recalled how Mangal Bagh and Naamdar created their own justice system, complete with vigilantes, courts, and jails. "Mangal Bagh sent his people to one of the spots notorious for drug peddlers, and fixed them all within a few days," said the official. The police turned a blind eye because they got a cut of the business. "If the police don't help, I would certainly look to Mangal Bagh to get rid of criminals and drug pushers," said the official, who himself is wary of the corruption and indifference of the police and other government departments. He was skeptical of the Sirat-e-Mustaqeem operation that, he said, scared people but yielded little. He pointed out that within a few weeks of the operation, Mangal Bagh and his men reemerged in Bara, Jamrud, and other parts of the Khyber agency, thereby refuting government claims that these "miscreants" would not return to the region again. "Agreed, they are running a parallel government—but is that a solution? Conditions that gave rise to Taliban in Afghanistan were also more or less the same," said another government official, who once served in the FATA secretariat.

What is clear is that the Taliban has capitalized on the absence of good governance and of swift justice. Common people, already reeling under backbreaking food inflation and a tormenting energy crisis, feel that politicians, criminals, drug traffickers, and officials have ganged up against them to deprive them of an honorable living. The Taliban and like-minded religious militants have successfully exploited these feelings while sowing fear in the minds of all government servants. Providing justice on the spot, prosecuting criminals, and ensuring fair play to victims of injustice are effective tools that the Taliban use to make themselves look like a God-fearing, formidable force that is eager to come to the public's rescue. Little attention, however, is paid to the consequences of their advances. Many frustrated people—and not just conservatives—overlook the problems that arise out of the Taliban code of life. It was the suppression of individual liberties in the name of a questionable puritanical brand of Islam that the Afghan and Pakistani Taliban practiced, and are hoping to put into practice again. This obviously does not augur well for Pakistan's tribal areas or for the country. It is a demoralizing thing to consider for the majority of people who find themselves at the receiving end of an overbearing and inefficient bureaucracy that is perceived as unhelpful, obstructive, and corrupt.

## Bajaur Agency

Bajaur is flanked by the Mohmand agency in the south and by the Afghan province of Kunar in the west. It is connected through the Malakand region to the northern areas of Pakistan that border China, giving it a strategic importance. The smallest of the seven tribal agencies, Bajaur is largely inaccessible due to its hilly terrain. Khaar is the administrative headquarters of the agency. It borders Afghanistan's Kunar province, which is a hotbed of Taliban violence. The alliance of religious political parties—the MMA—has great influence in this area, and two MMA politicians from this agency are represented in the National Assembly and one in the Senate.

Bajaur's proximity to Kunar fuels suspicions that Osama bin Laden and his deputy Ayman al-Zawahiri may be hiding in the area. A village in Bajaur came under an aerial attack, reportedly executed by the CIA, targeting Ayman al-Zawahiri, on January 13, 2006, killing eighteen people. Al-Zawahiri was not found among the dead and the incident led to severe outrage in the area. Interestingly, Abu Faraj al-Libbi, a senior member of Al Qaeda who was involved in an assassination attempt on President Pervez Musharraf, told interrogators after his arrest in May 2005 that he had lived in Bajaur for some time. Pakistan's Inter-Services Intelligence (ISI) arrested Libbi on May 2, 2005, in Mardau, a tobacco- and sugarcane-growing town along the Kabul River, some thirty miles north of Peshawar.

Bajaur was thought to be one of the most suitable places for setting up jihadi camps for the anti-Soviet campaign in the 1980s. Its population of about six hundred thousand is spread over seven subdistricts: Khaar, Mamoond, Sadozai, Brung, Qazafi, Naogati, and Chamarkand. Two major tribes, the Utman Khel and Tarklani, dominate the population here. They are further divided into subtribes: Mamoond, Salarzai, Alizai, Shamozai, Mandal, and Targhavi.

The agency plunged into violence and chaos in July 2008, when the Taliban, led by Maulvi Faqir Mohammad, came close to declaring it an independent state. Until late July, the civilian administration had practically lost control over Khaar, the agency headquarters, with the paramilitary Bajaur Scouts mostly restricted to their camp on the outskirts of town.

In early August, after Islamabad gave them the go-ahead, the Bajaur Scouts, led by Major General Tariq Khan, began a search-and-seize operation, backed up by Cobra helicopters. One after the other, they removed barriers that had been put up by the Taliban on the road connecting Khaar with Peshawar. The Pakistan army joined in four weeks later, with F-16 combat aircraft and heavy artillery that pounded Taliban positions around Khaar, forcing the entire leadership to flee into the Mamoond and Pashat valleys near the border to Afghanistan. The army-Scouts operation became more intense by the day: the difficult topography—forests, wild vegetation, and hills—worked as an impregnable shield and a perfect hideout for the militants, who kept attacking army posts and convoys. As the days passed, the area turned into a virtual battlefield, forcing almost three hundred thousand people to escape to safety.

When I went to Bajaur in late September 2008, it looked like a war zone: destroyed tanks on the road, bullet-riddled walls of mud compounds, and signs of army presence all around. The thunder of heavy machine-gun fire from Cobra helicopters greeted us when we reached Tangkhatta, on the outskirts of Khaar; the village on the Khaar-Peshawar road had served as a vantage point for the militants to ambush army and government vehicles. The army had taken this village and a big compound along the road on September 11, 2008. The compound was a typical one where small corridors connected several rooms and front yards; a hen clucked around her chicks, and more than a dozen pigeons were cooing to one another, unmindful of the battle that had taken many lives on that fateful day. Scattered quilts and clothes and bullet holes in walls bore witness to the bloody battle that took place there.

"Miscreants ambushed us thrice on that day," recalled Colonel Javed Baloch, who led the battle. The Taliban laid siege around them every time they attempted to retrieve the bodies of soldiers. A major, Asad Akbar, died in the fight. "We had to spend the entire night in the compound as we were caught between militants all around. Air support through the Cobra helicopters eventually forced the Taliban to retreat," Colonel Baloch said. "The choppers kept pounding militant positions as we rummaged through the shelled compound, surrounded by maize fields all around. Most of the crop is also gone because of the hostilities."

By November 2008, a large number of the families, men in particular, had returned, but the majority still lived in camps outside

FATA because the security forces were still fighting with the Taliban. Army officials claimed to have killed close to 1,600 militants by the end of November, at a cost of about 110 soldiers and officers. In a Cobra gunship raid in October, the army almost got Faqir Mohammad, the head of the TTP in the agency. Bajaur Scout officials said several mortars hit the car carrying him. "According to our human assets on the ground," said the official, "Faqir sustained injuries while at least one of his two sons was killed in the attack."

"Despite several reversals and heavy losses, militants use everything they can to survive and attack. Security officials are surprised by the combat tactics and the stiff resistance the battle-hardened fighters are offering. They simply dissolve into the local population after striking at targets," Major General Tariq Khan explained at the headquarters of the Bajaur Scouts, which is part of the Frontier Corps. "They use residential compounds and markets for defense," he added. Military officials interpret this as proof that Al Qaeda might be in cahoots with local Taliban, who frequently use improvised explosive devices, the suicide jacket being their most important and lethal weapon. It is not a ragtag militia we are pitched against, they argue. "They are fighting like an organized and well-trained army, using trenches and tunnels for vintage attacks and shelters," Major General Khan said.

The Bajaur region witnessed some "reverse infiltration"; until recently, Afghan and U.S. intelligence reports spoke of cross-border infiltration from Pakistan into Afghanistan, but Pakistani intelligence officials now claim armed militants from Afghanistan are entering FATA to stoke insurgency. "We detected close to two hundred armed men crossing from Afghanistan's eastern Kunar province into Bajaur," an FC official told me while driving through Khaar. He said Bajaur seemed to be attracting militants from other tribal regions, from across the border as well as perhaps from Iraq.

In tandem with the military operation launched in August, the authorities encouraged local tribesmen to resist the Taliban. The Taliban ambushed and killed three tribal elders—Malik Bakhtawar Khan, Malik Shah Zarin, and religious scholar Maulvi Sher Wali—who were on their way home after a meeting with government officials in Khaar in early September 2008. They had agreed to raise a lashkar, or militia, and had asked the government for support, journalists in Khaar told me during one of my visits to the region. The local tribesmen held the Taliban responsible for the killings and formed the lashkar under the leadership of Fazal Karim Baro. The Salarzai tribe stepped forward and raised three lashkars comprising some four thousand tribesmen for deployment at different locations. The government has denied supporting the lashkars. Yet given the context of the violence and the bloodbath that the Taliban have been perpetrating on people they consider "progovernment," support from the military and the civilian administration seems unavoidable. "We are not providing any money or weapons but assured them of all possible political backing," the army spokesman Major General Athar Abbas told me during a visit to Bajaur.

I met a few tribal chieftains on that same visit. They were wary of a military operation that had displaced scores of families. When I asked them why they had allowed the Taliban to take over, most went on the defensive. "No doubt we allowed them to find a foothold here, we were too timid," said Zarwali Salarzai. In fact, most locals welcomed the raising of tribal lashkars in Swat, the Bajaur agency, in the semitribal region of Darra Adam Khel, and in other parts of the tribal belt. Though they remained skeptical, the move did give them some hope and many joined the tribal army to take on the militants.

Once the Taliban recognized the emerging threat to their domination, they responded with violence. The militants in the Chamarkand district of the Bajaur agency kidnapped eleven elders of a tribal lashkar in October 2008, eight of whom were beheaded, and their bodies thrown on the main road. A suicide attack on an assembly of tribal elders of the Salarzai tribe the next month killed more than twenty tribal elders, including the head of the tribal lashkar in the area, Malik Fazal Karim Baro. About a hundred tribesmen were injured in the incident. Baro, a retired Bajaur Scouts officer, had been instrumental in raising the anti-Taliban squad in Bajaur. When the jirga of hundreds of tribal elders was in progress, a tribal boy—a teenager—came to the venue in a car. Getting out of the car, he went straight to the middle of the jirga and squatted near Fazal Karim Baro before blowing himself up. The militant group Karwan-e-Nimatullah emerged out of nowhere to claim responsibility for the attack.

In Buner (in the Malakand region) the local populace, largely on its own, raised an anti-Taliban lashkar in September 2008. Soon thereafter, they successfully chased and killed six militants who had attacked a police station near Kingargali, brutally killing eight policemen on duty. After that incident the people of Buner raised a formal lashkar of volunteers to contain the activities of militants in their area. Soon, residents of Maidan in Dir, where militants from Bajaur had taken shelter, followed suit. Following several rounds of talks, the militants had to leave the area. But the lashkar avoided flushing out the militants from their stronghold in Mula Said Banda and the Darra areas of Salarzai. It visited both areas once but met with resistance from some Taliban splinter groups. The ensuing clash left thirteen people dead, including eight lashkar men and five Taliban.

Lashkars were also formed in the Mamoond and Charmang districts of Bajaur. Mamoond is considered to be the bastion of the Taliban, and is the hometown of Maulvi Faqir Mohammad. It housed the main camp of the Tehreek-e-Taliban Pakistan. The lashkars worked as a form of social pressure on several militant groups, as it was now evident that the militants were losing local support.

On November 10, 2008, about a dozen Taliban commanders who were on the official wanted list surrendered to the administration at a jirga of Otmankhel tribes in Bajaur. Private TV channels quoted officials and locals as saying that the commanders had assured the jirga and the political authorities that they would not back the Taliban in the future. Locals said a jirga was also held in Khaar, where tribal elders handed over the wanted individuals to the political authorities. The Salarzai and Mamoond tribes held separate anti-Taliban jirgas in Bajaur the same day, vowing to continue their drive to purge the area of militants.

During the meeting, army and civilian government officials warned Mamoond tribesmen of full-fledged military action if they failed to take practical steps against the militants in their area. Officials vented their frustration at the noncooperation of some of the Mamoond subtribes, telling them they had been given enough time for action against the militants. Journalists based in Khaar told me that the army had even halted air strikes on Taliban strongholds, hoping Mamoonds would raise a lashkar to take on the militants. The areas of Mamoond and the Pashat valley close to the border with Afghanistan are hotbeds of Taliban militancy. The Tarklani tribe, of which Mamoond is a sub-tribe, is divided on both sides of the border. Locals believe that this tribe is providing support to militants, and thereby blunting all government efforts to neutralize them.

Life in Bajaur seems to have returned to some semblance of normalcy as a consequence of the presence of the army, the Frontier Corps, and the local militia. Beginning with the August 2008 assault on the TTP, the security forces did manage to clear and secure several areas, and restore relative peace, allowing many families to return. Several hundred militants were either killed or captured, while top-tier leaders such as Faqir Mohammad and Mulla Fazlullah (the head of TTP in Swat) managed to disappear in the mountainous valleys of Bajaur, both reportedly injured in aerial strikes between March and May 2009.

But the situation remains volatile, punctuated with skirmishes and clashes between the militants and security forces. The month of November 2009, in particular, witnessed fierce encounters with several dozen "miscreants" falling to army fire. Militants kept returning to attack security checkpoints to register their presence, an indication that the military has a tough task at hand, a task that is likely to keep it busy for years to come.

Although the military declared that it had wound up active operation in February 2009, it stays on in Bajaur because of its strategic location. The surge in militant activities in November 2009 appeared to be a direct consequence of the military operation in South Waziristan. In late November, a local anti-Taliban leader, Shahpoor Khan, became a victim of the terror campaign in Bajaur. Khan was returning home after offering prayers for Eid, a Muslim festival, when an improvised explosive device blew up his vehicle. Khan, in his early forties, was the successor to Malik Rehmatullah, who had been killed in a suicide attack at a mosque a year earlier. In another incident, in early November 2009, militants ambushed a car and executed two women schoolteachers. The purpose of such attacks was not only to silence opposition but also to distract the army's attention from military action in South Waziristan. The fragile conditions in Bajaur still keep some twenty-four thousand displaced people from returning home. Most of them have been living in a 3,500-tent camp some thirty-five kilometers southwest of Peshawar since the military operation forced them to abandon their homes.

Bajaur has been under the influence of numerous extremist groups, including Al Qaeda, the Taliban Islamic Movement, the Hezb-e-Islami of Gulbuddin Hekmetyar, the Jamaat al-Daawa ilal Quran wal Sunnah of Sheikh Jamilur Rehman, Tehreek-e-Nifaze Shariate Mohammadi, Jamiatul Mujahideen, Jamaate Islami, and Jamiat Ulema-e-Islam. An Al Qaeda affiliate called the Takfiris (Takfir wal Hijra), led by Mustafa Al Seerat Al-Suri, also has deep roots in the area.

The presence of radical groups who share an anti-Western, pan-Islamist agenda makes it a hot target that is under continuous U.S. satellite and human surveillance. The suspicion that Osama bin Laden, his deputy Ayman al-Zawahiri, and Gulbuddin Hekmetyar are hiding in the mountainous region keeps it under the special scrutiny of American, Afghan, and Pakistani intelligence.

The *New York Times* reported on November 10, 2008, that a Navy Seal team had stopped just short of raiding a suspected militants' compound in the Bajaur region of Pakistan in 2006. Quoting a former CIA official, the paper said an executive order was issued after the Bush administration had granted intelligence agencies sweeping power to secretly detain and interrogate terrorist suspects in overseas prisons and to bug telephone and electronic communications. (Targets in Somalia need the approval of the defense secretary, while targets in some countries, including Pakistan and Syria, require presidential clearance.)

The *New York Times* report stated: "An operation to send a team of Navy Seals and Army Rangers into Pakistan to capture Dr. Ayman al-Zawahiri, Osama bin Laden's top deputy, was aborted at the last minute. Zawahiri was believed by intelligence officials to be attending a meeting in Bajaur and the Pentagon's Joint Special Operations Command hastily put together a plan to capture him. There were strong disagreements inside the Pentagon and the CIA about the quality of the intelligence, however, and some in the military expressed concern that the mission was unnecessarily risky. CIA director Porter Goss urged the military to carry out the mission, and some agents in the CIA even wanted to execute it without informing Ryan C. Crocker, the American ambassador to Pakistan. Defense Secretary Donald Rumsfeld ultimately refused to authorize the mission."

Why is Bajaur a haven for militants? It is the birthplace of the banned Tehreek-e-Nifaze Shariate Mohammadi, the forerunner of the Pakistani Taliban. Sufi Mohammad launched the TNSM there in the early 1990s and successfully challenged successive governments in the Malakand region by setting up illegal courts run by his own mullas. Many fighters loyal to Gulbuddin Hekmetyar are also known to have found sanctuary in Bajaur because of their ideological and ethnic affinity to local tribes.

Following his futile attempt to save the Afghan Taliban from the U.S.-led onslaught with the help of thousands of ill-trained and ill-equipped volunteers, Sufi Mohammad was arrested in Miranshah in late 2001 and put behind bars for seven years without being formally charged. The aging cleric was released in late April 2008 in the hope of restoring peace in the neighboring volatile Malakand/Swat region, where his son-in-law Maulana Fazlullah briefly held sway until the army moved in in November 2007 to reclaim police stations and government offices that had been lost to Fazlullah's men.

Little did the authorities realize that with the passage of time, Sufi Mohammad had lost relevance in the face of the rising influence of Faqir Mohammad in Bajaur and Fazlullah in Swat and Malakand. While Sufi Mohammad was in jail, his son-in-law had taken charge of his movement, with most of Sufi's followers vowing allegiance to him.

He set up an FM station illegally, brought Taliban fighters from FATA to Swat, cooperated with the Afghan Taliban, and created a following for himself. With money flooding in, he started challenging the writ of the state and is currently the Al Qaeda leader in the region, though his whereabouts are much disputed.*

In the post-9/11 years, Bajaur first shot into the limelight on January 13, 2006, with an extremely controversial U.S. missile strike on a suspected Al Qaeda hideout. The predawn strike, apparently a combination of Predators and high-flying bombers, hit three residential compounds in Damadola village. Initially U.S. media reports said that the attack had killed at least five high-level Al Qaeda figures, including Ayman al-Zawahiri, Osama bin Laden's deputy. But events later proved this to be untrue and questions emerged as to the evidence on which it was based.

The Associated Press quoted a Pakistani security official as saying that a dinner at which al-Zawahiri was expected had been planned for the night of January 12.[15] A local cleric, Maulvi Liaqat, was at the dinner, but he left around midnight, unnamed Pakistani officials said. After the air strike, Liaqat was again at the scene, and he had the bodies of the Arab militants pulled from the rubble and taken away. A second cleric, Maulvi Atta Muhammad, took away the Pakistani militants, reported the *New York Times*.[16] Maulvi Liaqat was among thousands of fighters who went to Afghanistan as part of Maulana Sufi Mohammad's group to fight the United States and its allies in October 2001 and stayed with Hekmetyar's party in Afghanistan's Kunar province.

The missiles were deadly accurate. Despite the pitch darkness of the night, they not only located the three targeted houses on the outskirts of the village of Damadola Burkanday but squarely struck their *hujra,* the large rooms traditionally used by Pashtoon tribesmen to accommodate guests.[17] Unfortunately, though the technology that

---

*Fazlullah was one of Baitullah Mehsud's deputies, but he was also an active local leader for Al Qaeda. He used the TTP umbrella to promote Al Qaeda's agenda.

guided the missiles to their targets at 3:00 a.m. was faultless, the intelligence that had selected those targets was not. Even as American military and intelligence sources spoke of the possible death of Ayman al-Zawahiri, the man considered to be the brains behind Al Qaeda's strategy, Pakistani officials denied any "foreigners" had been killed in the U.S. missile attack. Some officials had initially said that "preliminary investigations" suggested some foreigners were present in the area.

In Damadola itself, locals said they had never sheltered any Al Qaeda or Taliban leaders, let alone al-Zawahiri, the instantly recognizable fifty-four-year-old Egyptian-born former doctor. "This is a big lie . . . only our family members died in the attack," said Shah Zaman, a jeweler who lost two sons and a daughter. "They dropped bombs from planes and we were in no position to stop them . . . or to tell them we are innocent. I don't know [al-Zawahiri]. He was not at my home. No foreigner was at my home when the planes came and dropped bombs."

Haroon Rashid, a member of Parliament who lives near Damadola, told me that he had seen a drone surveying the area hours before the attack. The dead were reported to include four children, aged between five and ten, and at least two women. According to Islamic tradition, they were buried almost immediately. One Pakistani official, speaking anonymously, told the *Observer* that hours before the strike some unidentified guests had arrived at one home and that some bodies had been removed quickly after the attack. This was denied by villagers.

U.S. and Pakistani officials said that the missiles were launched from American pilotless drones, which had previously been used to target senior Al Qaeda figures. Sheikh Mansoor, who was alleged to be Al Qaeda's third in command, was killed in a "standoff" missile attack around a month earlier while on his way to condole the death of Mohammad Haqqani, the thirty-year-old son of Jalaluddin Haqqani, who was himself killed in a drone strike in mid-February. Several eyewitnesses spoke of seeing planes and illuminating flares over the village, which, if true, would indicate the use of missiles from planes guided in by special forces teams on the ground, rather than CIA-operated drones.

The government lodged a formal protest over the missile strikes with the American embassy in Islamabad several days later. Only a week previously, Pakistan had protested a similar attack on a suspected Al Qaeda hideout near Mirali, in North Waziristan, which killed at least eight civilians. On December 1, 2006, one alleged Al Qaeda operative, Abu Hamza, or Hamza Rabia, was eliminated in a deadly missile attack from across the border, most probably fired from a CIA-operated drone. The government claimed that Abu Hamza and a few others were killed by accidental explosions inside the compound they had been living in. Public rage over these attacks was mounting and the authorities thought official denial might assuage bruised egos: thus the decision to concoct the story of an accident.

On October 29, 2006, Bajaur once again made international headlines, this time with the death of eighty-three alleged Taliban militants bombed while "training" inside a compound in the Chenagai village. Once again, al-Zawahiri, Maulvi Liaqat, and Maulvi Faqir Mohammed seemed to be the prime targets.[18] Religious parties and their leaders, led by the local member of Parliament, Haroon Rashid, and tribal Taliban members insisted that most people killed in the strike were students of the seminary and had nothing to do with terrorism or militancy. Most religious parties blamed the attack on the United States, despite the fact that the Pakistani government insisted its security forces had carried out the operation following intelligence reports that the seminary was the hub of militant training.

Ten days later, a cloaked suicide bomber sprang the most audacious attack yet on the Pakistan army, charging into a training ground and blowing up at least forty-two soldiers limbering up for their morning drill at the army's main training center in Dargai in the North West Frontier Province.[19] The attack struck at the very pillar that props up the Pakistan state, the army, which is considered Pakistan's most feared and powerful institution. Security officials immediately launched a search for a second suicide bomber whose explosives apparently did not go off and who reportedly escaped on a motorcycle. No group claimed responsibility for the Dargai carnage, yet even the then interior minister, Aftab Sherpao, described it as a reaction to the strike on the Chenagai madrassa in Bajaur. The blame fell again on Baitullah Mehsud's men. He had not formed his TTP yet, but many of his cohorts already operated in close coordination.

This incident triggered widespread discussion of the Taliban spillover into urban centers and of the "futility" of the September 2006 peace deal in North Waziristan, which eventually fell through due to noncompliance by the Taliban. Missile strikes inside FATA added to the fury that already ran high among locals. "This is a disaster. We all recognize the gravity of the situation. It's a nightmare to have an army being attacked on its own soil and by its own people," Aftab Sherpao told me later. "After those two incidents [Damadola and Chenagai] the doors to peaceful negotiated settlements are closed. I am afraid we are on a war course in the tribal areas," a senior army intelligence official told the *Washington Post*.[20]

To this day the Taliban-led intimidation of the local population in Bajaur continues unabated. Most music shops and haircutting salons have been closed and their owners have switched to other businesses.[21] In early May 2008, the TTP spokesman Maulvi Omar set a two-month deadline for growing beards and warned people at large as well as barbers of strict punishment in case of noncompliance. He said shaving beards was "against sharia law."[22] Taliban vigilantes regularly check private and public transport vehicles for cassette and CD players (which they consider un-Islamic). On several occasions they seized cassettes and players from several vehicles and smashed them on the spot. Masked gunmen warned clean-shaven commuters to grow a beard or face punishment. They ordered passengers to remove musical ring tones from their cell phones and not to use mobile phones with built-in cameras.

Besides its contempt for nongovernmental organizations, seen as agents of Western obscenity, Faqir Mohammad's TTP opposes antipolio vaccination drives and the use of iodized salt. They consider them "un-Islamic and suspect they lead to impotency," said a local resident.[23] Yet, following social pressure by local authorities, the Taliban did allow a three-day antipolio campaign in late July 2008. Agency surgeon Dr. Jehanzaib Dawar told reporters that around 593 teams had been formed to administer polio drops to children during the campaign. But the Taliban influence and propaganda proved to be a major obstruction to the vaccination drive. Local health department officials said that initially the refusal rate hovered around 5,000 a year ago but continued engagement helped bring down the rate to 2,500 in 2008.[24]

Within one year of its creation, the TTP in Bajaur had overshadowed and outpaced the TNSM. In a glaring display of their authority and their obscurantist and offensive agenda, TTP militants executed a woman after accusing her of being a spy for the United States and a prostitute. The body of the unidentified woman was found dumped beside a road near the town of Khaar. According to a Reuters report of June 11, 2008, the note found by the body said, "This woman was killed because she was an American spy and a prostitute and those found doing such activities will face the same fate." A villager said the woman had apparently been strangled as there were rope marks on her neck. "I didn't see any bullet or knife wounds." It was the first execution of a woman under espionage charges. Taliban forces have killed close to a hundred alleged spies since the war on terror began in late 2001.

In late July, Maulvi Faqir suffered a blow when four of his influential commanders protested the July 18 killing of the rival commander shah and several of his comrades by TTP commander Omar Khalid in Mohmand, and resigned from the organization. "Innocent mujahideen were killed in Mohmand. Mujahideen do not kill innocent people," Salar Masood, a spokesman, said in an expression of solidarity with those killed.[25] Masood charged the TTP with "deviating" from the real cause of fighting the Americans inside Afghanistan. "We took up the matter with Baitullah Mehsud but he did not take our concern seriously," the spokesman said. "We will form our own group—Tehreek-e-Taliban Al Jihad—to continue jihad against the United States," Masood said on the phone from an undisclosed location in the Bajaur region.

# 8

# Mohmand, Kurram, and Orakzai

Following a surge in U.S. drone attacks on militant shelters in Waziristan in late 2008 and the advance of the Pakistani military in and around various parts of FATA, the Mohmand, Kurram, and Orakzai agencies have succumbed to extreme violence. During much of 2009 and the early part of 2010, these smaller tribal regions remained on the boil. Militants' reactions to the government-sponsored mobilization of local lashkars (tribal armies) accounted for scores of deaths in these agencies, as the TTP sent suicide bombers to disrupt lashkar meetings and mow down gatherings of elderly tribesmen. This had a terrible effect on the civilian administration, much of which was forced to leave to save its skin. Taking advantage of the situation, a number of TTP and Al Qaeda fighters took refuge in these agencies after the military began seizing terrorists' dens in South Waziristan in October 2009. "With AK-47s and rocket launchers slung over their shoulders, the militants have begun patrols through the new territory and have set up checkpoints," the *New York Times* reported in November. "They come to our houses and terrorize us," Fareedullah, a student at Weedara in central Kurram, told the paper. "They are abducting our elders and stealing our cars. We have no way of rising up against them, and there's no government here to help us. . . . Kurram is in trouble."

The Mohmand agency, with its rugged and secluded terrain, served as a natural sanctuary for Taliban and Al Qaeda fighters, providing shelter and training, as well as a launchpad for their insurgent activities inside Afghanistan. In Mohmand, the Taliban launched itself by initiating a vicious crackdown against outlaws in the area, whipping, executing, and imprisoning people found to be in violation of the sharia—as interpreted by the Taliban. Al-Zawahiri is reportedly married to a woman from Mohmand who lives with her father in the border area between Mohmand and Bajaur.

The Kurram agency is home to roughly 450,000 Muslims, about one-third of them Shias. Parachinar is the administrative headquarters of the agency, which is dominated by two tribes, the Turi and Bangash. Turis are Shia; Bangash are divided between Shia and Sunnis. The arrival of several hard-core Sunni militants from the Middle East and Africa in the early 1980s injected an element of sectarian conflict in Kurram and the continued infiltration of Sunni extremists has since ruined the peace of the agency, turning it into a hotbed of sectarianism. The agency has witnessed some of the most barbarous mass killings—including instances of people being thrown into wheat thrashers.

Like Mohmand, Kurram offers an isolated sanctuary for the Taliban and Al Qaeda fighters. The emergence of the Taliban in Afghanistan and the subsequent war on terror precipitated sectarian tensions and led to the most brutal extermination of rivals, as well as protracted pitched battles between the Shia and Sunni populations between 2007 and 2010, the three worst years in the agency's history.

The violence in the Kurram agency has spilled over to the neighboring Orakzai agency over the past two years. Local residents say that the Taliban is carrying out its anti-Shia campaign in a very calculated way under the command of Hakimullah Mehsud and Noor Jamal, also known as Mullah Toofan.

## Mohmand Agency

The agency takes its name from the Mohmand tribe which resides there, numbering approximately 350,000. Ghalanai is the administrative headquarters. Mohmands are a very powerful and influential tribe and are known to be natural guerrilla fighters. One of the important mythic themes among Mohmands is the descriptions and details of the wars in which they have fought. Indeed, they are widely known to have given more trouble to the British than any other tribe. Another distinguishing mark is the importance that they give to their clerics and divine leaders—they fought most of their wars under the leadership of their mullas. More recently, Mohmand tribal leaders challenged the joining of Pakistani and U.S. forces to comb the area in 2003. Trouble erupted after U.S. and Afghan troops intruded into an area that Pakistani authorities claimed was their territory. The exchange of fire between the Pakistani and Afghan border security forces in June 2003 triggered a U.S. intervention, which paved the way for Pakistan army units to conduct search operations in the area.

On October 22, 2007, six small Taliban groups agreed to merge into Tehreek-e-Taliban Mohmand (TTM) in the Mohmand agency, naming Omar Khalid, who was then Baitullah Mehsud's deputy in Mohmand, as their leader. They formed a sixteen-member consultative shura and the spokesman of the new organization, Abu Nauman Sangari, told journalists that all six groups would work together for peace. Omar Khalid's real name is Abdul Wali Raghib and he is an ISI-trained jihadi who fought against Indian troops in Kashmir, but retreated into Mohmand after Musharraf's January 12, 2002, ban on militant outfits.

The TTM is essentially an offshoot of the TTP. It follows the Afghan Taliban's vision of sharia justice, adjudicating matters according to the group's own interpretation of Islamic laws and levying punishments, such as the beheading of criminals, in the area under its influence. Rampant crime, injustice, abductions, and an extremely inefficient and helpless administration provide the militants with a conducive environment for enforcing their agenda.[1] Under Khalid's leadership, the TTM practically controls the entire agency. It was involved in the abduction of ten paramilitary personnel, who were eventually released on the intervention of local elders in the summer of 2007.

Following on the heels of the bloody siege of the Red Mosque in Islamabad in July 2007, TTM zealots ordered female teachers and girl students to wear the veil. Only days later a woman teacher was murdered by unknown gunmen, triggering apprehensions that the TTM did it to strike fear in the hearts of government schoolteachers. If this was their goal they succeeded because the murder resulted in the closure of more than a hundred girls' schools in August. In November 2007, the Mohmand Taliban caught some criminals during a crackdown and later slaughtered them one after the other in the presence of thousands of people. It happened on the eve of Eid, the feast celebrating the end of Ramadan. The bodies were left on the spot for more than twenty-four hours to teach other bad people a lesson. In the last week of January 2008, the TTM shot some eight officials dead and took hostage another eight for ransom. In late April 2008, in the Muchnai area, they killed another five criminals accused of theft. They shot one dead, whom they had caught alive, in front of hundreds of people.[2]

On May 26, 2008, TTM militants and tribal elders signed an accord pledging to maintain peace in the Mohmand agency. In return, several militants who had been arrested on charges of terrorism and attacks on security personnel in the tribal region were released.[3] Under the accord, the militants undertook to remain peaceful and refrain from targeting security personnel and government installations. Prominent tribal elders attended the jirga, held at the residence of the tribal chieftain Malik Zahir Shah Qandahari in Lakaro. The militants gave their word to the jirga that they would not interfere in government activities and would not obstruct development projects.[4]

Qandahari secured the promise that girls and women teachers, including all government staff, would be allowed to go to school.[5] The Taliban also assured security to government employees. At the same time, it announced that NGOs would not be allowed to resume work in the area and accused them of "spreading obscenity." Taliban and pro-Taliban forces are antagonistic to NGOs and oppose them universally. They consider them to be agents of the West, used to invade local culture and misguide innocent Muslims. Scores of Afghan and foreign NGO workers have either suffered imprisonment or lost their lives at the hands of the Taliban and other militant outfits, all of whom accuse the NGOs of engaging in espionage for the U.S. forces.

TTM's zealots have a following of at least two thousand armed militants who act as vigilantes against criminals. "The killing of innocent people, kidnapping for ransom, blowing up check posts and attacks on government targets and officials are routine," observed an Islamabad-based think tank, the Center for Research and Security Studies.

By July 2008, the Taliban was in complete control of the agency. The writ of the government hardly went beyond the small town of Ghalanai, the administrative headquarters of Mohmand. Its border with the eastern Afghan provinces of Nangarhar and Kunar was practically unmanned, thereby giving free passage to the militants commuting between Pakistan and Afghanistan.

When I traveled to Mohmand in late 2003 and again in 2004, the military and civilian authorities seemed to have established control over most areas. They had begun some development work there and were building new metaled roads or passable tracks where none existed before. Meetings with tribal elders yielded largely positive impressions. The region had remained unattended by the government until Afghan troops intruded into the agency in pursuit of militants in the summer of 2003. This incursion caused a row over the border, which had never been clearly demarcated in this region. Only with the intervention of the U.S. military command based in Kabul could the dispute be set aside for a while.

As it turned out, there was much simmering underneath the façade of contentment. Despite government and military claims, by July 2008, the Mohmand agency had almost fully fallen into the hands of the TTM.[6] "Omar Khalid is the strongest and most influential Taliban leader after Baitullah Mehsud and Maulvi Faqir," residents of Ghalanai said.

His only significant challenger was the Khalid Sahib Shah group, which was closely linked to Lashkar-e-Taiba. It was formed in the early 1990s as a group focused on the Kashmir militancy. Fully sponsored and backed by the Pakistani intelligence apparatus, the group was also financed by the Saudis because it follows the Salafi school of thought, known as Ahle Hadith. Based in Muridke, near Lahore, Pakistan's second largest city, they do not control territory the way the

Taliban does, but their fighters are among the most lethal, best trained, and most feared. They are widely believed to be behind the November 26, 2009, attacks in Mumbai.

The Khalid Sahib Shah group and the TTP (the TTM's umbrella group) share a broad political agenda—opposition to the United States and its allies—and both draw support from Al Qaeda. The rivalry between the two groups is mostly local. What distinguishes the TTP is its well-funded and organized structure, whereas the Khalid Shah group is much smaller, with limited territorial authority in the Mohmand agency.

The two groups were running separate training centers and had set up checkpoints on roadsides, but were otherwise not infringing on each other's turf. The situation turned ugly in mid-July 2008, when Khalid Shah militants ambushed the local TTM commander, Qari Shakil, on his way back to his residence in Khwezo village, considered to be the stronghold of the Khalid Shah group. Shakil was injured in the attack and his double-cabin pickup truck was destroyed. The incident enraged Omar Khalid and his fighters, who lost no time in storming Khalid Shah's shelters at Ashrafabad, a small town in Mohmand. Later in the afternoon, they attacked a big training camp in the Khwezo area where, sources said, around a hundred people were present.

A spokesman for the TTM later claimed to have captured Khalid Shah along with his 120 fighters, and said their shura would decide his fate and that of his militants. After what appeared to be a mock trial, Shah and several of his colleagues, including his deputy, were executed a couple of days later, on July 18.

The two groups clashed for several days—unchallenged by security forces—executing and butchering each other's prisoners, forcing a mass exodus from the area. The law-enforcement agencies acted as silent spectators and this conveyed their helplessness.[7] Sources in Ghalanai later told us that the fight had clearly stemmed from the TTM's suspicion that Shah had been collaborating with the authorities. Since many suspected the LeT, his parent organization, of close links with the ISI dating to the jihad in Kashmir, such doubts were inevitable.

Because the execution of Khalid Shah and his men painted the

TTP in a bad light, Baitullah Mehsud asked for an explanation. "The ameer has asked Omar Khalid to explain the murder of Shah sahib because Baitullah had considered him our ally," Qari Hussain Mehsud, the TTP spokesperson, told a journalist on the phone in my presence.[8] Mehsud told Khalid, "Shah group is our ally and his death is a big loss for all of us," the journalist quoted Hussain as saying.

"Any group not showing allegiance to the Tehreek-e-Taliban Pakistan will not be tolerated in the Mohmand agency," Khalid had told reporters in his first press conference after taking over the headquarters of the rival jihadi outfit.[9] A week later, Maulana Fazlurrehman Khalil, the maverick head of the outlawed Harkatul Mujahideen, reportedly prepared a draft agreement for peaceful coexistence in the agency.[10] The agreement proposed that all followers of the deceased commander Khalid Shah would live and fight under the guidance of the TTP. On the face of it, both sides agreed to coexist peacefully in the interest of their larger political objectives. In essence, though, its strong organizational structure and bigger manpower gave the TTP advantage enough to prevail.

Before this confrontation TTP militants were training in Kared, in the Lakrot subdistrict, near the controversial Turangzai Sahib shrine and the mosque they had renamed the Red Mosque in solidarity with the embattled Red Mosque in Islamabad. Initially, a few dozen militants participated in the training, which focuses on ambush techniques, hit-and-run skills, assembling assault rifles, planting and detonating bombs, and first-aid and survival techniques. The housing in the camps was shabby but had all the basic facilities. The recruits were largely from FATA, but some had also joined from the southern part of the Punjab. The actual number of trainees varies and largely remains secret. According to some estimates, at first about forty zealots took part in the training, but this later swelled to hundreds.

Militants began by training in the dark after sunset, but the inaction of the administration emboldened them to brandish weapons even during the day. Citizens' complaints fell on deaf ears.[11] After two months of intensive training, the TTM began sending out threatening letters to barbers, drug dealers, and video shop owners of the area, ordering them to stop their non-Islamic businesses. In May 2008 a local newspaper reported, "Now the militants appear in a uniform wearing war-jackets and long boots. They march through the bazaars to show their strength and uniformity and have started confronting security forces, and chasing criminals. These incidents are still occurring."[12]

In this, Mohmand was not alone. Swat, Kurram, Bajaur, and South Waziristan witnessed similar scenes, but with the passage of time the open display of Taliban power has waned in the face of increased Pakistani military presence and the constant satellite-based surveillance of the Waziristan region by the Americans. In February 2009, the army and paramilitary forces—the Frontier Corps—occupied several prime locations in Mohmand. Occasional gunfights between TTP zealots and security forces kept the situation tense and forced several thousand families to flee for safety.

In 2010, Mohmand remained in the grip of violence and uncertainty, with militants reportedly popping in and out, fleeing from the army incursions in the Waziristan, Bajaur, and Khyber agencies. The explosive conditions paralyzed daily life in Mohmand, leaving many people with no option but to move out to safer places in the vicinity of Peshawar, Charsada, and Mardan. In December 2010, security forces lost more than two dozen personnel to terrorists; around one hundred innocent women and children were also killed in two different attacks that month.

## Kurram Agency

Kurram's Shia population comes from three tribes: the Turi (by far the largest, and exclusively Shia), and the Bangash and the Mangal (both mixed Sunni-Shia). Other smaller tribes, such as the Chamkani, Masuzai, Alisherzai, and Zarmusht, are mostly Sunni. The agency is hemmed in on the west by Paktia, an Afghan province; in the south by North Waziristan; in the northeast by Khyber; and in the east by the Orakzai agency.

The emergence of the Taliban in Afghanistan and the war on terror have accentuated sectarian tensions, which began with the influx of Sunnis in the early 1980s. The arrival of hard-core Sunni militants, such as Lashkar-e-Jhangvi, Sipahe Sahaba Pakistan, and Harkatul Mujahideen, most of whom settled down there after the government banned their radical outfits, added fuel to the fire. With Pakistani and Afghan Taliban trying to extend their tentacles into Kurram, the agency witnessed occasional pitched battles between Shia and Sunni populations. This resulted in the closure of the main roads that connect it with other agencies and main towns like Hangu, Kohat, and Peshawar.

Kurram witnessed unusual violence through most of 2008 and 2009, with Sunni militants threatening the minority Shia population. The Shias inhabit the valleys, while most of the Sunnis live in the hills. Taliban militants used the local Sunni population and their vantage points in the hills overlooking Shia settlements to unleash terror on the Shias. The Sunni-Shia conflict rendered most of the Kurram agency a no-go area—even the security forces found it difficult to operate. It has been a humanitarian disaster. Taken together with the huge displacements caused by the conflict in Waziristan, Mohmand, and Bajaur, the flight of hundreds of thousands from Kurram, largely Shia Muslims, marked one of the biggest internal displacements Pakistan has suffered in decades. Some commuters have had to take long detours for their businesses in neighboring towns, sometimes passing through the Afghan provinces of Paktika and Nangarhar. In the February 2008 national elections, a Shia candidate, Riaz Hussain Shah, escaped two assassination attempts, one of them a suicide attack on his election rally that killed sixty people. In the second attempt, Shah survived but his guards were killed.

Despite a string of peace efforts, skirmishes between the combatants have continued. On June 9, 2008, Shia-Sunni representatives reached a cease-fire agreement, and vowed to work toward peace. Three months later, in October, a grand jirga consisting of parliamentarians, tribal elders, and the political administration of the Kurram agency brokered a peace deal between the warring Turi (Shia) and Bangash (mostly Sunni). Interestingly, the jirga was finalized and signed in Islamabad, the federal capital, following several rounds of consultations. Under the agreement, signed on October 16, 2008, by a fifteen-member committee from each side and twenty-three representatives from neighboring Hangu, the warring tribes agreed to swap prisoners and remove the bodies of those killed during clashes and buried temporarily on "enemy territory." Both parties also agreed to remove roadblocks and vacate bunkers and hand them over to the Frontier Corps. They submitted undertakings worth $75,000 (PKR 60 million) each in case either party violated the accord. This meant the onus of maintaining peace fell on both rival camps, who agreed to stay in touch to ensure peace was maintained.

Following the peace deal, roads that connected Kurram with Hangu and other towns were finally opened after a year and a half. The road closure had resulted in severe food and medical crises, sending prices of basic items such as wheat, flour, and sugar sky-high and forcing thousands of families to emigrate to safer towns, such as Hangu and Kohat. Although an uneasy calm prevailed in Kurram after the peace deal, underlying sectarian tensions and acrimony continue to simmer.[13]

During much of 2008, government officials and security forces continued to be targeted by the Taliban. Besides the human losses—as many as 1,600 deaths in two years—the conflict has displaced thousands of people. Those who could afford to move did so, for safety or for business or even to put their children in school. The tribal feud, wrapped in sectarian color, sucked in teenagers as both sides recruited fighters as young as fifteen, many of whom were reportedly asked to perform barbaric tasks, such as beheading rivals, a new, post-Iraq phenomeon and an indication of the new reach of Al Quaeda in Pakistan.

## Trouble in Hangu

The trouble in the southern NWFP district of Hangu, the last town short of the tribal areas of Kurram and Orakzai, is directly related to the strife in the Kurram agency. The Taliban shuttle regularly between Parachinar, the administrative headquarters of the Kurram agency, and Hangu.

Hangu had been tense even before the flare-up in Kurram in July 2008. Early that month tensions rose when local police attempted to demonstrate their authority over the area by conducting a flag march on the Tal-Hangu road that meanders into the Kurram agency. The march alarmed the TTP militants on the outskirts of the city, who took it as a form of intimidation and consequently ambushed a Frontier Constabulary convoy in Zargari on July 12, killing seventeen men. The police retaliated at once, killing some of the invading Taliban and capturing a dozen of them, including Rafiuddin, a deputy of Baitullah Mehsud.

The same day, furious over losses, the Taliban raised a band of four hundred volunteers and laid siege to a police station in one of the subdistricts, Doaaba. The Taliban continued the siege for more than twenty hours during which they blew up the transformer that supported the power supply to the police station.[14] The local administration eventually called out the army for rescue. But the moment the Taliban heard of the advancing army units, they retreated. The army then launched a search-and-destroy operation, removed barriers on the main roads that had been put up by the insurgents to strike terror into the hearts of locals, and helped the police regain their position all over the district. The entire district was placed under curfew for about two weeks to maximize surveillance and minimize movements of insurgents.

The Taliban soon mounted a counteroffensive and began attacking army, paramilitary, and police targets. In one of the ambushes, twenty-nine FC personnel were taken hostage. The militants threatened to execute the hostages one by one if the military did not abort its operation. They also refused to allow the bodies of the FC personnel killed on July 12 to be removed. An assembly of local tribal elders managed to secure the bodies and delayed the feared execution of the hostages.

Apparently under the pressure of locals, the army wrapped up its operation on July 24 and retreated from Hangu. Almost the same day, eight of the twenty-nine hostages were set free, which hinted that some kind of deal had been struck with the militants. But while the tribal elders were deliberating and negotiating with the militants, the militants still held at least fifty government officials and paramilitary personnel, and the brother of the Hangu district mayor went missing along with three other friends. "The operation objectives have been achieved," said Major General Athar Abbas, the spokesman for the Pakistan army.[15] He said that areas like Zargari, Shanawari, Doaaba, Torawari, and Yakhkandao had been cleared of militants.

It was of course a tactical statement focusing on the present, because militants, following losses, had fanned out in different directions to regroup. Attacks on government and security forces later demonstrated that the Taliban threat was omnipresent and needed a long-term strategic response rather than surgical strikes, which bring with them shock and awe but whose impact soon vanishes.

The TTP threatened retaliatory strikes against the provincial government for its crackdown. It set a five-day deadline for the government to resign or face attacks on official targets across the province. Ameer Haider Hoti, the NWFP chief minister, laughed off the threats and brushed aside the TTP deadline: "While we pursue the course of dialogue with those ready to lay down arms and work for peace, we will not be intimidated by unreasonable militants."[16]

The provincial government engaged local tribes to fend off the Taliban threat. As a consequence, as many as eight tribes with an overwhelming Sunni majority in the Hangu district agreed not to provide shelter to the Taliban or any other militant outfit and to cooperate with the government.[17] The decision was taken at a jirga held at the Hangu district coordination office and attended by representatives from numerous tribes. A local elder, Nazim Malik Jaleelur Rehman of the Darsamand Union Council, told the BBC that all the tribes had agreed not to shelter militant outfits, and that every tribe would be responsible for maintaining law and order in its area with the help of the government if required.

Kurram and Hangu are not the only places simmering with Sunni-Shia tensions. Gilgit, a mountain valley on the old silk route in the far north of Pakistan, and the towns of Jhang and Multan in central Pakistan have also witnessed this rivalry. But scant administrative machinery, the jihadi culture that cuts across the border, and the tribal nature of life make places like Kurram ideal for followers of both sects to indulge in violence.

## Orakzai Agency

A small agency with a population of about 240,000, Orakzai is primarily inhabited by the Orakzai tribe. The other important tribe in the area is the Daulatzai. Shias and Sunnis live side by side in Orakzai, although seldom in peace. Regular sectarian clashes have diminished the effectiveness and influence of the Orakzai tribe. This is the only agency that does not share a border with Afghanistan. The former governor of the NWFP, General Ali Mohammad Jan Orakzai, belongs to this tribe. Some senior bureaucrats in the civil services of Pakistan also hail from this tribe, giving them influence in the corridors of power in Pakistan. Despite a comparatively higher literacy rate, the agency was the first one in which Taliban militants banned nongovernmental organizations from operating, declaring them anti-Islamic. The possession of televisions has been declared a crime here under the influence of the local Taliban.

A deadly suicide attack in the Khadezai area of the Upper Orakzai agency in October 2008 on a gathering of hundreds of local tribesmen— busy discussing a strategy to counter Taliban militants—was a potent reminder of the terrible toll Taliban and Al Qaeda militants are now exacting across FATA and elsewhere in Pakistan. A suicide bomber drove an explosive-laden Datsun pickup truck into the crowd and blew himself up, thereby causing the truck to explode. Earlier in the spring, terrorists had attacked a similar gathering in Darra Adam Khel, near Peshawar, killing at least forty-two people. And over the summer, the TTP slaughtered twenty-two people from the Bhittani tribe in South Waziristan, part of a jirga which had been convened to negotiate peace. The TTP took most of the twenty-eight-member jirga hostage and eventually executed twenty-two of them, alleging that they belonged to criminal gangs. Tribal, social, religious, and moral traditions and norms no longer restrain militants; they pursue their political agendas without compunction.

The suicide attack in the Orakzai agency targeted a gathering of the Ali Khel tribe that had assembled after the Friday prayers. Local television channels quoted eyewitnesses as saying that at least thirty-two people died on the spot after the massive blast, which left a five-foot-deep crater in the ground. Television channels aired devastating images of human body parts and personal belongings scattered all around. The tribesmen, backed by the authorities, had gathered to raise more tribal militias in Orakzai to drive out the Taliban and Al Qaeda from their area. A day earlier, members of the jirga had destroyed three Taliban hideouts, including the houses of two Taliban commanders in the Dabori area, and fined four Taliban members roughly $2,500 (PKR 200,000) each.

Kamran Zeb, a top government official in Orakzai, told Reuters, "The Lashkar had taken a decision to destroy militants' headquarters in the region. Shortly afterward, this attack took place." On October 5, the same tribal assembly had decided not to allow "outsiders" into the area. They said anyone found sheltering "outsiders" would be shot dead and would have his house demolished. The jirga asked tribesmen not to brandish arms and not to cover their faces. It went on to form a committee to destroy the Taliban training camp in the area.

Though the Shia population in the Orakzai agency is just 15 percent, the sectarian conflict in neighboring Kurram has spilled over into the relatively small agency, as sympathizers and supporters from Kurram reach out to help their respective counterparts in Orakzai. In September 2007, for instance, in a major sectarian clash spread over fifteen days, at least seventy people lost their lives. Since early 2008, most of the Orakzai agency, including Sunni-majority areas like Dabori Ghalju and Masoodzai, have remained under virtual Taliban control. Government forces and political authorities have little influence there. That even the former governor, Ali Mohammad Jan Orakzai, cannot visit his hometown reveals the gravity of the situation.

The Taliban initially launched themselves in the area with a vicious crackdown against outlaws, executing five people after convicting them. In April 2008, the TTP arrested nine criminals and shifted them to Waziristan for punishment. To press their agenda, local Taliban issued a decree the next month banning women's education and barring NGOs from the Orakzai agency. "From now on we will not allow girls and community schools and NGOs to operate in the Orakzai agency," Taliban leaders told a jirga in the Dewray area of the agency.[18]

The tribal elders and clerics gave in to the militants in exchange for their agreement to allow government officials to resume their jobs and facilitate service delivery, including the distribution of salaries. They issued warnings to NGOs, instructing them to fold up their operations and vowing to hand out tough punishments in case of any violations. Kidnappers, robbers, and other criminals were instructed to surrender before the Taliban shura or face punishment according to the sharia.

In most cases, local elders and clerics buckled under the pressure of armed militants. Once the Taliban swept in, most local residents and government officials simply caved in and began adapting themselves according to the militants' will. But when the government sent in troops and paramilitary forces and urged them to stand up to the militants, they picked up some courage and began discussing ways of countering the armed gangs.

In early August 2008, tribal elders of the agency reached an agreement with the government, undertaking not to shelter or protect militants, criminals, or foreign elements. The elders promised that the agency's soil would not be used against the Pakistan army, nor would anyone be allowed to enforce a parallel government.[19]

In an environment that is politically loaded and morally devoid of respect for compromise and understanding, this agreement soon collapsed. Agreements may exist on paper with several influential local chiefs abiding by them, but the real problem lies with the militants, who rarely feel themselves to be bound by their agreements. Their exploitation of traditional Sunni-Shia rivalry has allowed them to co-opt locals in the tribal areas and turn them against the government and their own leaders, and to destabilize the region to their advantage.

By March 2010, the situation in Kurram had improved somewhat, with the Pakistan army in control of high grounds and critical access roads between and around Hangu. It was now able to escort commuters between Hangu and the Kurram agency. Some locals even began traveling on their own. For several months, Orakzai and Kurram swarmed with those TTP leaders and activists who had fled the military operation in South Waziristan, but by late March, most had either moved back to their areas or taken refuge elsewhere. As a consequence, local TTP commanders, such as Toofan Mullah, seemed to be in control of certain areas, playing hide-and-seek with security forces. A number of DVDs, purportedly filmed in Orakzai and Kurram, are in circulation in the area as well as in major towns, such as Hangu, Peshawar, and Charsadda. Most of them contain horrific scenes, including the beheadings of alleged spies and informers, amputations of limbs of alleged thieves and robbers, and floggings of adulterers. These videos serve as terror multipliers, but there is little the authorities can do to halt their propagation.

Local residents say the TTP has lost strength in the Kurram agency as a result of the military's advance on critical locations, yet the organization still seems to exercise control over people and territory in Orakzai, with almost one-third of the area under its direct or indirect influence. Despite military claims of success, Kurram, Orakzai, and Mohmand remained in the grip of TTP-led violence throughout 2010, causing nearly two hundred thousand people to flee from their homes. A definitive end to the cat and mouse game between the military and the militants is nowhere in sight.

Hakimullah Mehsud turned this triangular region into a hotbed of sectarian violence. More than one million refugees from Waziristan, Bajaur, Mohmand, and Swat forced to live in camps are the living proofs of an ideological proxy war between Iran and Saudi Arabia that is likely to take Pakistan awhile to overcome.

# 9

## Swat Is Burning

In the summer of 2007, two couples from Lahore, accompanied by their children, traveled up to the scenic ski resort Malam Jabba in Swat for a peaceful weekend. After spending the day there, they came down to Mingora, the administrative center of the Swat valley, to stay in a hotel. At around 2:00 a.m., a band of about a dozen Taliban knocked at their doors and asked them to leave.

"Don't spread obscenity here, just leave the place," one of the militants thundered while swinging his gun. The two frightened women took refuge in one of the bathrooms. But the Taliban ordered them to come out and even shot several times at the door. As a result, the women got a bullet each. Terrified and bleeding, they eventually opened the door. Amid the cries of their wailing, terrified children, the women, bleeding from gunshot wounds, packed up their families and fled. Their husbands were verbally abused and knocked about but were then allowed to escort their wives and children out. The hotel staff were silent spectators.[1] The families had to travel for about two hours before they got treatment at a government hospital in Mardan, some sixty kilometers from Peshawar.

This episode is reminiscent of the early days of the Taliban in Afghanistan, when zealots used to drag men out of their beds for not offering prayers or not sporting beards, or would whip women for traveling alone. But this happened in Mingora, often compared to Switzerland for its beautiful mountain scenery. It offered a glimpse of what was to come in the ensuing weeks; by mid-November, the entire Swat valley, once a favorite destination for tourists, had turned into a battlefield, the local people caught between the military and the militants of the Tehreek-e-Taliban Pakistan.

In the next eighteen months forty educational institutions were targeted in the Swat valley. Most school buildings were badly damaged by bombs or mortar shells. On June 25, 2008, the worst day for schools, militants burned or bombed ten schools in the district. A local lawyer and social activist, Shaukat Saleem, told journalists at the Peshawar Press Club that Taliban militants had even occupied several schools in the Malta subdistrict of Swat. Saleem said that out of the roughly 2 million inhabitants of the Swat/Malakand region, up to 700,000 were of primary school age and government enrollment hovered around 528,000. Damage or destruction to female educational institutions, he said, had deprived around 148,000 girls of an education.

By February 2009, as many as 182 schools, predominantly girls' schools, stood largely in ruins because of Taliban attacks. Locals say that because of the insecurity and fear that the Taliban had instilled in people's minds, schools even in safer areas had been closed down. About four hundred hotels were also shut down or damaged, including the beautiful Malam Jabba Hotel, situated amid picturesque hills.

Taliban militants targeted prominent educational institutions in the valley, including the Sangota Public School and College, which was attacked and damaged on October 6, 2008. Established in 1952, the missionary school was a gift of the British government to the then ruler of Swat and had about a thousand pupils on its rolls. Initially boys and girls studied together but since 1998 admissions have been restricted to girls only.

Throughout 2008, the Taliban kept targeting female educational institutions, apparently to express their rejection of what they call "Western education" for girls. But based on my experiences with the Afghan Taliban in Kandahar and elsewhere in Afghanistan, and my understanding of the TTP ideology, it seems to me safe to assume that these Taliban are not interested in education at all. It stands low down on their list of priorities. The TTP in Swat, led by Maulana Fazlullah, offers little rational explanation when asked why it opposes the education of girls. They duck the question, saying the answer lies in the enforcement of the sharia. But the sharia has little to say specifically about girls' education. The Quran emphasizes the value of the pursuit of knowledge for all, and gender is not mentioned. It is the narrow-minded mullahs and extremely conservative clerics who like to see women confined to their homes, as if their only function was to serve men. Ironically, Muslim Khan, the TTP spokesman for Swat who is now in government custody, denied any hand in the destruction of these schools and announced that his organization would reconstruct all damaged girls' schools at their own expense.[2]

To go back to the events of 2007: in mid-September, within weeks of the Mingora hotel incident, militants overran vast swathes of the Swat valley, seized about a dozen police stations, and declared the imposition of Islamic sharia. People watched in awe as TTP zealots checked to see whether their orders were being followed. Besides the army and government installations, TVs, VCRs, music shops, barber shops, and girls' educational institutions were all under TTP attack. The Taliban staged several public incinerations of video and music equipment to demonstrate how much they loathed these "tools of obscenity and immorality." They even sent leaflets to private institutions, such as banks, barring employees from wearing jeans and trousers, described as "symbols of the immoral West." Buoyed by his success, Maulana Fazlullah set up several sharia courts to dispense justice to "criminals." In early November, one of the courts punished three alleged criminals by flogging them in public. "After the government's indifference, we have set up our own Islamic court to dispense justice to the people and today is the beginning of the struggle for a cherished goal [enforcement of sharia]," Sirajuddin, the then spokesman for Maulana Fazlullah, told the media afterward.

The criminals were caught "red-handed" while trying to kidnap two women from Matta tehsil the previous month. Maulana Shah Dauran, head of the private Islamic court, who also does a regular program on Fazlullah's FM radio station, read out the crime the three men had allegedly committed as well as the punishment they had been awarded, adding that the punishment was "reformatory" and not under the penal code. Eyewitnesses said the three men had not been allowed to register a plea before they were lashed. Maulana Fazlullah's armed guards warned the media against photographing or taping the punishment.

"We are reporting these incidents to the provincial government with the warning that the cleric in Swat could spell trouble for the entire province if left unchecked. But the provincial government simply ignored the warnings," a senior intelligence official told me in Peshawar in December 2006.[3] The MMA, a religio-political alliance made up of many conservative clerics, had by than controlled the province for almost five years but it had done little to contain the activities of militant groups, many of which have good relations with ministers and local leaders. Most politicians were reluctant to take action for fear of reprisals. The Taliban was in effect running a parallel administration in Swat and Malakand; their local leaders would write instructions to government officials for trade permits, postings, and transfers of officials and even summon government functionaries for explanations.

As things spiraled out of control in November 2007, the army launched the Rahe Haq operation and a cat-and-mouse game between the Pakistan army and TTP militants began. Once the army moved in, it became almost impossible for the militants to hold on to the scores of police stations they had occupied for several weeks. One by one, the militants abandoned all the police stations and disappeared into the mountains, moving from one town to the other, leaving their footprints and then speeding away in four-by-four compact trucks. Small in numbers—not more than three thousand according to some counts—they still managed to terrorize people and seize places at will. These small bands gave the police and the military a difficult time, affecting general life and businesses. The government, educational institutions, banks, shops, and commercial centers remained closed for months, or conducted limited business out of fear of getting caught between the military and the militants.

Janikhel and Peochar appeared to be Fazlullah's strongholds, but strangely, the army stayed away from these valleys, which are surrounded by high mountains. In a briefing at headquarters in Rawalpindi, General Ahmed Shuja Pasha, former director general of the military operations in Swat, who became the head of the ISI in October 2008, declared these areas to be the local Taliban hubs. He explained that their formidable topography—high mountain passes and narrow gorges—made it difficult for the army to operate there. Those who have flown over the 1,360 kilometers that the frontier provinces share with Afghanistan will understand the challenges with which the environment and terrain confront the army. "A nightmare for those who move through these gorges and passes and a haven for those who want to ambush," said the general. General Pasha complained that some twenty informal but often frequented routes between Pakistan and Afghanistan, and another 350 unfrequented passages as well as nine divided villages on the 2,560-kilometer border, impede efforts aimed at checking and controlling illegal cross-border movement. Another obstacle in the way of an all-out offensive, he explained, is that the militants live among the population, making it extremely hard for the army to launch attacks.

"A very difficult and worrying situation for us," the general concluded, while explaining how the army was fanning out to clear the areas of militants. General Pasha also vented his frustration over the inaction by the local government, which he believed simply left the TTP unchallenged to spread its wings in the entire region.

In April 2008, authorities decided to release Sufi Mohammad, the aging cleric who founded the TNSM, the forerunner of the TTP, in the hope of bringing peace to Swat and Bajaur. But Sufi Mohammad's authority had been eclipsed during his seven years in Pakistan's jails and his more ruthless son-in-law now controlled the militants in Swat. The government announced with great fanfare the signing of a peace agreement with Sufi Mohammad in May, but no one in the region believed it would be honored.

Sufi Mohammad's release achieved little as far as restoring peace in Swat, Malakand, or Bajaur. In fact, Faqir Mohammad, who now controlled the TTP in Bajaur, openly scoffed at Sufi Mohammad's purported deal with the government. "Talks with Maulana Sufi Mohammad will not help the NWFP government bring peace to Swat. The

government should hold talks with Fazlullah instead of Sufi Mohammad," Faqir Mohammad said at a press conference in Khaar.[4]

Faqir Mohammad and his colleagues remain wedded to the goal
of evicting foreigners from Afghanistan. Addressing a gathering of
about five thousand tribesmen who had come together for the funeral
of a local journalist in the Bajaur agency, the militant leader expressed
unrelenting opposition to the U.S.-led forces: "We will not attack government positions and whoever indulges in such an attack will be
treated as an enemy . . . but we are Muslims and the enemy of infidels
and will continue our jihad in Afghanistan as long as the foreign allied
forces are there."[5]

Although General Pasha announced that he was wrapping up the
military operation in Swat in early 2008, the army had to remount its
efforts on July 30, after scores of security personnel were abducted and
several government installations attacked. The army claimed to have
killed close to a hundred militants, including two important commanders, but more than two dozen civilians and fifteen soldiers also
fell in the cross fire.

Maulana Fazlullah had warned that his group would carry out
suicide attacks if the government relaunched a military operation in
the valley.[6] Fazlullah, with his back to the cameras and most of his face
covered with a white shawl, hurled the threat during a televised press
conference in the remote mountainous Taran area of the Kabal subdistrict. At the same time, he announced the suspension of talks over
the implementation of the accord reached on May 21 with the provincial government.

As the military began pounding militant positions at various
locations in early August, Fazlullah made good on his promise: eight
security forces personnel were killed and six others injured when a
remote-controlled device blew up the van carrying them in the Hazara area of the Kabal subdistrict. Muslim Khan, the TTP spokesman
for Swat, claimed responsibility for the Hazara attack and said it
was a reaction to the military operation. "We avenged the killing of
innocent civilians by the security forces in unabated shelling," Khan

told the media on the phone from an undisclosed location. "We will carry out suicide and bomb strikes in response to attacks on the Taliban."

Elsewhere, the militants torched six more educational institutions, including the Swat Public School, a private girls' college in Mingora, and a primary school in Matta on the same day, while two bridges, one at Allahabad on the Kalaam Road and the other at Khwaza Khela, were damaged by mortars. In the Darmai area of Matta, militants abducted two nephews of a police official, Jamaluddin, warning him to quit his job, failing which the victims would be executed. Local authorities imposed a limited curfew in and around Mingora to restrict collateral damage in the operation, thereby bringing daily life and business activities to a halt.

To further rub salt into the government's wounds, TTP's Bajaur chief, Maulana Faqir Muhammad, and the organization's spokesman, Maulvi Umar, convened a joint press conference on August 5, 2008, at Inayat Kalay near Khaar, the administrative headquarters of Bajaur, to threaten the government and military with retaliation.[7] "We can instigate our fighters into action across the country if the government does not stop the ongoing military operation in Swat," Umar warned.

By late 2008, the TTP had mounted an unassailable insurgency in Swat, where the entire security apparatus—police, paramilitary forces, and intelligence—had existed for decades. How could a small army of vigilantes take over the entire Swat valley, in the presence of this security infrastructure? General Pasha offered few convincing answers. Nor could local residents offer a satisfying response to the question of how they had managed to terrorize an entire population. Fear of reprisals, once again, was probably a major piece of the puzzle.[8]

Several factors seem to have combined to empower the militants. Initially, the army appeared to be hesitant to take them on. The extremely poorly trained and badly paid police were never a match for the zeal of the insurgents, who were well trained and driven by their Islamist ideology. The provincial police were deficient in numbers in most areas, with less than twenty policemen for each police station.

Above all, despite official claims of "relentless crackdowns on the militants," doubts about the role of some government agencies abound. Locals believe there is a nexus between intelligence agencies and the militants. Army and intelligence officials deny any linkages. "How can we protect groups that are killing and butchering our own personnel and government functionaries?" asked General Pasha during one of our discussions. People in the affected areas who have witnessed the rise of Taliban forces take such claims with a big pinch of salt. The historical relations between intelligence agencies and militant groups have shaped and fueled the situation, allowing the Taliban to entrench themselves practically unchallenged.

Pakistanis are now facing a bitter reality: the prospect of a TTP insurgency spiraling into other areas. In November 2008, three incidents occurred within the space of thirty-six hours in Peshawar. A suicide attack outside the Qayum Stadium on November 11 killed five during a ceremony to mark the successful completion of the regional games; Stephan D. Vance, who headed the "Livelihoods" project of an American group working on USAID-funded schemes in FATA was gruesomely murdered the following morning; and an Iranian diplomat based in the city was abducted. There was another attack about thirty kilometers north of Peshawar when a suicide bomber rammed an explosives-filled bus into the gates of a school. Many locals saw the string of attacks as a direct consequence of the Pakistan army's crackdown on militants. Few believed they would be the last.

### The Awami National Party (ANP) and the Targeting of Politicians

In August 2008, the Provincial Assembly of the North West Frontier Province witnessed an emotional and fiery debate on the situation in Swat. Those bemoaning the breakdown of law and order were ministers in the provincial cabinet. "Swat is burning. Innocent people are being killed," the minister of forests, Wajid Ali Khan, said during his speech to the assembly. That Khan openly broke down during the session was a manifestation of the toll that the constant threats had taken on him and other Members of the Provincial Assembly (MPAs). Another MPA followed with an emotional speech of his own. "We cannot go to our constituencies for fear of being killed . . . whether it is mosques, women and children, or young and old, none of us is safe." Ayub Ashari, the minister for science and technology, was arguing that the government had lost its writ in Swat. As MPAs vented their anger and frustration over the alarming situation, the body of Ahmed Khan, the brother of a politician, was found in the Kabal subdistrict of Swat. He had been kidnapped by militants a few days before and executed. The same day, the bodies of two youngsters from a political family who had been kidnapped about a week earlier were found in Aligrama, with their throats slit.

Only a few days before, some two hundred armed Taliban had besieged Swat's Shah Dheri suburb in the early hours and, after a brief exchange of fire, entered the compound of Iqbal Anmed Khan, the elder brother of the ruling Awami National Party MPA. They overpowered the servants and security guards and shot him dead along with two of his sons and seven servants in the courtyard of the residential compound. The entire family had locked themselves inside the house, but the Taliban broke open the locked gates. They told the women to stay inside, and led the men into the courtyard, where they were all killed. After the cold-blooded murder, the militants blew up the house with explosives, killing all those inside, including women and children. Waqar Ahmad Khan could not even attend the funeral ceremony of his brother and young nephews after relatives advised him to stay in Peshawar for security reasons. Later, their family hotel in Swat also came under militant fire.

One after the other, leaders of the ANP, an ethnic Pashtoon nationalist party that is the lead partner in the coalition led by Benazir Bhutto's Pakistan People's Party, which has been in power since February 2008, received threats: resign from the government or face the consequences. The head of the party, Asfandyar Wali Khan, the grandson of Bacha Khan, known as "Frontier Gandhi," narrowly escaped death at the hands of a suicide bomber at his residence on October 2. (Abdul Ghaffar Khan was famed for his pacifist politics before and after the creation of Pakistan in 1947.) The TTP claimed responsibility for this as well as the November 11 suicide attack outside the Qayum Stadium in Peshawar (the ANP minister Bashir Bilour was the target). The bomber had blown himself up near Bilour's car, but luckily, Bilour was not in it. Afzal Khan, another veteran ANP leader, also faced the wrath of the Taliban, which shelled his home in Swat. Fortunately, Khan, who has practically retired from politics, escaped unhurt.

Such is the level of fear created by Taliban militants that all assembly members, many district mayors, and most leaders affiliated with the ruling political parties have abandoned Swat and taken refuge in Peshawar and Islamabad. Two members of the national legislature, the ANP's Muzaffar-ul-Mulk (alias Kaki Khan) and the PPP's Syed Allauddin, and all seven ANP-affiliated members of the provincial assembly cannot visit their homes and constituencies due to the danger of suicide bombers and target killers tasked to eliminate them. Even if they dare, they do it in a highly clandestine way. The district mayor, Jamal Nasir, left Swat in early 2007 after surviving an attempt on his life. Civil and police officers are reluctant to serve in Swat and more than 350 policemen have given up their jobs. The Swat district government system, therefore, remains paralyzed, crippled by long curfew hours and chronic lack of representation.

This situation obviously is the result of a deliberate effort to create fear and to undermine the legitimate government. The militants' objective is to intimidate ANP members into resigning from office. They also want to replace the relative secularism of the PPP with their brand of draconian Islamic sharia. After the departure of Pervez Musharraf, the ANP and the PPP of Benazir Bhutto earned the wrath of the TTP and its affiliates for their policies; the militants perceive them as agents of the United States of America, who are out to demolish Islamist forces.

The secularist ANP used to look to Moscow for political guidance and had close links with the Afghan government before the Soviet invasion and occupation of Afghanistan in December 1979. Post–9/11 events, however, seem to have influenced the ANP's outlook and opened it up to Washington. The warm relationship between American diplomatic missions in Pakistan and the ANP after the February 2008 general elections have not only raised eyebrows in the country but also alarmed the TTP for a very simple reason: the ANP leadership has been calling for the elimination of terrorist sanctuaries in the tribal areas and supports the military operation in FATA, Swat, and Malakand.

The TTP and its affiliates view the ANP's support of the military as a sign that they have joined an international alliance against "Islamist forces," and hence their violent reaction. It was probably because of these suspicions that the peace accord between the Swat-TTP and the ANP-PPP coalition government signed in May 2008 collapsed amid absurd claims and demands by the militants. The failure of the agreement underscored the fact that the conflict in Swat could not be resolved through conventional methods.

Over time, other political parties have come to see the Pakistani Taliban's new assertiveness as a threat to their own interests. Altaf Hussain's MQM controls the city of Karachi (population fifteen million), Pakistan's largest commercial center and the doorway for the country's external trade via the Arabian Sea. Ethnic Pashtoons constitute a good chunk of Karachi's population, more than three million. Most of them are settlers from FATA and the Frontier Province (NWFP), among them big traders and transporters, particularly from Waziristan. Although most of these Pashtoons joined mainstream Karachi political parties, a substantial number not only sympathize with various Taliban and Islamist groups but also serve either as financial conduits or mobilizers of parallel funding for them. It was against this backdrop that Altaf Hussain's colleagues in Karachi began raising a hue and cry about the "Talibanization of the city" in the summer of 2008, expressing fears that this disturbing trend might disrupt the peace. In a telephonic address to his people from London, Hussain urged his followers to rise and resist the "Talibanization of Karachi." He also petitioned foreign countries for help in fighting the Taliban. Although hollow on substance, Hussain's outburst did provoke the Taliban into equally emotional and provocative responses. "Once we are given the go-ahead by Baitullah Mehsud, Karachi's residents and Mehsud could take control of the city whenever," said Maulvi Umar, a spokesman for the TTP who is now in government custody.

## Decapitating the Pakistani Taliban

All through 2008, Pakistan reeled under a medium-intensity insurgency, with the Taliban influence growing rapidly. The state virtually lost territorial control to Taliban militants not only in most of FATA but also to a great extent in the Swat region, formerly a peaceful and bucolic part of the North West Frontier Province. Beginning from North and South Waziristan, the Taliban movement spilled over to the Mohmand, Orakzai, Kurram, and Bajaur agencies. In early summer, militants from the Khyber agency almost converged on Peshawar, assisted by other militants from another semiautonomous region, Darra Adam Khel, triggering fears the provincial capital might be within the grasp of the militants.

The army responded with force and carried out several operations in Darra Adam Khel, which connects Peshawar with the highway to Karachi—the lifeline for Pakistan's external trade—through a tunnel. The Japanese-funded tunnel remained closed for several weeks following its brief seizure by Taliban militants, who attempted to blow it up in January. Militants and the military traded heavy fire for days, until the army forced the Taliban out of the area and reopened the strategic tunnel, which is also a vital link between the southern parts of the NWFP and its capital, Peshawar, through the Indus Highway.

Meanwhile, American CIA-run pilotless drones kept lobbing precision missiles into Al Qaeda hideouts in Waziristan. In 2008, the CIA replaced the Predator with the Reaper, a more lethal unmanned aerial vehicle. Unlike the Predator drone, the new Reaper can fire Hellfire missiles and drop five-hundred-pound bombs. Throughout 2009, Reapers continued lobbing Hellfire missiles on suspected hideouts—more than five dozen attacks on targets in South and North Waziristan, including one on August 5 that took out the icon of terror, Baitullah Mehsud, the founder of the TTP. His death would incite TTP loyalists and inspire a rash of suicide bombings in his name. No one knew what impact the elimination of the TTP's charismatic leader would have on the group.

Following almost three weeks of speculation, Hakimullah Mehsud—charismatic, bold, brash, and at twenty-seven one of Baitullah Mehsud's closest confidants—finally met with four journalists at an undisclosed location on August 25, 2009, along with fellow tribesman Waliur Rehman Mehsud. He claimed that the shura had unanimously made him the new emir of the TTP, while Waliur Rehman was appointed to lead the Mehsud Taliban in South Waziristan. Azam Tariq, whose real name is Raees Khan Mehsud, was appointed TTP spokesman. Until his elevation to the post of emir, Hakimullah had led TTP operations in Khyber and Mohmand, and guided the anti-Shia campaign in Kurram and Orakzai, where he spent most of his time until assuming his new responsibilities. His selection as Baitullah Mehsud's successor was not uncontested, and Pakistani intelligence officials told me that Al Qaeda and the Afghan Taliban had played a role in resolving differences between various TTP commanders.

The record violence that Peshawar and the tribal regions witnessed in the months of October and November 2009 suggested that the TTP under Hakimullah Mehsud was out to avenge its leader's death. But the army quickly pushed back. Until it swept into the narrow, mountainous valley surrounding Sararogha on November 3, 2009, the village had served as the South Waziristan headquarters of the TTP. Militants had seized the town in a surprise raid on a paramilitary fort on January 25, 2008, instantly executing half of the two dozen Frontier Corps soldiers, a move that filled the inhabitants with fear and forced them into silence. Now the army retook the town and its southern ridge, Point 1345, which overlooks Sararogha and the road to the edge of the valley. The fight for this ridge was fierce and bloody, with one colonel losing one of his legs to gunfire from TTP militants. Officials claimed to have killed more than 550 militants in the campaign while suffering close to 100 casualties themselves.

Because access to the area—dubbed the "den of terror" by many army officials—was extremely limited and the military choked all arteries leading in before launching the operation, independent verification of the army's claims is almost impossible. The entire civilian population evacuated the area, leaving the military and the militants to wrestle each other.

Stones and debris still litter the ground of the fort—the result of heavy artillery fire the army used while entering the town. "It all started from here, the challenge to the state of Pakistan," Brigadier Muhammad Shafiq, the commanding officer, told me during a recent visit. "Sararogha has turned into a symbol of the TTP terror in the region."

The suicide attack on the CIA's base in Khost, in eastern Afghanistan, on December 30, 2009, which killed seven CIA officials, triggered a wave of retaliatory drone strikes in Waziristan. The Chapman forward base was the main staging post for the CIA officers responsible for coordinating and carrying out drone strikes inside Pakistan. Hakimullah Mehsud emerged in early January in a video together with the Jordanian doctor who carried out the attack. Mehsud claimed his men had first hosted and then facilitated the doctor's transport into Afghanistan. More than a dozen strikes in January 2010 suggest the CIA had begun getting solid intelligence on the whereabouts of TTP militants who took shelter in North Waziristan following the Pakistan military's move into South Waziristan in October.

In the early hours of January 16, 2010, Hakimullah and his associate Qari Hussain—considered the master strategist for the TTP—narrowly survived a drone attack on a compound they had stayed in for the night in Shaktoi, a town on the border between North and South Waziristan. Initial reports broadcast news of their deaths, but in an audio message a day later Hakimullah said he was alive and kicking. A source close to him said the militant's car was hit in the attack and he had sustained some injuries.

After several weeks of speculation, Taliban sources quietly conceded Hakimullah's death. Azam Tariq, the TTP spokesman, confided this to Pakistani journalists based in Peshawar and Dera Ismail Khan in early March, thereby confirming the second fatal blow to the TTP within six months.

A fresh string of suicide attacks in different parts of the Frontier Province and two deadly strikes in crowded markets in Lahore on March 12, 2010, underscored that the TTP had now begun drawing support from proscribed organizations, such as Lashkar-e-Jhangvi. Five low-intensity bomb explosions in upscale localities the same day stunned the city of Lahore. In phone calls to journalists in Peshawar on March 13, both Azam Tariq and Qari Hussain, the dreaded trainer of suicide bombers, claimed responsibility for the Lahore attacks and said that since "the government of Pakistan has become a puppet of the U.S.," they would continue attacking its interests.

Tariq warned that failure to halt operations against the Taliban would lead to more attacks. "Our two thousand suicide bombers, who have already spread across the country, will act against security personnel and government installations," he said in a statement released to the press.

From North and South Waziristan to Lahore and Karachi, radical Islamist forces have ganged up against the state and the people of Pakistan. This challenge forced the military into a new round of undeclared operations in Mohmand, Orakzai, and Kurram in the spring of 2010. To hit TTP militants and their hideouts in Nairobak and Ferozkhel villages, the army deployed the air force this time, heavily bombarding suspected militant strongholds.

Officials categorize the "Talibanization" of Pakistan as the biggest challenge to the government, but locals seem to differ: the biggest challenge, to their mind, comes from neglect, official apathy and incompetence, a corrupt police, and a slow legal system that often works in favor of the haves and punishes the have-nots. The common people believe that if Islamabad and the military wanted to block the Taliban, militants would not have a free run in these areas. Most suspicions fall on the intelligence agencies.

During the Musharraf era, the seeming inaction of the security forces was seen by many people as proof that the armed forces were playing a set match with the militants to convince the United States that the situation was dire and that Pakistan would need substantial financial support to fight it. Many people in Swat and elsewhere still believe this.

General Ashfaq Kayani, the chief of army staff since Musharraf's long-deferred resignation from the position in 2008, told a group of journalists during a meeting at his Rawalpindi residence in late January 2009 that he had heard this argument over and over again. But, he asked, why would our soldiers kill their own people? Why would the intelligence agencies support Taliban militants who are executing people indiscriminately? The general was confident and convincing when he brushed aside this widely held belief. I met him again on September 27, 2009, at his Rawalpindi residence, and he echoed his remarks. "I have heard about these perceptions but I see little rationale behind them," Kayani reiterated. He pointed to the roughly four hundred officers and soldiers who had lost their lives during the Swat and Bajaur operations in one of the highest soldier-to-militant fatality ratios in combat—and on their own soil.

Pakistan's support for the Taliban regime, and its involvement with many of the militant gangs that participated in the first Afghan jihad and in the incursion into Indian-occupied Kashmir, has had its consequences. Islamabad is widely seen as a supporter of militant Islam. The majority of residents in the tribal regions and many people elsewhere in Pakistan continue to believe that the army is in cahoots with the militants. But since 2007 the Pakistani Taliban has been deliberately and aggressively targeting the Pakistan army. On October 10, 2009, it lay siege to the military's general headquarters in Rawalpindi, just south of Islamabad, and hundreds of Pakistani soldiers have been killed in various operations. So a gradual transition within the military establishment appears to be under way. Interviews with senior officers and a number of army and government officials seem to suggest that the security establishment has learned the hard way that militant groups are dangerous and unreliable partners. They can be allies in destruction but can't be counted on to help build a peaceful and constructive future.

What was clear, as of February 2009, was that both peaceful and military means had failed to normalize the situation in Swat, and that the continued turmoil warranted a critical review of policies. General Kayani promised to go for a new approach, that is, to clean up and secure the area and to stay to help the civilian administration reestablish itself. This sounded like a formidable task. His strategy depends on the combination of military action with political leadership and civilian administration. The army usually does the surgical operation and secures the area, but unless political representatives and the civilian administration step forward, the army cannot stick its neck out for very long. If it does, people will begin to view it as an occupation force, a perception that dents the image and intentions of the army in the long run, and that would put it in grave danger of shoring up the very insurgency it seeks to quell.

By early 2011, conditions in Swat and other areas of Malakand had substantially improved and reconstruction was under way with the help of USAID and other donors. More important, most of the political figures who had left the city returned to lead the reconstruction efforts. The floods in the summer of 2010 badly affected settlements along the Swat River and made it all the more crucial for politicians to go back to help their constituents. Some criticized the government for failing to move quickly to counteract the ravages of the flood. The military once again took the lead in relief efforts, after the floods ravaged millions of acres of land and directly affected almost 20 million people from the north to the south.

# 10

# Al Qaeda Brings
# Suicide Bombing to Pakistan

Suicide bombing is a relatively new phenomenon in Pakistan that emerged a few years after the ouster of the Taliban regime in Afghanistan. It was an unwelcome and unremarked upon repercussion of the Iraq war. In 2006, there were six such attacks; in 2007, the number went up to fifty-six and in 2008 at least sixty-one fanatics blew themselves up in this way. With more than one suicide strike a week, these attacks and bomb blasts claimed 2,116 lives, including 558 law enforcement personnel, and injured 3,962 in 2007, according to a document compiled by the Ministry of Interior for the cabinet in January 2008. By 2009 there were eighty-seven suicide attacks and 3,025 victims of terrorism in Pakistan.

Most of the attacks on law enforcement personnel were carried out in FATA and the adjoining settled districts. North and South Waziristan have become the principal training ground for Pakistan's suicide bombers. Militants and their recruiters prey on boys as young as twelve and brainwash them on the virtues of the life "hereafter" and this idea—essentially an Al Qaeda tactic—has snared many innocent, ordinary, disgruntled youngsters in Pakistan's tribal areas. Initially, Arab Al Qaeda zealots led the mission, but it has subsequently been taken over by members of the Haqqani network and by the TTP. Strangely, despite the occasional pronouncement by a handful of clerics, no major religious leader has ever openly condemned suicide bombing. Of the few clerics who dared to denounce suicide bombing, one was executed under mysterious circumstances.

In May 2008, Noor Ahmed Wazir told me in Peshawar that three of his cousins from Miranshah, in North Waziristan, had already been through suicide attack training at a camp near Shawal, run jointly by TTP's Qari Hussain and Siraj Haqqani, the son of the Afghan war veteran Jalaluddin Haqqani.

The squad of suicide bombers headed by Qari Hussain had a special status. Boys not older than seventeen are restlessly waiting for their turn to strike against targets and embrace martyrdom. Baitullah Mehsud believed that the suicide bombers (fidayeen) were a force that could never be defeated. "They are my atom bombs. If the infidels have atom bombs, I have them too," he boasted in the presence of journalists who met him at a deserted government school in Spinkai, a desolate Pakistan village in South Waziristan, in May 2008. "When these 'fidayeen' are told that 'hoors' (beautiful girls) are waiting, looking out of the windows in paradise to embrace them, these youngsters they all clamor to be the first to go on a mission. They want to see how many 'hoors' out there are really waiting for them in paradise," said one of the Taliban fighters.[1]

Soon after Operation Zalzala launched in May 2008 to flush Baitullah Mehsud's followers out of South Waziristan, the Pakistan army took local and foreign journalists to a bombed house at Spinkai to show them "evidence of suicide bomb factories." Several days of fighting had left twenty-five militants and six soldiers dead, but the army claimed it had broken the back of TTP militants.

Brigadier Ali Abbas said his troops had recovered twelve detonation-ready suicide jackets, and many others were being prepared (using ball bearings and steel nails) at a camp that military officials said was a government-run school. The school was part of a large compound just outside the village that included a small mosque.[2] Major General Tariq Khan, the commander of the division that captured the area, told visiting journalists, "It was like a factory [and it] had been recruiting nine- to twelve-year-old boys and turning them into suicide bombers; [it also] manufactured IEDs." At another location military investigators found film footage on a DVD that they believed depicts children at the school being taught suicide training.[3]

The general said that during operations in the area, soldiers had rounded up more than fifty boys who were undergoing suicide attack training. Many of the boys had been kidnapped. Most of them were from the ethnic Pashtoon belt of the NWFP and some were locals from South Waziristan. "The boys were handed to an NGO, Save the Children, to be looked after," said General Khan.[4]

Several suspects picked up by intelligence and security agencies in October and early November 2008 made startling revelations during interrogation. One young suicide bomber from Dera Ismail Khan, who collapsed as he approached a paramilitary camp on the outskirts of Swat in September, recounted the kind of fairy tales the trainers spun to entice children into becoming suicide bombers. "My ustad [teacher] told me I would rocket into paradise once I press the button," the boy explained, pointing to the trigger of the suicide jacket he had wrapped around his waist. A security official recalled that when the boy was taken to a military hospital for a checkup, he was visibly moved by the sight of the nurses dressed in white. He blurted out, "My ustad had promised me 'hoors' like these once I reached paradise."

Imran, alias Mansoor, a Taliban leader arrested during a shootout with security forces in the Mohmand agency in late October after serious injuries prevented him from escaping, told his interrogators that a militant group in Karachi persuaded him to move to Dera Ismail Khan, the gateway to South Waziristan, for training in manufacturing IEDs.[5] Following this training, Imran moved to the Mohmand agency and stayed with TTP commander Omar Khalid's people, preparing cars and jackets for suicide strikes. A mechanic, Farooq Sattar, used to visit the camp to pack explosives into cars destined for strikes. "We called him the Master Khudkush car [expert of suicide cars]," officials quoted Imran as saying.

With him in the camp were five Arabs, two of whom went down in a U.S.-missile attack while the other three were still in Mohmand living with Commander Abdul Hannan, the Al Qaeda point man in the agency. Their mentor was Sheikh Usman, who trained both Arabs and Pakistanis in the deadly art of making suicide jackets and IEDs.

All of them maintained good relations with Baitullah Mehsud, who, according to local sources, occasionally helped the Mohmand Taliban with cash and goods.

## Al Qaeda's Footprints

Before September 11, 2001, Al Qaeda did employ suicide missions as part of its global jihad, but in the aftermath of 9/11, and particularly since the Iraq war, the extremist interpretation of jihad has undergone a radical transformation, degenerating into a cult of suicide bombing. In their premartyrdom videos, bombers taunt their audiences with phrases such as "while you Americans love life, we love death." When these videos are shown on Western television, they evoke disgust, contempt, and at times mockery, and fuel anti-Islamic sentiment.

The basic mind-set of the new Al Qaeda and its affiliates glorifies violent martyrdom above all else. As the eminent Pakistani journalist Khaled Ahmed explained in an article in the *Friday Times*, the message given to young jihadis is: "You are not a good jihadi until you kill yourself in the act of killing many others."

The mujahideen did not carry out a single suicide attack during the ten-year-long Afghan war against the Soviets. The assassination on September 9, 2001, of the Afghan Northern Alliance leader Ahmed Shah Massoud by suicide bombers was the first such attack in Afghanistan. Until early 2004, when the resurgent Taliban mounted six suicide attacks against U.S. and Afghan forces, not a single follow-up attack had been reported in Afghanistan. But the subsequent years saw an explosion of suicide attacks in the country: 21 in 2005, 136 in 2006, and 137 in 2007. In 2006 there were 1,100 casualties from suicide bombings, and in 2007 the number rose to 1,730. The Taliban aimed at exposed targets: 900 Afghan policemen and 40 Afghan aid workers were killed in 2008 in various acts of violence, including suicide attacks.

New training techniques, including the use and manufacture of IEDs and suicide jackets, and support from narcotics trade tycoons continue to help the Taliban and Al Qaeda on both sides of the Durand Line to enlist recruits and acquire the hardware they need for attacks and propaganda. Money generated from drug trafficking and abductions for ransom also enable the militants to financially compensate families of young suicide bombers. Exact figures are hard to come by but a friend in Makeen told me that families receive between $1,200 and $3,000. That said, the payoffs are inconsistent and the money is less significant than the promise of a swift ascent to heaven.

"Despite allegations, there is no evidence that suicide bombers are paid to do the job," said Rahimullah Yusufzai, an analyst and expert on Afghan and tribal affairs. He had met with the families of three suicide bombers in the Shabqad area of the Charsadda district who told him that they did not receive any money after their young sons sacrificed their lives in Indian Kashmir and Afghanistan. Visits to the poverty-stricken homes of the bereaved families and interviews with neighbors supported this claim. The three young men killed themselves and many others due to their belief that they were dying for a worthy and holy cause.[6]

Intelligence officials discovered that most of the suicide bombers used in the roughly eighty suicide attacks inside Pakistan between January 2007 and July 2008 were Pakistanis and Afghans, many of them orphans or mentally unstable teenagers recruited from asylums, orphanages, schools, and Afghan refugee camps in Pakistan.

In a sensational interview with Pakistan's Geo TV on June 21, 2008, Mustafa Abu al-Yazid, alias Sheikh Saeed, who heads Al Qaeda's operations in Afghanistan, said that suicide bombing was allowed in Islam. He declared that the clerics who outlawed it were "lackeys of the government." The Egyptian militant gave an aggressive justification for suicide bombing, claiming it was a "legitimate weapon against the enemies of Islam."[7] On August 13, 2008, Pakistani officials announced that Mustafa Abu al-Yazid had been killed in Bajaur; this was thought by some to be an attempt to refute recent U.S. accusations that sections of the Pakistani intelligence services were still assisting Islamic extremists. On February 9, 2009, the Indian government received a video from al-Yazid in which he said that if India attacked Pakistan, Al Qaeda would hit back, taking everyone by surprise, as he was presumed to be dead.

Whether it was the attack on President Musharraf in December 2004 or on Prime Minister Shaukat Aziz in April 2005 or the massive detonation, probably by remote control, outside the Pakistan Ordnance Factories west of Islamabad in August 2008 or the truck that a bomber drove into an assembly of tribal elders in Orakzai in October 2008, all these bore the hallmarks of Al Qaeda, which has successfully expanded the Taliban agenda of taking on foreign troops in Afghanistan and brought the carnage close to home.

"We were told to fight against Israel, America, and non-Muslims," said seventeen-year-old Muhammed Bakhtiar, when asked why he wanted to become a suicide bomber.[8] Bakhtiar and his friend Miraj Ahmad left everything and everyone they knew in Buner to join a madrassa in Bunal, near Lahore. A man had then come to their boarding school and told them about Markaz-al-Daawatul Ershad, in Muridke, run by Jamatud Dawa, the charity linked to Lashkar-e-Taiba, which shares the Al Qaeda ideology.

"We read about jihad in books and wanted to join," said Ahmad. "We wanted to go to the Muridke madrassa so we would have a better life in the hereafter."

Once at the center, the boys had the option of becoming freedom fighters or suicide bombers. The students were taught Islamic studies in the mornings, and afternoons were reserved for sports after lunch. Jihad training was given in the evenings, two classes a night. "The jihadi man who brought us to Muridke told us we would become great by fighting jihad," said the clean-shaven Bakhtiar. "We knew we could never become great if we stayed in Buner. I wanted to become great."

When the parents of Bakhtiar and Ahmad learned the boys had missed a week at their boarding school in Bunal, they panicked. They contacted relatives and friends, but everything led to a dead end. Even their principal, Abdur Rahman, expressed ignorance about their whereabouts. "We don't support this; suicide attacks are murder; this is against

Islam," said Rahman. "Those boys went to Muridke by themselves, they should have been here taking their exams, and I no longer want them back in my school," he said.[9]

Eventually, the tribal elders intervened and brought Bakhtiar and Ahmad back home.

Bakhtiar and Ahmad were just a few of the lucky ones whose parents managed to locate and retrieve them from the Muridke seminar. But scores of youngsters, recruited from across the country, have simply lost their lives and souls to the jihad; most could neither be rescued nor extricated from the ideological web that had been spun around them.

### Overview of Suicide Bombings in Pakistan

The first suicide attack in Pakistan occurred in Islamabad in 1995, when a bomber rammed his explosives-laden truck into the Egyptian embassy, killing fourteen people. The bomber was Egyptian. The second suicide attack hit Karachi in 2002. There were twenty-two suicide attacks between 2002 and 2006, at which point the current epidemic began.

The full scale of Al Qaeda's involvement in the spiral of violence in Pakistan became evident in September 2007, when Zawahiri vowed in a public statement to avenge the government's crackdown against the religious militants in Islamabad's Red Mosque in July. Pakistani jihadis responded by staging multiple suicide attacks against the army, the air force, the ISI, and other government personnel. In the six months following the assassination of former premier Benazir Bhutto on December 27, 2007, militants carried out some twenty suicide attacks at various locations. Highly motivated youngsters staged at least fifty-six suicide attacks that year, a dramatic increase from the six in the previous year.

Until 2007 the strikes mostly targeted restaurants and public places frequented by foreigners. This abruptly changed after the seizure of the Red Mosque, when terrorists began targeting army, police, and intelligence facilities or army convoys in northern Pakistan, mostly in the NWFP and FATA. This trend climaxed with the raid and siege on October 10, 2009, of the general headquarters in Rawalpindi. Heavily armed attackers, riding in a couple of cars, simply hurled grenades to break the first security cordon and then stormed the GHQ building itself. There they neutralized the second line of security and swept inside the complex, seizing a block that houses Military Intelligence and taking forty-two hostages around midday.

The siege ended after eighteen tense hours, when all but three hostages were released. For the first time in its history, the mighty military establishment looked vulnerable. Subsequent attacks on Inter-Services Intelligence and Military Intelligence installations in Lahore and Peshawar underlined the new tactics the terrorists had adopted to create a sense of insecurity all over Pakistan. When the militants moved the war into urban centers, attacking civilians and the security forces alike in the latter half of 2008, the GHQ finally woke up.

Most of us have no illusions anymore about the consequences of past policies, a very senior general, commanding a corps, told me during a long private session in Islamabad in late December 2009. The general, who cannot be quoted directly because of institutional restrictions, said that as the insurgency picked up and terrorists began knocking out targets in Islamabad, Rawalpindi, and Lahore, the corps commanders favored an all-out campaign against the groups involved. A consensus was reached that all militants must be dealt with indiscriminately—however close they may have been to our institutions, he said.

The Iraq war helped popularize suicide bombing throughout the Muslim world and bears some responsibility for Pakistan's current predicament. The war had an enormous emotional impact in Pakistan. Most Pakistanis thought it was an unjust war, imposed on Iraq under a flimsy pretext. So the reaction to it was quite intense, especially among those who were wary or critical of the presence of American and NATO forces in Afghanistan. That is why almost every discussion of the Afghan war in Pakistani social and political circles invariably brings in the U.S. invasion of Iraq and its consequences for Pakistan.

But it was the second drone strike on January 13, 2006, targeting

Ayman al-Zawahiri in Damadola, a village in Bajaur, followed by another on October 29 that killed eighty-three students at a seminary in Chenagai, that was the real trigger. On November 9, the militants struck back with a suicide bombing at a paramilitary school in Dargai, some 150 kilometers northwest of Islamabad. (The bomber ran onto the training ground and blew himself up in the middle of exercising recruits, killing more than a dozen people.) The second major trigger was the operation targeting Islamabad's Red Mosque in July 2007.

Border cities like Peshawar and Kohat have borne the brunt of the violence. The NWFP witnessed the first suicide attack by a woman when, on December 4, 2007, a female suicide bomber blew herself up in a high-security zone in Peshawar. Except for killing herself, the suicide bomber, who was said to be in her midthirties, fortunately did not cause much damage, probably because of a last-minute attack of the nerves.

A suicide attack near a Shia mosque in the heart of Peshawar in early December 2008 killed close to fifty people, more or less a repeat of an attack of the same intensity in almost the same area a year before during the month of Shia mourning, Moharram. (A few strikes on mosques in Quetta, Rawalpinidi, and Multan were also sectarian in nature.)

Those involved in suicide attacks in Pakistan can be categorized as belonging to two types of radical organizations. The first is primarily sectarian—the most vociferous of these being the banned militant Sunni groups Lashkar-e-Jhangvi and Lashkar-e-Taiba. Their leaders fought in Afghanistan, first against the Russian troops and then against the U.S.-led allied forces. For ideological inspiration they look to Al Qaeda, although they were set in their sectarian ways days before this more recent affiliation. Pakistani intelligence officials have traced dozens of suicide bombings and attacks on Shia gatherings and mosques to Lashkar-e-Jhangvi activists who have linked up with Al Qaeda and expanded their focus since September 11. Lashkar-e-Jhangvi's links to Al Qaeda were established toward the end of the 1990s, when its founder, Riaz Basra, and several others were camping and training in Afghanistan. All were wanted on multiple criminal charges in Pakistan.

The second type of suicide attackers belongs to pro-Taliban groups who are linked to Al Qaeda and gathered together under the leadership of Baitullah Mehsud. This group's agenda differs from the others; while the former seeks to give a purely religious spin to their war, the latter pursues a purely political agenda, one that aims at destabilizing Pakistan through acts of terror that do not distinguish between government, army, tribal, or religious targets. The followers of the TTP and its affiliates are not concerned by the destruction of schools and hospitals or the loss of lives of innocent citizens in pursuit of their relentless, violent campaign.

### The Bomber Who Wavered

"We receive funds from Arab countries, therefore, we cannot carry out any attack there, and if we commit any wrong there, they will stop supply of funds to us." This was the response of Abu Nasir al-Qahtani, a suicide bombing trainer, when one of his disciples, twenty-one-year-old Mansoor Khan Dawar, asked him through his local teacher whether suicide bombing was Islamic and why only Afghanistan and Pakistan were the targets of such attacks.

Born in Hurmaz, a small village near Miranshah in North Waziristan, Mansoor was picked up by Taliban recruiters from a village mosque in the spring of 2006. "After several sessions at an isolated compound in Hurmaz, my teacher took me to Spinkai Raghzai for special training," Mansoor told one of my close friends based in Miranshah, whom I had sent in to interview youngsters who had undergone training for suicide bombing.

The camp was led by Qari Hussain, the TTP master-trainer of suicide bombers. If Mansoor Khan was to be believed, al-Qahtani, a Saudi national who had escaped from the Bagram prison north of Kabul during the summer of 2005, was staying with Hussain at that time.

After his escape from Bagram, al-Qahtani fled to North Waziristan. He joined forces with Abu Wafa, an expert in militant activities, and soon became active in the Afghan provinces of Khost, Paktika, and Paktia. "A recently released CD shows al-Qahtani imparting military training, guiding the fighters with the help of computerized maps to attack enemy bases and delivering a lengthy speech to wage jihad against 'infidels' in Afghanistan and Iraq," the Pakistani *News* reported shortly before al-Qahtani was recaptured in early November 2006 by Afghan and coalition forces in Khost.[10]

"When I met al-Qahtani, he soon impressed me with his thoughts on Islam and America and I decided to become a suicide bomber," Mansoor recalled. Mansoor was either unable to identify or perhaps did not want to name the place where he got his training. His description of the place, however, suggests the camp was located somewhere in the Shawal Mountains that form a natural border between Afghanistan and Pakistan.

"I completed my training in the mountains in twenty days. Most of the time we were either training or praying and the speeches by al-Qahtani were also very emotional and motivating," Mansoor said, explaining that he trained in a group of ten. "Our instructors would show videos of atrocities on Muslims and also teach us verses of the Holy Quran and Hadiths against the infidels." Once convinced that the young boy was ready for the suicide mission, his mentors told him to visit his parents before embarking on the "journey to eternity."

Mansoor's parents were surprised, but also greatly relieved to see him again after an almost four-week absence. But the boy seemed to be a different person; he had turned quiet and reclusive, arousing their suspicion. "After my father repeatedly asked me what I was up to, I told him about the training and the mission ahead of me, of my intention to carry out a suicide attack," said Mansoor, who appeared nervous at the time of this conversation.

His father—Abdul Ghani Khan, a low-ranking government official—then engaged him in a long discussion, trying to explain the positive and negative aspects of the jihad Al Qaeda and the Taliban were waging. He reminded his son of how the "Americans and their Arab hosts were enjoying their lives in Saudi Arabia and other Muslim countries." Why don't the militants target these Arabs and Americans? And is suicide bombing in accordance with the Islamic sharia? "If they give you and me a satisfactory answer, I will not stop you from blowing yourself up," Mansoor quoted his father as saying.

When the boy wavered a little, his father asked him to put these questions to his local teacher, who was a cleric at one of the mosques near Mirali, a town notorious for hosting foreigners. Mansoor traveled up to Mirali and put the questions to him. A little embarrassed, the teacher rang up al-Qahtani (he was fluent in Arabic) and informed him of Mansoor's dilemma.

That is when al-Qahtani said, "We receive funds from Arab countries, therefore, we cannot carry out any attack there, and if we commit any wrong there, they will stop supply of funds to us. But jihad in Pakistan and Afghanistan is lawful and even the Saudis believe so."

Mansoor returned home after spending another few hours with the teacher, still undecided and confused. Once he sat down with his father, the fog of confusion disappeared but his fear of the consequences of walking out of Al Qaeda made him shudder, he said.

His father eventually went to his teacher and managed to convince him that Mansoor was not firm anymore and could back out at the last moment of a suicide mission. The cleric somehow relented and allowed Abdul Ghani Khan to take his son back on condition that they leave the village. The family eventually moved to Bannu, a populous district of the NWFP that borders North Waziristan.[11]

## The Making of a Suicide Bomber

The ranks of suicide bombers swelled significantly after the September 6, 2006, peace agreement in North Waziristan, which bound local tribal elders to disallow the cross-border movement of militants to and from Afghanistan. The deal provided all shades of Taliban in North Waziristan with an opportunity to recuperate from their losses at the hands of the military in the preceding months, and to reorganize and enlist new recruits for their battle and suicide squads. The militants got breathing space and their fears of being hunted by the military diminished, at least for the time being. Many disguised militants also received compensation for damages to their property during the military operation.

Residents of Miranshah, Makeen, Wana, Shawal, and several other villages and hamlets in Waziristan often speak without condemnation, sometimes even with pride, of camps that motivate youngsters into blowing themselves up in the name of God and Islam. "The TTP and other outfits prey on youngsters and isolate them instantly if they find them fit for their mission," said Ehsan Khan Daur from Mirali. The would-be bombers are brainwashed to the extent that they begin to dream of the "glorious life afterward." They are prepared like grooms before the wedding ceremony, and emotionally "motivated" in such a way that most of these boys rarely bother to think twice before putting on the locally improvised explosives-laden jackets that they explode at the chosen site.

Enthusiastic teenagers are usually recruited from mosques or seminaries, where jihadis hunt for potential bombers. They are moved from safe house to safe house and receive various forms of training. Bombers, for example, are taught to duck their heads when they pull the switch so their head is blown apart and is unrecognizable. Meanwhile separate teams choose the next targets in Afghanistan—a job done jointly by the Taliban and Al Qaeda; the former provide the manpower and the latter the explosives training, teaching young jihadis how to pack them either in a jacket meant for a suicide mission or a vehicle for a strike on a bigger and politically critical target.

"If we kill Americans through suicide bombing, America will not become Muslim. If we kill Pakistanis through suicide bombing, Pakistan will become a more strict adherent of Islam." This, according to Khaled Ahmed, a Pakistani expert on Islamic militancy, is the thought process that "seems to be the driving force behind Al Qaeda's suicide bombing campaign."

Government investigators claim almost all the suicide bombers in Pakistan are young men in their teens or twenties. Sources within the ranks of the Islamic militants corroborate this, proudly saying that youngsters have responded most enthusiastically to the call to fight against the enemies of Islam.[12] Rehman Wazir, a resident of Wana, recalled how some youngsters from his village spent a few weeks at one of the camps run by Qari Hussain. "When they returned home, they were changed people, dreaming only of paradise," Wazir said. They had been assigned numbers and were told to wait for their turn, he said.[13]

Intelligence officials in Peshawar told me about Adnash Gul, a twenty-three-year-old who was intercepted in Dera Ismail Khan, one of the largest cities in the NWFP. Carrying a vest strapped with fifteen kilograms of explosives, Gul told interrogators he studied at a madrassa in Miranshah and was supposed to hand over the explosives-laden jacket to a man in Dera Ismail Khan.

Lack of basic facilities, a poor education infrastructure, and dismal employment opportunities make the tribal areas an ideal hunting ground for Islamic militants seeking young warriors. And they reap a rich harvest of teenagers, pumped with zeal for jihad.

## Does Islam Permit Suicide Bombings?

In April 2007 I wrote a couple of special reports for the weekly *Friday Times* on whether suicide bombing is permissible in Islam. I spoke with several religious leaders and scholars, whose responses were wrapped in "ifs and buts," rather than a straight appreciation or condemnation of suicide bombings. The following responses are insightful.

Qazi Hussein Ahmed, the mercurial chief of the Jamaate Islami, was reluctant to speak on the issue "because of its technicality." Munawar Hassan, the party secretary general and a fiery orator and demagogue, however, agreed to speak on behalf of the party.

"Pakistan supported infidels who carried out bombings on Bajaur and elsewhere. . . . General Musharraf and infidels are allies and that is why they are facing similar reaction. Why are they supporting infidels? Why are they providing logistic support to them against the Taliban?" Hassan asked. However, he had little to say on whether the wrongdoings of leaders justified the murder of common people.

It merits mention that Mufti Nizamuddin Shamzai, the late spiritual mentor of the famous Binori Mosque and seminary in Karachi, decreed in 1998 that killing Americans was justified. Lashkar-e-Taiba issued a similar proclamation soon after. This outfit had in fact launched a number of suicide attacks in the summer of 1998 in Indian Kashmir as a ploy to pressure the Indian government into retreat.

The ex-LeT chief Hafiz Saeed, put under house arrest on December 10, 2008, in the aftermath of the terror attacks in Mumbai, used to take pride in patronizing suicide squads for Kashmir. But talking to a private television channel on February 24, 2007, he said, "Killing innocent people is not permissible in Islam." This was a departure from the approach he and his colleagues had devised and implemented, because suicide attacks were at the heart of the LeT campaign in Kashmir.

Maulana Sami ul-Haq, former senator and chief of Darul Uloom Haqqania, a notorious seminary about one hundred kilometers northwest of Islamabad, said, "They will kill me if I dare to issue a decree against suicide bombings." But then he went on to rant in the typical conservative way. "It is a reaction to what has been going on worldwide," he said. "An international coalition is conspiring to suppress those who are fighting for their identity and freedom." He likened suicide bombers to a legitimate tactic of war. Haq's seminary shot to international prominence for its role in the Afghan jihad as well as its connections to Afghan Taliban leaders, many of whom had graduated from his school. As a self-proclaimed mentor, Maulana Haq would brag about his students' zeal and devotion to the cause of the Afghan Taliban and playfully evade direct questions to impress visitors. (Whenever questioned about the source of his funding he would quip, "There are multiple sources; after all, we are doing service to a national cause.")

Allama Sajid Ali Naqvi, the mysterious head of the now defunct Shia religio-political party Tehreek-e-Jafria Pakistan, which is suspected of promoting the Iranian brand of militant Islam, candidly considered the question and ended up with the same conclusion: "Generally, killing others by blowing one's self up is prohibited in Islam, but in particular circumstances you can't condemn such an act." Referring to a spate of suicide bombings that had erupted in Pakistan since mid-January 2007, Naqvi said, "Those attacks which are being carried out on a sectarian basis or against innocent people are completely un-Islamic, Islam doesn't permit them. But if these are carried out to achieve major goals, for instance, to defeat evil powers or their puppets, then one can't oppose it straightaway."

Hafiz Hussain Ahmed, a former member of parliament who once was the most vocal leader of the Sunni Deobandi Jamiat Ulema-e-Islam (JUI) of Maulana Fazlurrehman, was equally ambiguous. "No doubt, such strikes are condemned in any religion but instead of debating their legitimacy, we ought to look into the causes which force somebody, particularly youth, to end his life for such an act," he said, sounding like a pragmatic politician. Like General Pervez Musharraf, Ahmed is quick to enumerate the causes that he believes underlie anti-U.S. emotion in the Islamic world: "The situation in Palestine, Kashmir, Afghanistan, and Iraq does not let you issue a decree against such actions. . . . We have been saying that Pakistan's coalition with U.S.-led war on terror brought this menace in the country and that is why they must review their policy."

Mufti Muneebur Rehman is considered a moderate and liberal religious scholar and frequently appears on national television channels. Asked for an opinion on the legitimacy of suicide bombings, Rehman said, "The unlawful murder of any person is forbidden in Islam, whether it is a suicide attack or simple killing." Unlike others, he offered no caveat for this verdict.

"There is no word for suicide bombing in sharia. It is just unlawful killing that is forbidden," he said. "And would those who describe these attacks as a reaction to the turmoil in Waziristan tell us what was the sin of those clerics and people who were killed in the congregation of Nishtar Park [in Karachi in 2006] or elsewhere in similar attacks? Were these victims responsible for ordering the military operation in the tribal areas?"

Hanif Jalandari, chief of the Multan-based Wifaqul-Madaris (the central directorate for Deobandi seminaries), who lords over about 7,500 seminaries across the country, did not mince his words: "Islam doesn't permit any Muslim to attack another Muslim or those non-

Muslims living in a Muslim country. Recent suicide bombings in Pakistan are unlawful. It is not just the killing of a Muslim which is a sin, it is also a sin if one considers it legal, that is, sanctioned by Islam. It is an un-Islamic act and, according to Islamic scholars, such a man is not a Muslim."

Though suicide bombers kept striking at public places and targeted army and government officials in big numbers throughout 2007 and 2008 (with more than 106 attacks altogether), none of the mainstream religious leaders condemned them. Only Maulana Hassan Jan openly opposed suicide attacks. Jan, who had taught sharia law in Saudi Arabia and was an influential figure among Taliban leaders, issued fatwas (religious decrees), calling suicide bombings "un-Islamic." Most probably to punish him for his opposition to what most militant groups justify as a legitimate tactic, he was shot dead on September 15, 2007. Three people had asked him to accompany them to officiate at a wedding, but when he joined them, they shot him in the evening on the outskirts of Peshawar.

Against this backdrop, several religious scholars and clerics from twenty-eight religious groups gathered on October 14, 2008, at a conference in Lahore to discuss the issue of suicide bombings. The low-key Muttahida Ulema Council of Pakistan organized the meeting at the Jamia Naeemia madrassa in Lahore. At the end of the talks, the council came up with a decree, which was part of a twenty-one-point declaration. Point 13 of the declaration said: "It is the Ulemas' fatwa by consensus that suicide attacks inside Pakistan are haram [forbidden in Islam] and illegitimate." Taken at face value, the decree implies that such attacks are forbidden in Pakistan and permissible in other countries. When asked, none of the scholars offered any explanation as to why they specified that Pakistan was the only forbidden territory.

In a bitter stroke of irony, the head of Jamia Naeemia, Mufti Sarfraz Naeemi, was killed along with at least eight others when a suicide bomber struck his mosque after Friday prayers on June 12, 2009. Naeemi, sixty-one, was a liberal scholar who had taken the lead in denouncing suicide bombings. A moderate cleric of the Barelvi branch of Islam and an outspoken critic of the Pakistani Taliban, Naeemi had told Reuters a few weeks before his death, "The military must eliminate the Taliban once and for all, otherwise the Taliban will capture the entire country, which would be a catastrophe."

In a rare show of courage and unity, on December 19, 2009, dozens of religious scholars and clerics gathered in Islamabad to declare suicide attacks as un-Islamic and forbidden in Islam. In what appeared to be the first conscious move by the Ministry of Religious Affairs to try to rein in the spread of violent militancy, the participants reminded the assembled crowed that the Holy Quran forbids the killing of innocent people. "The sharia introduced by the Prophet Muhammad is complete and adequate for us and we do not need anything more. People committing terrorist acts and plotting or carrying out suicide attacks are not Muslims and are being used by our enemies to destabilize Pakistan," said the scholars, drawn from various parts of the country.

Hamid Saeed Kazmi, the minister for religious affairs, who himself survived an assassination attempt, said on the occasion that those attacking mosques and educational institutions could never be called Muslims because Islam does not permit such acts. Kazmi was referring to a December 4 attack allegedly by a splinter of Lashkar-e-Taiba on a mosque located in a high-security zone of Rawalpindi, where Pakistan's military establishment is headquartered. Armed forces personnel, both serving and retired, gather for prayers at the Parade Lane Mosque, as it is known, in great numbers on Fridays. The attack left forty-five people dead, including a serving major general, two of his sons, and four other brigadier- and colonel-ranked officers; a former chief of general staff, General Mohammad Yousaf, was also among the victims.

Despite its good intentions, the entire exercise meant little in concrete terms. At this point no religious decree or legal order will deter militants from executing their mission.

# 11

# The ISI Factor

The Inter-Services Intelligence, Pakistan's powerful spy service, has remained in the international spotlight since its significant expansion of power and prestige during the U.S.- and Saudi-funded anti-Soviet jihad in the 1980s, when it executed operations with the help of its proxies in Afghanistan. No state intelligence agency is as controversial. It is widely believed that the ISI conducts the covert war in Indian Kashmir and maintains ties with the Afghan Taliban. Many Pakistanis believe that the ISI watches them at all times and will punish them for stepping out of line, while the Indian and Afghan establishments hold the ISI responsible for the terrorist violence that takes place in their countries.

The ISI was founded in 1948 by a British army officer, Major General R. Cawthome, then deputy chief of staff in Pakistan's new army. Field Marshal Ayub Khan, the president of Pakistan in the 1950s, expanded its role as a counterintelligence agency. Since then its mandate has mushroomed. It is now tasked with collecting foreign and domestic intelligence; coordinating the intelligence functions of the three military services; surveillance over foreigners, the media, politically active segments of Pakistani society, diplomats accredited to Pakistan, and Pakistani diplomats serving outside the country; intercepting and monitoring communications; and conducting covert offensive operations.

The ISI's involvement in the anti-Soviet operation turned it into an overzealous organization that indulged in both domestic politics and foreign affairs. The triumph of that jihad encouraged them to try to repeat the experience of manipulating religious zeal to humiliate an overbearing power in the arena of Indian Kashmir. The muddle that followed the Red Army's departure from Afghanistan in February 1989 indelibly muddied the image of Pakistan, its army, and the ISI.

In time, the ISI would throw its weight behind the Taliban, hoping it would act as Pakistan's pliant satellite state in Afghanistan, and thus provide Pakistan the strategic depth it had long sought to its west in order to counter threats from the east. Pakistan's quest for political domination of Afghanistan gained momentum after Indian military intervention severed its eastern wing, turning East Pakistan into independent Bangladesh in 1971. The ISI has in fact been credited with creating and supporting the Taliban movement to realize the goal of securing strategic depth through a friendly government in Afghanistan.

## The Taliban Connection

The ISI receives flak from all over the world on two counts: its support for the postmujahideen militia in Afghanistan—the Taliban—and its close links with Muslim separatists in the Himalayan state of Kashmir. Let us first see how Pakistan responded to the emergence of the Taliban.

In 1993, when Benazir Bhutto returned to power for a second time and made Naseerullah Babar the home minister, Babar visited Herat to meet with Ismail Khan, the independent Tajik warlord supporting Ahmed Shah Massoud, and went to Kandahar to meet with the emerging Taliban and other warlords to discuss with them an end to war and the rehabilitation of the highways into Central Asia.[1]

Babar followed up by sending a convoy of trucks loaded with medicines through the Pakistan border post of Chaman, aiming to continue to the Afghan cities of Kandahar and Herat en route to Turkmenistan. He kept insisting that since Benazir Bhutto was on her way to the Turkmen capital, Ashkabad, he wanted the way clear for goods as well as a diplomatic convoy to show the world that the road was open.

"We thought that if this route was open to the Central Asian republics, they would be able to get their economic independence after depending on Russia for more than seventy years," Babar said of the rationale behind the caravan.

The convoy was dispatched against the advice of the foreign office and intelligence officials who had been warned by the Taliban leader Mulla Mohammad Omar to expect trouble from the warlords. "I met Omar in the second half of October at Spin Boldak, where he advised me not to bring the convoy because the situation was not fully under control," said a former ISI colonel. Predictably, the trucks were stopped right on the border by some rogue commanders of Professor Rasool Sayyaf, one of the seven key mujahideen leaders.

"We put pressure on Sayyaf, whose people had intercepted our convoy. I put all his family at Jalozai and let him know that they had to get the caravan released," Babar said. Jalozai is a deserted area near Peshawar that became infamous in 2001 for extremely poor standards of living when Afghans fleeing drought and hunger settled in the spot in late 2000.

The colonel returned to Mulla Omar for help and was advised to get safe passage guarantees from Afghan leaders whose commanders had erected at least forty checkpoints between Spin Boldak, the Afghan frontier town, and Kandahar. It took three days, and then the convoy moved from Chaman.

That was when regular contacts between the Taliban and the ISI were established. Until then, the ISI had bothered little about southern Afghanistan. Because southern Afghanistan traditionally had been promonarchy, and was not the hotbed of "jihad" against the Soviets, Pakistan never really devised a strategy for this region. That is why the Taliban emergence came as a surprise.

Contacts with the Taliban grew as its fighters took one province after the other, and swiftly moved north toward the capital. Once the Taliban entrenched themselves in Kandahar in late 1994 and looked set to storm past the opposition, the Pakistani establishment decided to extend whatever support it could to the new "hope" for Afghanistan. Islamabad saw it as a chance to ensure a friendly government in Afghanistan.

The first quarter of 1995 saw an influx of ISI and Pakistan army officials on a variety of missions. By 2000, the ISI presence in Kandahar had grown to about half a dozen officers, with a string of local informers, including officials of Mulla Omar's secretariat and his Ministry of Foreign Affairs.

In February 1995, while on an assignment to cover the then "mysterious" movement and its leaders in their bastion of Kandahar, I saw several plainclothes Pakistan army officers cross the border, starting from Spin Boldak and making their way to Kandahar. One could easily distinguish these officers from the rugged Afghans; their gait, appearance, and overall demeanor were visibly different.

Led by Naseerullah Babar and inspired by the "access-to-Central-Asia" vision of Foreign Minister Sardar Assef Ahmed Ali, the Pakistani establishment rushed to extend whatever support it could to the Taliban. This was Benazir Bhutto's second government, the Soviet Union had been shattered, and with the emergence of the ethnic Pashtoon Taliban, Pakistan's civilian and military establishment thought the time for reaching out to resource-rich Central Asia had perhaps arrived. A friendly and peaceful Afghanistan offered the shortest access route to Turkmenistan's Daulatabad oil and gas fields. Hence Pakistan's eagerness to explore and exploit possibilities of establishing contacts with Central Asia via Afghanistan.

## Nation Building in Afghanistan

One of the major things Babar did was revive the Afghan Trade and Development Cell (ATDC) at the Ministry of Foreign Affairs in Islamabad. The initial annual funding for the cell amounted to Rs 300 million, which by 2001 had shrunk to a paltry Rs 40 million.

Babar also ordered several practical steps to help the Taliban rehabilitate its tattered infrastructure. Engineers from Pakistan's Water and Power Development Authority (WAPDA) were sent to Herat, Kabul, and Jalalabad to repair and make operable the power stations. Experts from the telecommunications department were sent across into Taliban-controlled areas and provided with a high-frequency telephone system accessible through code numbers for the Pakistani cities of Peshawar, Quetta, and Islamabad. They also helped restore the internal phone network.

Aviation experts from Pakistan were supposed to upgrade some of the Afghan airports for international flights, and its engineers did carry out some work at the Kandahar airport. The National Bank of Pakistan and the Utility Stores Corporation were to open branches in Afghanistan. The Ministry of Foreign Affairs set up the Afghan Trade and Development Cell that was responsible for all bilateral financial and development matters.

In all, by summer 2001, Pakistan had provided more than a hundred high-frequency phone lines to Afghanistan. Kabul, Jalalabad, Mazar-e-Sharif, Kandahar, and Herat were all accessible through the Pakistani phone network. More than 60 percent of the connections were with the Taliban's ministry of foreign affairs, aviation, and the core leadership, including Mulla Omar. Pakistani officials in Afghanistan told me that plans were afoot to increase connections to 1,500 to improve communication.

In Kabul I was told that at least five connections were with the embassy of Pakistan, at least twenty-five with the Taliban government departments and ministries, the official Bakhtar news agency, and Ariana Airlines. In Kandahar at least four lines were serving Pakistani diplomats, and a minimum of fourteen were at the disposal of Taliban leaders and ministers. Out of the five connections in the western town of Herat reached from Islamabad as local numbers, the governor, the mayor, and the corps commander shared one number each and two were with Pakistani diplomats.

The lines from Peshawar connected Kabul and Jalalabad through a radio satellite high-frequency system with Pakistan and the rest of the world through the old Afghan telecommunication network Mukhabirat. A high-power satellite booster with solar batteries atop the Lattaband Pass between Jalalabad and Kabul was also installed to ensure better communication.

Residents in Kabul, Jalalabad, and Kandahar had interesting stories to tell about the users of these phone lines. Many Taliban leaders/ministers who had Pakistani phone connections used them as public call offices after office hours as an additional source of income. "That is why their bills are running into tens of thousands of rupees, which they pay very regularly," a Pakistan Telecom official said during a chance meeting in Kabul in early 2001, pointing to the heavy bills the connections in Afghanistan were running.

"They are also charging ten Pakistan rupees a minute for incoming calls from Europe and the Gulf, where thousands of Afghans have either found refuge or are working and call up their relatives in these big towns," said a Pakistani diplomat posted in Afghanistan for many years.

The September 1999 analysis by the Defense Intelligence Agency contains quite a damning account of Pakistan's role as the real host of Bin Laden and his Al Qaeda members in Afghanistan. It says Bin Laden's Al Qaeda network was able to expand under the safe sanctuary extended by the Taliban following Pakistan directives. If there is any doubt on that issue, consider the location of Bin Laden's camp Zahawa targeted by U.S. cruise missiles in August 1998. Positioned on the border between Afghanistan and Pakistan (in Paktia province of Afghanistan) it was built by Pakistani contractors, funded by Pakistan's Inter-Services Intelligence (ISI) directorate, and protected under the patronage of a local and influential tribal leader, Jalaluddin Haqqani. However, the real host in that facility was the Pakistan ISI.[2]

Human Rights Watch (HRW) conducted an examination of their own into Islamabad's military assistance to the Taliban. "In April and May 2001, HRW sources reported that as many as thirty trucks a day were crossing the Pakistan border," it concluded. "Sources inside Afghanistan reported that some of these convoys were carrying artillery shells, tank rounds, and rocket-propelled grenades. Such deliveries are in direct violation of UN sanctions. Pakistani land mines have been found in Afghanistan; they include both antipersonnel and antivehicle mines. Pakistan's army and intelligence services, principally the Inter-Services Intelligence Directorate (ISI), contribute to making the Taliban a highly effective military force. While these Pakistani agencies do not direct the policies of the IEA (Islamic Emirate of Afghanistan), senior Pakistani military and intelligence officers help plan and execute major military operations. In addition, private-sector actors in Pakistan provide financial assistance to the Taliban."[3]

Sources for this part of the report were a 1997 UN secretary-general's report, as well as an unnamed military expert with experience in Afghanistan. Part of it was based on what Anthony Davis had been reporting for *Jane's Intelligence Review* (JIR). Interestingly, Davis wrote in one of his JIR 2001 reports that there was no "incriminating evidence available on the Pakistan military's involvement with the Taliban." In its comment on the "presence of Pakistani military advisers performing command and control functions for the Taliban offensive prior to and following the fall of Mazar-i-Sharif in August 1998," the HRW relied for confirmation on an e-mail communication in September 1998 with a Pakistani source.

The HRW also relied on interviews with Western diplomatic sources and military experts, and with journalists and other observers in the region in 1999 and 2000. HRW spoke with a Taliban official in Kabul in 2000 who confirmed that senior Pakistan army and intelligence officers were involved in planning Taliban offensives. All these sources requested anonymity.

Pakistan was also helping the Afghans to rehabilitate their agricultural sector. One prime example is the Ghaziabad farm outside the eastern town of Jalalabad, where lack of care, water, and fertilizer had left the vast olive, almond, and orange orchards barren.

"We provided them with seven hundred thousand olive plants, and are also training their farmers and agronomists at a couple of places in Peshawar," Arif Ayub, the Pakistani ambassador, told me during an interview in summer 2001 at his embassy office in Kabul. He said agricultural training was given to the Afghans to rehabilitate these orchards, and the results of this training had been very encouraging. They were also doing road repairs. Interestingly, Ayub was the first Pakistani diplomat who refused to grow a beard before or after arrival in Kabul; almost all other diplomats and support staff grew beards to avoid trouble from the Taliban.

"Agriculture is one innocent sector in which we believe we can and should help the Afghans," said another Pakistani diplomat, adding that the Afghans had flooded the Pakistani mission with requests for training and guidance in the agricultural sector. But with Pakistan itself facing financial problems, the budget of the country's foreign ministry allocated for Afghanistan during the 2000–2001 fiscal year was less than $700,000.

## The ISI Rules the Roost

At the height of their interaction with the Taliban regime, ISI functionaries and the army representatives posted inside Afghanistan had greater access to the Taliban nucleus of power than the civilian diplomats.

"We have had to wait for weeks to get an audience with Mulla Omar or his closest aides but the army people get the appointments instantly," said one of the Pakistani diplomats posted in Kandahar. He was wary of the fact that the Pakistan army officers would sometimes hold meetings with the Taliban leadership on their own, without taking the senior-most civilian diplomats like the consul general in Kandahar and the ambassador in Kabul into confidence.[4]

"ISI officials always excluded civilians from their meetings with Afghans. On several occasions we came to know about their meetings only afterward," said one of the senior-most diplomats posted in Kandahar during the Taliban rule.

Those were days when ISI functionaries, particularly those posted there, considered Afghanistan a crucial hotbed for militants fighting in Kashmir. Major militant groups—Lashkar-e-Taiba, Jaish-e-Mohammad, and Harkatul Mujahideen—ran their training facilities in the Taliban-controlled areas. They all enjoyed unusual access to the Taliban power centers as well as to Pakistani ISI officials. I recall an interesting exchange of arguments with one of the military officials posted in Kandahar in early 2001; once he ran out of arguments in support of Pakistan's Taliban policy, the officer said, "We also have to think of the struggle in Kashmir." This, in a way, was an indirect admission that because the Taliban was taking care of the militants active in Kashmir, Pakistan would have to live with them.

Senior intelligence officials used to stick their necks out by regularly visiting the Taliban stronghold of Kandahar. One of the officials, Faiz Jeelani, a major general, would fly to Chaman in a helicopter and then be picked up by the Taliban on the way to Kandahar, where the ISI had taken over the consular section in the summer of 2001, a Taliban official told me at his Kandahar residence in March 2001. Tayyab Agha and one Mulla Ahmedi from Ghazni, both trusted aides of Mulla Omar, would attend most of the meetings, along with the Kandahar governor Mulla Hassan Rehman and the deputy defense minister Mulla Akhtar Usmani. Not many civilian officials would even come to know about these consultations.

After a meeting that Moinuddin Haider, Pakistan's interior minister, had with Mulla Omar in March 2001, one of Omar's aides took a Pakistani intelligence official aside and asked, "Does he really know what he is talking about? He is clueless about what is going on." The aide did not elaborate but the incident underlines the close links that existed between the Pakistan army officials and the Taliban. It also reveals that the military and intelligence community kept civilian diplomats out of their dealings with the Taliban leadership. Whether the latter ever listened to Pakistan is questionable because, as one diplomat put it, "most Pakistanis were seen as untrustworthy partners who could betray the Taliban whenever the crunch came." Some intelligence officers would become loyal to a fault.

Colonel Sultan Ameer Imam, a former ISI officer involved with the Afghan mujahideen ever since Pakistan agreed to play host and teacher to the Muslim resistance on the instance of the CIA, briefly trained Mulla Omar as a young mujahid in the mid-1980s near Quetta, the capital of Pakistan's southwestern Balochistan province. Following his retirement from the army, Imam, who one Pakistan foreign secretary described as an "asset for his long involvement in Afghanistan and tremendous rapport with scores of Afghans," served as the consul general in Herat until the fall of the Taliban.

According to officials at one of the border posts in Balochistan,

Imam visited Afghanistan in the second week of October 2001, just a couple of days after the American and British planes had launched Operation Enduring Freedom. It was a time when no Pakistani official was supposed to enter Afghanistan because all the diplomatic staff had been recalled after General Musharraf broke off relations with the Taliban on September 19, 2001, and pledged unconditional support to the U.S.-led war on terror. Imam later told me at his apartment in Rawalpindi that he went on a private visit, just to gauge the situation. He denied that his visit had anything to do with the ISI or any other government agency.

## The Kashmir Connection

Complaints about the ISI have not been restricted to Afghanistan; Kashmiri militants have no qualms in talking about the extent of ISI's influence and support. Driven by the desire to free Kashmir from Indian rule, these jihadis took Pakistan army officers at their word: for god-fearing, staunch, and practicing Muslims. "I was really disappointed to know that the officer who used to sermonize us on the Quran and the teachings of Islam and criticized the West had TV sets and music systems at home," said a militant of an ISI officer who had good rapport with his organization.[5]

During a visit to the ISI headquarters in the mid-1990s as prime minister, Benazir Bhutto was given a presentation by the Kashmir cell on how the mujahideen were being trained and infiltrated into Indian Kashmir.[6] "Are we really doing this?" asked a baffled Bhutto, who until then had parroted what the Ministry of Foreign Affairs would tell her—that Pakistan was only extending political, moral, and diplomatic support to Kashmiris.

Bruce Riedel, then an aide to President Bill Clinton, gave a detailed account of how distraught and wary Nawaz Sharif appeared when he went to Washington on July 4, 1999, to seek the president's help in diffusing an alarming situation that had arisen out of the Pakistan army's occupation of certain peaks in the Kargil sector of Kashmir.[7] The army and the ISI kept the civilian government out of the loop as it planned on an ambitious assault into Indian-controlled land in Kashmir.

The Kargil conflict took place between May and July 1999 in the Kargil district of Kashmir and elsewhere along the Line of Control (LOC), the 520-kilometer border that divides Kashmir between India and Pakistan. The infiltration was code-named Operation Badr. Its aim was to sever the link between Kashmir and Ladakh, the neighboring province in India, and cause Indian forces to withdraw from the Siachen Glacier, thus forcing India to negotiate a settlement of the broader Kashmir dispute that has dogged bilateral relations since both countries became independent of British colonial rule in 1947.

The Kargil war began when the Indian security forces found out that Pakistani soldiers and Kashmiri militants had occupied vintage positions on the Indian side of the LOC. During the initial stages of the war, Pakistan blamed the fighting entirely on independent Kashmiri insurgents, but documents left behind by casualties and later statements by Nawaz Sharif and his chief of army staff General Pervez Musharraf acknowledged involvement of Pakistani paramilitary forces. The Indian army, later supported by its air force, recaptured a majority of the positions on the Indian side of the LOC. With the help of international diplomatic mediation, the limited war came to an end. Pakistani forces withdrew from Indian positions but not before taking heavy casualties, which some army officials rank as high as six hundred soldiers.

One of the objectives of the Kargil incursion was to internationalize the Kashmir issue, by linking the crisis in Kargil to the larger Kashmir conflict but this attempt, vociferously protested by India, found few backers on the world stage. A tactically brilliant move turned out to be a strategic disaster, with not a single nation siding with Pakistan. The entire G8 and the European Union supported India and condemned Pakistan. China, a longtime ally of Pakistan, insisted that Pakistan pull its forces to the preconflict positions along the LOC and settle its border dispute peacefully.

Censured by the international community for violating the Line of

Control, Pakistan's prime minister, Nawaz Sharif, was compelled to sign a pullout agreement in Washington on July 4, 1999, in the presence of U.S. president Bill Clinton. Nawaz Sharif's army chief of staff, who had masterminded the Kargil incursion, was none other than General Pervez Musharraf. General Musharraf cited Sharif's decision to pull back from Kashmir and give in to international pressure as one of the reasons for his coup five months later.

Even in Pakistan, critics remember Kargil as a black spot in the country's history, mounted within weeks of Indian prime minister Atal Bihari Vajpayee's historic bus journey across the border into the city of Lahore in February 1999. The advance amounted to a massive breach of trust and permanently set back relations. For the first time, Pakistan received an international rebuke for violating the Line of Control accord, and the Clinton-Sharif statement permanently sanctified the LOC as a de facto border between the two countries. Pakistan's image nose-dived, and it was seen across the world as a pariah state using militants to serve its ends. The Kargil episode also sowed the seeds of disagreement between Nawaz Sharif and General Musharraf, who eventually deposed Sharif in a bloodless coup on October 12, 1999. This pushed the country into further international isolation. Its diplomats struggled to rehabilitate Pakistan's image but with a military dictator in power, they found little resonance internationally—until the 9/11 terror attacks shocked the world and overnight changed Pakistan's strategic importance. It was a boon for the despot Musharraf and began his reversal of fortune. From the adventurous head of a rogue army, he went on to become a crucial ally of President George W. Bush when he agreed to shun the Taliban and become part of the international coalition against terrorism.

While this realignment between Islamabad and Washington was under way, the ISI continued to maintain good working relations with the Kashmiri militant groups. The Indian government and security agencies began mobilizing tens of thousands of troops, amassing at least six strike corps close to the border. Pakistan responded in the same vein, bringing the two armies in an eyeball-to-eyeball conflict in January 2002.

Once again, the world watched with concern as the nuclear-armed neighbors indulged in saber-rattling, triggering fears of a war that could engulf the entire region, if not the world. As they were relying heavily on Pakistan for their operations in Afghanistan, British and U.S. diplomats once again sprang into action to de-escalate Indo-Pak tensions. Temperatures eventually cooled down in September, when both countries agreed to demobilize troops to their pre-January 2002 levels.

Under intense U.S. pressure, Musharraf banned six Kashmir-focused militant outfits, including Lashkar-e-Taiba and Jaish-e-Mohammad. Following the announcement, the authorities arrested more than two thousand activists of various militant groups, announced the seizing and freezing of their bank accounts, and sealed their camps. But their break with the ISI was not yet visible.

The ISI's Kashmir tactics suffered another blow when Christina Rocca, the U.S. assistant secretary of state for South Asia, visited Islamabad in May 2002, followed by Richard Armitage, the deputy secretary of state, both on a mission to pressure Pakistan into changing gears on its support for Kashmir. Rocca's visit coincided with the killing of more than three dozen Kashmiris in Srinagar, and before she arrived in Islamabad the ISI called up all the components of the United Jihad Council (UJC) for a briefing. "International pressure on us is becoming increasingly unbearable. You will have to halt the operations across the Line of Control," one of the participants recalled being told in a personal interview on the outskirts of Islamabad.

Indian bellicosity had raised the temperature and was the other reason a senior army officer gave the UJC members to slow down their movement. "Alarmed by the warning, we asked whether there was any change in the Kashmir policy. No, it is just a change of tactic for the next three months. We will see afterward," one of the Kashmiri militants quoted an officer as saying to reassure the entire Kashmiri militant leadership.[8] "We were told to hold back and wait for better times," the head of a Kashmiri outfit told me at his Rawalpindi residence later that year. As a result, the infiltration across the Line of Control significantly slowed down.

As General Musharraf responded positively to India's demand for "actions and not words" on the issue of infiltration, by mid-June in 2003, the cross-border movement dropped by three-fourths. Even the radio communication center near the world's second highest peak, K2, was cut off for fear of interception by American satellites and Indian surveillance. "We are really going to suffer this summer and fall as far as launching is concerned," an anxious militant in charge of operations for one outfit told me at his Islamabad seminary-cum-guesthouse.

## U.S. Suspicions and Accusations

The U.S. administration's suspicion and mistrust of the ISI is rooted in thirty-two documents that the U.S. Defense Intelligence Agency (DIA) of the Pentagon compiled in September 1999 and placed for public scrutiny in 2002, on the first anniversary of the September 11 attacks. These documents clearly show that the U.S. State Department and the DIA knew of the role of the ISI in sponsorsing not only the Taliban but also Al Qaeda.[9]

After General Musharraf seized power on October 12, 1999, the documents say, the presence of Pakistani intelligence in Taliban-controlled territory increased, and Afghanistan became a veritable Pakistani colony, facilitated by the past ties of many Taliban mullahs with Pakistan's military-intelligence establishment. Yet the Bush administration chose to close its eyes to the complicity of Pakistan and projected General Musharraf to the international community as a frontline ally in the war against terrorism.

Relentless American pressure in 2003–4 forced President Pervez Musharraf to demobilize most Kashmiri militant outfits, order the closure of many camps, and restrict them from carrying out operations on the other side of the Line of Control, the de facto border between India and Pakistan in Kashmir.

Since becoming an essential element of the international antiterror war, the ISI has undergone quite a transformation: It stopped funding the operations of groups battling Indian forces in Kashmir and curtailed its tentacles in Afghanistan. Out of strategic considerations, the organization maintains contacts with the Kashmiri outfits, but most of the Afghan-related officers now interact with the FBI. Even retired ISI officers are working for the U.S.-agencies. Yet suspicion abounds that within the ISI several elements are still maintaining contacts with the Haqqanis, Mulla Omar, Hekmetyar, and several Pakistani militant outfits.

The spotlight fell on the ISI again after the deadly attack on the Indian embassy in Kabul in July 2008 and the November 26 terror attacks in Mumbai, which the Indian authorities claimed were carried out with the consent of the ISI. On July 30, 2008, the *New York Times* published a piece during Prime Minister Yousuf Raza Gilani's Washington visit that linked the agency with Al Qaeda-affiliated groups operating in the border regions. Only two days earlier, President Bush and Gilani had exchanged vows to cooperate in the war on terror, but the *Times* dropped a bombshell on the entire entourage, greatly dampening the spirit of the visit.

The report said some CIA officials had traveled secretly to Islamabad on July 12 and presented evidence to Pakistan's most senior officials showing that members of the ISI had deepened their ties with some militant groups operating in FATA that were responsible for a surge of violence in Afghanistan, possibly including the suicide bombing earlier that month of the Indian embassy in Kabul, which killed forty-one people.[10] "The decision to confront Pakistan with what the officials described as a new C.I.A. assessment of the spy service's activities seemed to be the bluntest American warning to Pakistan since shortly after the Sept. 11 attacks about the ties between the spy service and Islamic militants. The C.I.A. assessment specifically points to links between members of the spy service, the Directorate for Inter-Services Intelligence, or ISI, and the militant network led by Maulvi Jalaluddin Haqqani, which American officials believe maintains close ties to senior figures of Al Qaeda in Pakistan's tribal areas," wrote the *New York Times*.

Two days later, Siraj Haqqani, the most active son of Jalaluddin

Haqqani, did some damage control. "I have nothing to do with the ISI," he said in a statement issued from somewhere in North Waziristan.[11] Sources in Peshawar, who are familiar with the jihadi leadership, claim that most of Hekmetyar's leaders and activists are quietly living in Peshawar. His family members have even attended weddings of relatives. "I would say that the intelligence agencies do know about these people but are probably keeping quiet as a policy of tolerance," a Pakistani journalist with close links to Hekmetyar's Hezb-e-Islami said, requesting anonymity.[12]

Prime Minister Gilani also denied the existence of any links between the ISI and the militants. In the aftermath of the September 11 attacks and especially since September 19, 2001, when Pervez Musharraf declared "unconditional support to the international coalition against terrorism," the CIA and the Federal Bureau of Investigation (FBI) have been heavily dependent on the human assets of the ISI for operations and surveillance in the war on terror.

Two days before Gilani's meeting with Bush in Washington, Lieutenant General Martin E. Dempsey, the acting commander of American CENTCOM forces in southwest Asia, visited Rawalpindi, headquarters of the Pakistan army, to discuss the situation in the tribal areas. General Dempsey also met with Pakistani commanders in Miranshah, where units of Pakistan's 11th Army Corps and the paramilitary Frontier Corps are headquartered, for discussions on the deteriorating security situation in the region. Even today, North Waziristan remains the focus of the U.S. and NATO forces because they consider it the hub of Al Qaeda and other foreign fighters. Pakistani troops and U.S. drones continue to target mosques and seminaries directly or indirectly associated with Al Qaeda.

According to a statement issued by the Inter-Services Public Relations (ISPR), Dempsey met with General Tariq Majeed, then chairman of the Joint Chiefs of Staff Committee, a largely ceremonial position, to convey his concerns. Majeed bluntly referred to the six missiles that the U.S. forces had lobbed into Azam Warsak, in South Waziristan, the same morning. The attack was the fourth in July.

As far as Pakistan's army was concerned, the "uninformed strikes" were not welcome at all. "Expressing concern over repeated cross-border missile attacks/artillery and mortar firing by coalition and Afghan forces, General Tariq Majeed said that 'our sovereignty and territorial integrity must be respected,'" the ISPR stated. It quoted Tariq as telling Dempsey, "Any violation in this regard could be detrimental to bilateral relations."[13]

"It was a very pointed message saying, 'Look, we know there's a connection, not just with Haqqani but also with other bad guys and ISI, and we think you could do more and we want you to do more about it,'" one senior American official said of Dempsey's message to Pakistan.[14] Al Qaeda was not specifically mentioned because evidence of the direct involvement of Al Qaeda in operations is scanty and because most attacks on U.S. and NATO targets inside eastern Afghanistan have been carried out by Haqqani's and Hekmetyar's militants. The *Los Angeles Times* quoted an American counterterrorism official as saying there were "genuine and longstanding concerns about Pakistan's ties to the Haqqani network, which of course has links to Al Qaeda."[15]

Six months earlier Mike McConnell, the director of national intelligence, and Michael V. Hayden, the CIA director, had made a similar trip to Islamabad, meeting with President Pervez Musharraf and other army officials to seek for the CIA and U.S. forces based across the border "greater latitude" to operate, particularly in the Waziristan region, which the U.S. military believes serves as the base for Taliban and Al Qaeda terrorists.[16]

Two days after its first bombshell, the *New York Times* published an even more damning report. This time it said American intelligence officers had conclusive proof that the ISI had helped plan the bombing of India's embassy in Kabul: "The conclusion was based on intercepted communications between Pakistani intelligence officers and militants who carried out the attack, the officials said, providing the clearest evidence to date that Pakistani intelligence officers are actively undermining American efforts to combat militants in the region."[17]

The *Times* also reported that there was new information showing that members of the Pakistani intelligence service were providing militants with details about the American campaign against them, in some cases allowing them to avoid missile strikes in Pakistan's tribal areas. Such reports embarrassed Pakistani leadership and amounted to a devastating public indictment of the ISI.

Pakistani government and military officials brushed aside the U.S. administration's allegations. "All elements sympathetic to Taliban and the likes of them have been shunted out and we stand committed to the war on terror," Major General Athar Abbas, head of ISPR, said.[18] Senior intelligence officials also put up a strong defense of their policy toward Pakistani and Afghan militants, explaining why it was in their interest to keep a door open to Haqqani, just as the British government kept up contact with some Taliban leaders in southern Afghanistan.[19]

In private conversations with Pakistani intelligence officials, I was told that the American claims about the telephone intercepts were based on circumstantial evidence. Suicide attacks are usually carried out in complete isolation of such communication, they said. Nobody would be so foolish as to leave such a clear trace of their involvement.

What is true is that Pakistan is deeply perturbed about India's growing ties to the Afghan government and its establishment of as many as five consular offices in the country, which it believes are being used as intelligence hubs. "The Indians set up one of these missions in Kandahar, just across the border, and that one is really driving the Pakistanis crazy," said a U.S. official on return from a fact-finding mission in South Asia. Pakistan security and intelligence officials suspect that the Indian embassy and its four consulates in Jalalabad, Kandahar, Mazar-i-Sharif, and Herat are being used to fuel and fund the insurgency in the tribal area and Balochistan, where Baloch nationalists are reportedly receiving aid from Indian sources.

The American visitors were told that the government of Pakistan had sought help from Taliban commanders such as Sirajuddin Haqqani for the release of its ambassador Tariq Azizuddin, kidnapped by Baitullah Mehsud's network in Afghanistan, after the Karzai administration failed to secure his release. (Azizuddin himself refused to divulge how his ninety-seven-day-long ordeal at Taliban hideouts in

Waziristan came to an end, yet he admitted several channels worked overtime to secure his release.[20]) It was pointed out that before opening new channels of communication with the Taliban in Helmand province in March, the British and NATO forces had been talking to leading Taliban leaders through Michael Semple, the acting head of the European Union mission to Afghanistan, and Mervyn Patterson, a senior UN official.[21] The Afghan government unceremoniously expelled both Semple and Patterson in January 2008 on charges of maintaining contacts with the Taliban and thereby undermining "the war on terror." The point was, if you can do it, why can't we?

In my discussions with Afghan president Hamid Karzai and his deputy interior minister, Abdul Iladi Hadi, in June 2008, their arguments were deeply embedded in the belief that the ISI was manipulating militants like Baitullah Mehsud and Fazlullah to destabilize Afghanistan.

Without naming the Pakistani military or the ISI, Karzai believes these organizations are still backing militants. "I don't hold the civilian government responsible but I just address the prime minister of Pakistan when I want to convey a message and I get the response to it when the prime minister speaks," Karzai said in an interview at his palace in Kabul.[22]

Interviews with locals and a survey by the Center for Research and Security Studies (CRSS) in April–May 2008[23] revealed that Muslim separatists were openly trained in Pakistan-administered Kashmir and FATA at least until March 15, 2004, when the Pakistan army lost dozens of soldiers and officers in a bloody encounter with the fighters of the Islamic Movement of Uzbekistan (IMU) at Sheen Warsak near Wana. This was the beginning of a very gradual break between the military and the militants.

Residents of the Waziristan region and other FATA areas identified Islamist militant groups such as Jaish-e-Mohammad (JEM), Harkatul Mujahideen, Lashkar-e-Taiba, and Lashkar-e-Jhangvi as beneficiaries of the military and ISI-led establishment's largesse. They believe that these outfits either ran their own complexes in FATA or depended on the hospitality and help of local Taliban and mujahideen groups. The perception is that intelligence agencies look the other way when local and Afghan Taliban and Al Qaeda operatives and leaders meet, move, or murder pro-government Pakistani and Afghan officials and tribesmen.

Certainly it is true that in the past the ISI has protected Al Qaeda operatives living in Pakistan. Ahmed al-Khadir, a close associate of Osama bin Laden, was wanted for the 1995 bombing of the Egyptian embassy in Islamabad. In the summer of 2001, after weeks of highly risky surveillance work, Egyptian investigators tracked down al-Khadir to a safe house in Peshawar. The Egyptians notified the ISI chief, General Mahmood Ahmed, who promised swift action.

"It was swift, but not in the way the Egyptians had expected," Time magazine reported on May 6, 2002. "That night last summer, the Pakistani security forces never turned up. Instead, a car with diplomatic plates full of Taliban roared up to the Peshawar house, grabbed al-Khadir, and drove him over the Khyber Pass to safety in Afghanistan—beyond the Egyptians' grasp. Put bluntly, the Pakistani spy agency . . . had betrayed the Egyptians." The next day, the ISI called up and said, "The man gave us the slip," a diplomat recalls. "It was a lie," Time magazine reported.[24]

In June 2008 the U.S. think tank RAND Corporation concluded in a report that Pakistani intelligence agents and paramilitary forces had helped train Taliban insurgents and had given them information about American troop movements in Afghanistan.[25] The study, Counterinsurgency in Afghanistan, found that some active and former officials in the ISI and the Frontier Corps provided direct assistance to Taliban militants and helped secure medical care for wounded fighters. It said NATO officials had uncovered several instances of Pakistani intelligence agents' providing information to Taliban fighters, even "tipping off Taliban forces about the location and movement of Afghan and coalition forces, which undermined several US and NATO anti-Taliban military operations." No time frames were given, though—an important in omission.

The study was funded by the U.S. Defense Department, and was apparently used as a reference during Prime Minister Gilani's U.S. visit. A statement by Ahmed Mukhtar, Pakistani defense minister, can be taken as confirmation of this. "The Americans told us that vital intelligence is leaked ahead of operations, and that people within the ISI do it on purpose," Mukhtar told the media after meetings with U.S. officials, including U.S. Defense Secretary Robert Gates. He vigorously denied the allegation and insisted that Pakistani intelligence agencies were fully cooperating with the United States and NATO.

"There are umpteen examples in the past where action has been taken against these insurgents, or, for that matter, foreigners," Pakistan military spokesman Major General Athar Abbas said in response to the RAND Corporation report. "Therefore, we reject this claim of sanctuary being aided by Pakistan's army or intelligence agencies."

The current Pakistani ambassador to the U.S., Husain Haqqani, has maintained in several articles and in his book *Pakistan: Between Mosque and Military*, written during his stay with American think tanks, that Pakistani military and intelligence services have for decades used religious parties as a convenient instrument to keep domestic political opponents at bay and for foreign policy adventures, such as the jihad in Afghanistan and the insurgency in Kashmir. "The religious parties provide them with recruits, personnel, cover and deniability. . . . They trained the people who are at the heart of it all, and they have done nothing to roll back their protégés," states Haqqani, who served rival governments in Pakistan in the 1990s.

Some Pakistanis will jokingly call Haqqani the American ambassador to Washington for his antimilitary pronouncements. His vocal support for the Kerry-Lugar Act, with its rebukes and benchmarks, made him unpopular at home. This may be one reason why he did not accompany Hillary Clinton on her visit to Pakistan in October 2009, a clear departure from tradition, as Pakistani ambassadors usually accompany high profile dignitaries on visits to their country.

The big challenge facing Pakistan is to convince the world that the ISI is safeguarding only the legitimate interests of the country. It will require a lot of persistence to prove that the ISI is working against, and not for, radical fundamentalist groups, which now pose a direct threat to Pakistani society.

"If the FBI and MI6 are here in the region to look after their interests how can the ISI remain oblivious to the situation in its neighborhood?" said General Talat Masood, a defense and political analyst. "It must get rid of the sympathizers and supporters of Al Qaeda and Taliban but it would fail in its duty if it left its job to foreigners."[26]

William Pfaff, a journalist for the *International Herald Tribune*, echoed this question in a recent article. "The American generals seem to be saying to Pakistan: You henceforth will ignore your own national security interests and devote yourself to our interests, whatever the cost to you. You will hand over all of the Taliban leaders and men in your country, and place your army under our strategic control. Otherwise we will bomb your cities," Pfaff wrote in an article on December 15, 2009, which was reproduced by Pakistan's *Daily Times*.

Why General Petraeus and Vice President Biden think this a good idea, as they do, reportedly, I cannot for the life of me tell you. I think it is a way to wreak further havoc in the region and do fundamental damage to the United States.

## Subversion in Bangladesh and the Mumbai Attack

The ISI has been linked by its detractors to violent struggles in Bangladesh, Sri Lanka, and Nepal. America's STRATFOR intelligence analysis service reported in April 2007 that "Pakistan is fuelling the growing Islamization in South Asia and had a strong nexus with Bangladesh intelligence agencies in laying a militant trap for India which is fighting a growing Maoist movement." The STRATFOR forecast, titled *India: The Islamization of the Northeast*, observed that instability in neighboring Bangladesh is giving foreign powers (China, Pakistan) an opportunity to exploit a whole range of secessionist movements to prevent India from emerging as a major global player.

The ISI, in cooperation with Bangladesh's Directorate General of Forces Intelligence (DGFI), appears to be investing a considerable amount of resources into solidifying India's militant corridor. There are growing indications, says the report, that these two agencies are working clandestinely in Bangladesh to bring all the insurgent outfits based in India's northeast together with insurgents in neighboring countries under one umbrella. "The ISI has facilitated cooperation between the United Liberation Front of Asom (ULFA) and other northeastern militant outfits with the Liberation Tigers of Tamil Eelam (LTTE) in Sri Lanka, Islamist militant groups in Kashmir, Islamist groups in Bangladesh and a growing number of Al Qaeda-linked jihadist groups operating in the region."[27]

The Indian government has continually blamed most acts of terrorism in Kashmir and elsewhere in India on the ISI. In early 2003, it promised in Parliament to present a white paper on the ISI's activities inside India, but it reversed the decision four years later, saying the move would jeopardize national security. Former Indian prime minister Atal Bihari Vajpayee openly spoke of the "nexus that exists between the ISI and Bangladesh," which, though denied by the Bangladesh government, kept reverberating in the media, vitiating the bilateral relationship.

On November 26, 2008, multiple bloody strikes, including on the Taj and Oberoi Trident hotels in Mumbai—eleven in all—once again shook the entire region. The three-day carnage was the work of several attackers who had traveled from the port city of Karachi in Pakistan. These acts of terror provided Indian officials and the media with another opportunity to point a finger at the ISI. The electronic media in India whipped up a frenzy that aroused fears of yet another war between the two now nuclear-armed nations.

Fortunately, India had voted out the ultranationalist BJP, and its new prime minister, the Congress Party's Manmohan Singh, decided to resist the cries for revenge. Despite the massive hue and cry accompanied by demands to teach Pakistan a lesson, better sense did eventually prevail. Singh joined the chorus for a while but then toned down his rhetoric, probably realizing that two nuclear-armed states can ill afford to engage in tit-for-tat retaliations that could easily spin out of control. Senior officials in Washington and London also kept urging New Delhi to resume talks.

Once again in the eye of the political storm, the ISI rejected allegations of links, and the Pakistani government offered to help its Indian counterpart get to the plotters. New Delhi immediately broke off relations and refused to resume talks until the culprits were brought to justice.

The culprits, in this case, were leaders of the outlawed Lashkar-e-Taiba, including its maverick chief Hafiz Saeed. Based on statements by Amir Ajmal Kasab, the lone survivor of the Mumbai attacks, the Indian authorities demanded the immediate arrest and punishment of Saeed and his commander, Ziaurrehman Lakhvi. Pakistani officials denied any link with the terrorist outfit and kept asking for evidence and access to Kasab.

Officials requesting anonymity told me in Islamabad that operatives working for a local ISI detachment in Karachi might have been aware of the LeT plan to attack Mumbai. But headquarters never knew of it. If this was indeed the case, it was a remarkably stupid move. Most probably nobody in the senior ranks of the ISI would have let the militant group go ahead with its planning in view of the already volatile relations with India and the raging insurgency inside Pakistan.

In September 2008, Richard Boucher, the U.S. assistant secretary of state, told Reuters that the ISI "needs reform but there is no indication of this happening yet." The Mumbai terror attacks two months later provided Boucher with another opportunity to publicly criticize the ISI. Indian leaders insisted that the Lashkar-e-Taiba terrorists involved in the attacks and their masterminds acted under ISI instructions. But he had little evidence to back up his claim beyond the assurance of Indian security officials. On numerous occasions, Prime Minister Manmohan Singh himself has spoken of a "thin line between the state and nonstate actors," when responding to the Pakistani position that the terror acts were perpetrated by nonstate actors.

Total denial in Islamabad was met by Indian insistence of the ISI's involvement. Throughout 2009, the saber rattling and trading of accusations continued. Prime Minister Singh kept up the pressure by asking for a definite move against LeT, one of the most vicious militant groups fighting the Indian forces in Kashmir. LeT was also blamed for the December 13, 2001, attack on the Indian parliament in New Delhi, which Indian leaders and officials believe was orchestrated by the Pakistan army.

The Indian view that the perpetrators of the Mumbai attacks had the support of Pakistan's state agencies is supported by the Afghan establishment and Pashtoon nationalists on both sides of the Durand Line, and this breeds suspicions and fuels resentment in both countries. The Indians and Afghans are paranoid about the role of the ISI in the region, which they see as the root cause of all evils. Sadly, things are not quite so simple.

When I put India's claim before General Kayani in September 2009, he briskly quipped: "We cannot outsource our national defense to private groups." On the same occasion, in an indirect reference to the involvement of the ISI with Kashmiri militant groups, he said, "It is a thing of the past, we cannot afford it anymore."

When he took over the top position at the ISI in October 2004, Kayani did try to clean the stables, opening the doors of the agency to the media (selectively), and firing and reshuffling officers whom he believed were a problem. The U.S. Army establishment lauded his efforts, and encouraged the general into more openness and greater coordination with its own spy network.

What is clear today—based on personal interviews with members of Kashmiri militant organizations—is the growing distance between the ISI and the field operations of these outfits. While old contacts with organizations such as Hezbul Mujahideen, Harkatul Mujahideen, and Lashkar-e-Taiba may be intact, the microscopic surveillance by the CIA and FBI, through an elaborate chain of contacts, restricts the ISI from conducting business the way it did until 2004. The Kaloosha operation served as a wake-up call to the military and intelligence establishment, and marked a turning point in their relations with militant outfits.

Most Kashmiri-focused militant leaders now live an extremely low-profile life either in Islamabad or Muzaffarabad, the capital of the Pakistani part of Kashmir. They usually avoid contacts with the media and most of their training camps now serve as shelters for hundreds of youthful fighters who were recruited all over Pakistan. Total disengagement would probably be difficult and dangerous. Abandoning tens of thousands of extremely motivated and brainwashed fighters could theoretically deliver many into the hands of the terrorist networks that are now rattling Pakistan with suicide bombings and attacks on the security establishment.

"We feel so handicapped and cut off now that the contacts [with the military establishment] are diminishing," the head of one of the Kashmiri organizations said to me when I asked about the nature and level of relations in the last six years or so. During a meeting that took place in November 2009 at a guesthouse in Islamabad, the bearded chief spoke of the difficulties his group was facing in keeping its boys (fighters) motivated while restraining them from crossing into Indian Kashmir. He complained about financial difficulties and said that the agency was not attending to them anymore.

The Indian army has largely confirmed the marked reduction in infiltration from Pakistan, probably explained through a decision by Islamabad to draw down the regular army in the parts of Kashmir under its control, replacing them with special police. A ministry of external affairs spokesman in New Delhi informed the press on December 18, 2009, that as many as thirty thousand troops (two divisions of infantry formations) had been pulled out of Kashmir, an indirect admission that the infiltration and threat level from Pakistan had receded.

### Rogue Elements: Is the ISI Still Supporting Terrorism?

The ISI has remained under close Indo-American scrutiny for nearly ten years. In October 2006, the Council on Foreign Relations quoted experts as saying that the ISI had supported a number of militant groups in the disputed Kashmir region, some of which were then on the State Department's foreign terrorist organizations list. Though the level of assistance to these groups has varied, Kathy Gannon, who covered the region for decades for the Associated Press, said that support in the past consisted of money, weapons, and training. A few weeks earlier, the BBC received a leaked copy of a report from the British Defense Academy, a think tank run by Britain's Ministry of Defense, which stated that "indirectly Pakistan (through the ISI) has been supporting terrorism and extremism—whether in London on 7/7, or in Afghanistan, or Iraq." Just days later, Mumbai's police chief claimed to have proof that the ISI had planned the July 11, 2006, bombing of the Indian city's commuter rail system, which was carried out by Lashkar-e-Taiba.

In a sort of rebuttal, a short-tempered President Musharraf underscored the importance of his nation's role: "Remember my words: if the ISI is not with you and Pakistan is not with you," he warned Americans, "you will lose in Afghanistan."[28] On October 1, in an appearance on NBC's *Meet the Press*, Musharraf acknowledged that some retired ISI operatives could be abetting the Taliban insurgency in Afghanistan, but he would not concede to any active involvement of current operatives. On several occasions, though, Musharraf admitted that ethnic, cultural, and ideological sympathies, and monetary motivations did play out in the field, on remote check posts where soldiers or officers sympathetic to Islamist militancy might look the other way when insurgents pass through for a cross-border operation or are on the run from U.S.-NATO forces.

Musharraf's anger was understandable. His help to the West had made him unpopular with his countrymen as well as a target of assassination attempts by Islamic militants, all of which had served to destabilize Pakistan. And now he was distrusted by the very Western powers he was helping. This was Musharraf's dilemma: neither his Western allies nor the radical Islamists trusted him. Hard-liners within the ISI, particularly those who had made their careers entirely within the agency and who had gone ideological as a result of their association with militant groups, smelled a rat. For them, cooperation with the United States amounted to selling Pakistan's soul to the devil. The man who had raised his fist at a public rally in Kashmir on February 5, 2000, to declare that "jihad runs in our blood" had undergone a partial transformation. Much before he gave up the presidency in August 2008 in the face of a united opposition, Musharraf had begun to distinguish between good and bad jihadis, branding the latter as "enemies of Islam and of mankind."

The Pakistan army's and the ISI's stock rose in 2003 as they gradually and reluctantly expanded their cooperation in the war on terror and turned over close to eight hundred Taliban and Al Qaeda operators, known or suspected. But this cooperation started souring, particularly after the U.S. invasion of Iraq, as the United States and its coalition partners increasingly accused the ISI of playing a double game by protecting the agents it had once cultivated.

While Musharraf and Kayani seem to have realized that salvation lay in cutting off support for militant groups, it was an uphill task to untie the knots within the command structure of the ISI. "A state within a state" is how most people allude to the agency, and rightly so; scores of officers and field operatives violated the mandate of their leadership and the instructions of their immediate superiors by extending direct or silent support to the very groups the ISI and CIA were jointly hunting down. "Rogue elements" is the term most often used for these dissenters within the organization. One by one they have been picked off and sent out to pasture, and gradually, the majority of officers appear to be coming around to the view that they need to change their perspective on Pakistan's national interest, shaped until recently by the concentration of half of the Indian military strike force along the border with Pakistan.

This doesn't mean that all of those inside and outside the agency who believe in an Indo-Israeli-American "axis of evil" conspiring against all Muslim countries have been rooted out or completely neutralized. This conspiracy theory appeals to millions of disgruntled Pakistanis, those who buy into what the ruling elite—politicians, landlords, generals, and industrialists—tell them to deflect their attention from pressing issues of governance, corruption, and service delivery, conveniently passing the buck and blaming external factors for the miseries of Pakistan. Scapegoatism has a long history in Pakistan and sadly fits into an insensitive ruling elite's scheme of things.

## A Bad Marriage: Cooperation with the CIA and FBI

The ISI has come a long way since its initial reluctance to cooperate with the United States and NATO in the immediate aftermath of 9/11. Under the new terms of cooperation with the United States in late 2001, General Musharraf was compelled to purge the ISI of its Islamic leanings. Still, many believe the changes were initially only skin deep. With the CIA/FBI gradually entrenching itself in various parts of Pakistan and actively collaborating with the Pakistani military and intelligence establishment, many within the Pakistani intelligence community began to feel insecure. By mid-2004, the Kashmir cell was officially wrapped up, the Afghan cell revamped, and many overzealous senior and midcareer operatives were sent into early retirement.

The terms of cooperation flowed from Pakistan's promise of "unconditional support" to the antiterror coalition. The CIA and FBI set up a number of electronic surveillance facilities to monitor telecommunications within Pakistan. The Capital Development Authority, Islamabad's municipal services institution, was asked to vacate a whole block located exactly in the rear of the ISI headquarters and the Americans moved in some time in early 2003, with the latest eavesdropping gadgetry. Scores of ISI officers were deputed to the CIA/FBI on a permanent basis and the rival agencies began to work together on at least five special task forces, set up in Islamabad and four provincial capitals, for special search-and-seize operations. The three agencies also formed new Joint Interrogation Teams known as JIT. These teams jointly interrogate Al Qaeda or Taliban militants, assisted by Pakistan's civilian Intelligence Bureau.

A former darling of the ISI, Colonel Sultan Ameer Imam was unofficially declared persona non grata, and state institutions were told to keep him at a distance. A few friends working at state-run think tanks told me how their superiors—under instructions from Musharraf's office—advised everybody to stay away from Imam and the likes of him. The colonel, who wears a saintly look with his long, hennaed beard, white turban, and loose white salwar kameez, was one of the

officers who had trained former mujahideen. Even the Taliban leader
Mulla Omar had gone through him, and this was one reason why
Colonel Imam was very close to the Taliban shura. Imam was serving
as Pakistan's consul general in the western Afghan city of Herat when
9/11 happened, and he along with other Pakistani diplomats were
asked to return home.

Agents of the purged ISI were quick to seize the killers of the *Wall
Street Journal* journalist Daniel Pearl, one of whom, Omar Saeed Sheikh,
was released from Indian jail in exchange for the freeing of passengers
hijacked on an Indian Airlines plane in December 1999. (Sheikh challenged his conviction and the case is still pending.) And in early April
2002 more than sixty Al Qaeda operatives were arrested in Faisalabad,
along with Abu Zubayda, Al Qaeda's third highest ranking member.[29]
But the accusations only grew, as did punitive actions by the coalition
forces in Afghanistan and in Pakistan's tribal areas.

Most CIA veterans agree that the relationship between the CIA
and the ISI is like a bad marriage, in which both sides have long
stopped trusting each other but would never think of breaking up
because they have become so mutually dependent.[30] Some former spies
even talk about the ISI with a mix of awe and professional jealousy.
But a web of competing interests complicates the relationship. "The
top American goal in the region is to shore up Afghanistan's government and security services to better fight the ISI's traditional proxies
(the Taliban and former mujahideen) there. Inside Pakistan, America's
primary interest is to dismantle a Taliban and Al Qaeda safe haven in
the mountainous tribal lands," wrote the *New York Times.*

The *Times* noted that even the ISI "has difficulties collecting information in the tribal lands, the home of fiercely independent Pashtun
tribes. For this reason, the ISI has long been forced to rely on Pashtun
tribal leaders—and in some cases Pashtun militants—as key informants. Given the natural disadvantages, C.I.A. officers try to get any
edge they can through technology, the one advantage they have over
local spies. The Pakistan government has long restricted the areas
where the C.I.A. can fly Predator surveillance drones inside Pakistan,
limiting paths to approved 'boxes' on a grid map."

## The Quetta Shura

The "Quetta shura" is the term used by those who wish to underscore that key Afghan Taliban leaders are using Quetta, the provincial capital of Balochistan, as their command and control headquarters for militant activities inside Afghanistan, with which Pakistan's southwestern province shares a 1,360-kilometer-long border. Pakistani authorities have been under pressure from the United States for quite some time to dismantle Taliban structures in Quetta. As late as December 2009, U.S. officials in Islamabad and Karachi openly talked about the presence of key militants in Quetta, saying that members of Al Qaeda could be a part of the "shura," or government, operating out of the city.

Quetta, surrounded by hills on three sides, is spread over 1,024.3 square miles. With a population close to eight hundred thousand, it is Pakistan's ninth biggest city, barely fifty miles from the border with Afghanistan. One of the Afghan Taliban's former chief spokesmen was seized from Quetta in 2005, and Mulla Omar is widely believed to have reassembled parts of his government there. Its proximity to Kandahar, the birthplace of the Afghan Taliban movement, and to Zahedan, the Iranian border town, make Quetta an important marketing and communications center for trade with neighboring countries. The strategically vital city also lies on the Bolan Pass route, which was once the only gateway to and from South Asia.

Ever since the Taliban's defeat in December 2001, Quetta has remained in the news. The majority of the city is ethnic Pashtoon, enhanced by the presence of at least three hundred thousand Afghan refugees, displaced during the civil war in Afghanistan. Most affluent Afghans remained in the city, occupying big settlements including the Pashtoonabad neighborhood, which is reportedly home to hundreds of influential Afghan families. Quetta, therefore, mostly wears the look of a Taliban city; black-turbaned, bearded men stalk the roads and markets in the traditional loose dress worn by all Pashtoons between Quetta and Kandahar. It makes them all look like members of the Taliban, something very striking, particularly for maiden visitors or foreigners. Pakistan's army and ISI officials question the U.S. push for a harder line in Quetta, calling it propaganda and a pressure ploy. If the United States had real actionable intelligence on the Quetta shura, they say, it would have acted long ago. If the ISI helped catch people like Khalid Sheikh Mohammad (from Rawalpindi), Abu Zubayda (from Faisalabad), and Taliban leader Mulla Dadullah's brother (from Quetta), why wouldn't it extend similar support to capture or fix the Taliban leadership?

What most foreigners overlook is the extremely porous border and thin administrative and security infrastructure that allows militants and tribesmen to move easily across the border. As many as nineteen tribes live on both sides of the border and that makes it easier for members of the Taliban or Al Qaeda—whose faces are little known in public—to move in and out of shelters and guesthouses in Quetta or border towns such as Chaman, Mand, and Panjgoor. Islamists, say security officials, also use Pakistan's border with Iran, which is poorly guarded. The ISI currently holds dozens of Turkic men and women, as well as Chechens, Arabs, and Iranian Balochis, who were intercepted while attempting to cross into Afghanistan or Waziristan via Balochistan. Al Qaeda, they believe, is fully at work to recruit people in the restive province and engage them in missions inside Afghanistan or Pakistan.

The American defense establishment evoked hostile reactions with its suggestion immediately after President Barack Obama's December 1, 2009, speech at West Point that drone strikes be extended to cities such as Quetta, where the Afghan Taliban is widely believed to maintain their command and control structure. "This will be extremely counterproductive; we may not be able to control the commotion even if one Hellfire missile is fired into Quetta," a very senior army commander responded, when I drew his attention to the growing chorus of attacks on the Taliban Quetta shura. Here, too, American officials have linked the ISI to Taliban leadership, saying that the Pakistani agency was preventing conclusive action against the shura. But the general I spoke to said that this was far from the case, and that reservations had to do with their understanding of the explosive situation in Balochistan, where a low-grade insurgency has been under way for a decade. "In our meetings with national security adviser Jim Jones and the Central Command chief General David Petraeus, we have challenged them to pinpoint any location in or outside Quetta and we will follow them for action," he said. Another extremely highly placed source quoted General Kayani as telling General Jones, "Sending drones and missiles into Quetta will be disastrous."

Only days before, General Petraeus had conveyed similar concerns to his Pakistani interlocutors. He told local TV channels, including Express TV, that the United States would pass on "actionable intelligence on the Quetta shura" with the hope of actions against its members. During these interviews he underlined that U.S. intelligence "has not seen any evidence in the past two years of any interaction between the ISI and some of the militant groups operating in the border region." But the off-the-record American view of the ISI is different from what one hears in public.

## Who Controls the ISI?

In 2001, Benazir Bhutto called for a truth and reconciliation commission to investigate the conduct of Pakistan's intelligence agencies at home. She bemoaned the fact that "now we have seven intelligence agencies playing politics right down to the tehsil [village] level . . . this has led to the destabilization of political governments, the collapse of the economy and has undermined our standing in the international community," Zulfiqar Ali Khan, who served as Pakistan's ambassador to the United States during her first government in the late 1980s, recalled during our meeting at his Islamabad residence in January 2001.

Bhutto was particularly incensed over the role the ISI and the Military Intelligence, both army outfits mandated with internal and external security operations and counterintelligence, played against her party. Listing the names of former army chief, General Aslam Beg, ex-ISI chief Hameed Gul, and General Asad Durrani, she claimed that the ISI and MI had doled out money and promised incentives to lure MPs away from the party while she was in office because the army establishment was uncomfortable with her foreign policy and security agenda.

Benazir Bhutto had appointed Zulfiqar Ali Khan, a former air force chief, to head an inquiry commission in 1989 to look into the working of various intelligence agencies, including the ISI, the Intelligence Bureau (a civilian intelligence gathering outfit), the Federal Investigation Agency (FIA), and the Special Branch of the police and to recommend measures to improve their performance and keep them away from the political arena.[31] Khan had suggested scrapping the political wing of the ISI, a demand that reverberates within Pakistan even today.

Similar exercises were undertaken earlier as well: General Yahya Khan (who briefly ruled Pakistan from 1969 to 1971) did it for Field Marshal Ayub Khan; Rafi Reza, a former federal secretary, conducted a study for Zulfiqar Ali Bhutto; and Sahabzada Yakub Khan, former foreign minister, did it for General Zia ul-Haq. But there was little movement on the implementation of these commissions' recommendations, simply because the military-led security establishment towered over all other institutions.

Even General Pervez Musharraf, a few months after seizing power in October 1999, had desired better coordination among various intelligence outfits. "Musharraf had suggested that the interior ministry should act as the main coordinator for all the intelligence agencies for the effective utilization of resources and for depoliticizing them," recalled Ansar Abassi, a senior Pakistani journalist.[32] Political expedience, however, came in the way of any effort at reform.

The aftermath of 9/11, which once again sucked the ISI into the Afghan imbroglio, made it more difficult for Musharraf and his civilian partners to even think of reforming the intelligence apparatus. On the contrary, while the ISI stepped forward to help dismantle the terror networks that had taken root in Afghanistan, the agency also turned inward and indulged in unprecedented wheeling and dealing with political parties, to the benefit of General Musharraf. It reportedly heavily manipulated the formation of the government born out of the October 2002 elections. The ISI has now become accustomed to tipping elections, intimidating candidates, and buying votes and it is doubtful whether even a change of command could radically alter its fundamental outlook in the short term.

While he was prime minister, Nawaz Sharif handpicked serving generals to head the ISI but neither could save him in 1991 or 1999, when he angered the military establishment by seeking civilian supremacy over the armed forces through constitutional amendments. On both occasions, the ISI chiefs, who are supposed to report to and support the prime minister, sided with the general headquarters, led by the chief of the army staff. "The reason is that the ISI is a military institution wedded to the military's institutional outlook and concerns about power and security. All its staff look up to the army chief and not the prime minister or defense minister for their promotions and careers," concluded the *Friday Times*.[33] In Pakistan's political context, a purely military organization is not likely to be comfortable with the civilian leadership, which has been struggling (in vain) to establish its credentials as a responsible and sincere stakeholder in the country's political system. The perpetual imbalance in the civilian military equation continues to distort the political landscape: in the struggle for supremacy the most organized institution—the army—almost always emerges on top vis-à-vis a fragmented, shortsighted, and polarized political elite.

In July 2008, a few hours before embarking on his trip to Washington, Prime Minister Gilani made an ill-conceived attempt to put the ISI under the Ministry of Interior. Theoretically, the ISI reports to the prime minister, or head of government, and it actually did so from October 1999 to December 2007, when General Musharraf headed both the government and the military. A force almost exclusively drawn from the military, the ISI never trusted civilian prime ministers like Benazir Bhutto and Nawaz Sharif, who accused it of plotting against the governments and undermining their authority. Thus the attempt—a faux pas at best—to tame it through the Interior Ministry.

A federal minister, who spoke on condition of anonymity, confirmed to me later that President Zardari had advised the prime minister to subject the ISI to civilian authority. This was probably one of the reasons why the army and the ISI fell foul of Zardari within weeks of his becoming president on September 9, 2008. The ISI had been keeping track of Zardari's hasty moves and statements, including his decision to send ISI chief, General Ahmed Shuja Pasha, to India within days of the Mumbai terror attack in November. For several hours most TV channels ran the breaking news that Pasha was being sent to India as a confidence-building measure and that arrangements were being finalized for his visit to New Delhi. But around midnight the news died, and the trip never materialized. The army hit back on both occasions, and within hours the notification was withdrawn.

"Two emergency calls from Rawalpindi to London forced Prime Minister Gilani to change the decision of placing the Inter-Services Intelligence under the Interior Ministry within a few hours, causing serious embarrassment for him," the *News* said. Bad timing and poor advice notwithstanding, the reversal of the orders not only tarnished Gilani's image in and outside the country but also exposed the hidden tensions between different state organs responsible for national security. The generals, both at the ISI and at general headquarters in Rawalpindi, found it hard to swallow the prospect of being made accountable to civilian bureaucrats, and thus the maneuvering behind the scenes that scuttled their "subjugation" to the Ministry of Interior.

"We were preparing for our Friday prayers when we got to know about the decision—many couldn't help smiling and laughing," a brigadier working at ISI headquarters told me a few weeks later. They were all incensed over the government's decision to dispatch the ISI director to India to explain the agency's position on the Mumbai terror attacks.

"The situation was simply too explosive. We could not afford to have exposed our chief to a ballistic Indian media in a moment of rage and anger," a very senior army official told me during a discussion in Islamabad in July 2009. Journalists would have pounced on him like vultures. "We had to correct that decision; it could have triggered a revolt within the army," said the official, adding that a visit under normal circumstances would be helpful but not in the immediate context of an event that had kicked up war hysteria in India.

Pakistani foreign ministry diplomats, analysts, and politicians alike hold the ISI responsible for Pakistan's foreign policy failures, which they believe stem from a suspicious mind-set deeply mired in the cold war tactics of securing a safe border in the west through a friendly government in Kabul, keeping India bogged down in Kashmir, and keeping those politicians and intellectuals in check who are averse to a big standing army. But equally corrosive is the ISI's determination to muzzle any debate as to whether the country needs such a big army at all, and to intimidate the intelligentsia.

I wrote an article in 1996 for the *Friday Times* on how poorly the intelligence agencies operated in Pakistan-administered Kashmir. As a result, the ISI put me on a "security risk list" and barred me from all army-related functions and ceremonies. The ban was finally lifted in 1998, after I approached the ISI through highly placed sources and convinced the generals that what I wrote was in good faith.

I was lucky in that I escaped unharmed. But the case of Najam Sethi, the chief editor of the *Friday Times*, exemplifies how those considered "anti-Pakistan" are treated. He was picked up in April 1999 by Civilian Intelligence Bureau operatives and was eventually handed over to the ISI, who kept him in illegal detention for several weeks. One of the tools that allows the ISI to pick up people is the Pakistan Armed Forces Act, which is applied to civilians to keep them quiet. Luckily, in Sethi's case, for the first time the Supreme Court rejected the government position that the army can arrest a person under the act and detain him indefinitely. Sethi was released under tremendous international pressure, but had he been a lesser-known journalist, he might have come out a shattered man.

The ISI rarely allows civilian governments to devise an independent Afghan or India policy. In fact, the military, from the time of General Zia ul-Haq onward, has never really allowed politicians to think on their own on these two fronts. The Afghan war provided Zia and his associates an opportunity to expand the ISI into a monolithic organization with tentacles reaching into all provinces of Afghanistan. As the disengagement from Afghanistan got under way following the Soviet pullout in February 1989, the militants that the CIA and

ISI had gathered for the jihad began realizing that they could act else-where. Soon they would be fighting in Azerbaijan, Bosnia, Tajikistan, and Kashmir.

Apart from money and guidance from the ISI, these groups received a lot of funding from the Arab world, a fact borne out by the Arabic fluency of some of the top leaders. Gulbuddin Hekmetyar, Burhanud-din Rabbani, and Professor Abdurrab Rasool Sayyaf are all conversant in Arabic, probably because of their close ties to the House of Saud, the rulers of the Saudi royal kingdom. Similarly, several leaders engaged in the Kashmir insurgency are fluent speakers of Arabic, and regularly visit Saudi Arabia. I know a few of these leaders personally, and they told me that after the ISI froze funding following U.S. pressure in 2003, they managed to get financial resources from some Middle Eastern countries to keep their "body and soul together."

Most ISI officials I have been speaking to privately no longer deny their past involvement with militant groups such as the LeT, JeM, or HM. They also acknowledge previous contacts with Mulla Omar, Haqqani, and Hekmetyar, and even some of their Pakistani admirers, currently known as the Pakistani Taliban.

"Since the March 2004 Kaloosha operation the outlook on these militants has changed quite a bit," a senior ISI official told me in early February 2009. "Nobody wants the dark-age Taliban-style rule in Pakistan. Why would we support such forces which have now become a direct threat to our own existence?" he asked. He pointed out that sons and daughters of scores of senior ISI and army officers were studying abroad or at prestigious Pakistani institutions. Why would they want radical and obscurantist militants to rule their country?

The army and the ISI deny any direct links with the LeT. When I confronted army chief general Ashfaq Kayani on this issue during a long consultative session he had arranged on September 27, 2009, for a few analysts who belong either to the Frontier Province or FATA, draw-ing his attention to allegations from New Delhi about the relations between the security apparatus and the LeT, the general quipped: "We cannot outsource our national defense; that is a thing of the past."

When I met with General Kayani again in January 2009, along

with a group of analysts, we discussed the issue at length. One could not wish for Afghanistan what one did not want for Pakistan, Kayani said, in what was perhaps the first candid response by a serving army chief. "We have been misunderstood as far as the notion of strategic depth is concerned. All we have been interested in is a stable and peaceful Afghanistan, a border that we don't have to worry about. I don't think anybody had ever even dreamed of occupying and treating Afghanistan as Pakistan's surrogate," he said. "But we must be mindful of what is happening in our immediate neighborhood."

Kayani went on to explain how the ISI, under his command as director general (between October 2004 and October 2007) and as the army chief since November 2007, has undergone a transformation in outlook and approach.

While Musharraf relied on the Military Intelligence for domestic political objectives, Kayani took the ISI-CIA/FBI collaboration to new levels, though the task of changing the pulse of this institution was not easy at all—nudging senior cadres away from anti-Americanism represented a formidable challenge. Their views were shaped by rampant conspiracy theories, including ones of America's alleged desire to transform the Pakistani security institutions to the benefit of India. Many Pakistanis across the sociopolitical spectrum, as well as a big section of the intelligentsia, share this view.

"Our security establishment is not ready yet for rapprochement with India," a three-star general admitted when I spoke to him in December 2009 in Lahore. Even now, from a soldier's point of view, India represents a far bigger threat than a ragtag army of a few thousand fanatics scattered over an inhospitable region. The soldiers observe that half of India's strike corps, with several thousand tanks and combat aircraft, is deployed within ninety miles of the border, a far greater threat than the militants, and it will take time to change that perception. But the new army chief has started the process.

General Kayani told us that regardless of the past relationships, the ISI must move on in the national and regional interest. "We cannot allow the likes of Baitullah Mehsud and Maulana Fazlullah to dictate to us on issues such as religion and governance. Neither do we want

Afghanistan to descend into obscurantism," he explained. "We must calibrate our future planning with the future plans of the U.S. and NATO forces. They may leave Afghanistan in a few years, but we have to live with the people whom we are attacking right now."

Senior ISI officials at its walled headquarters in Islamabad, however, insist that as a counterintelligence outfit they have to perform their primary tasks. "Outsiders cannot deny us the right of doing what they themselves do," said an official, pointing to the CIA, the MI6, Mosad, and Indian intelligence outfits, which he said operate wherever they deem fit.

Only the months and years to come will demonstrate to what extent the ISI has really changed in outlook and approach, and whether the U.S.-led efforts to reform this institution will bear fruit.

Extricating the army and the ISI from their cold war mind-set will not only require time and deftness but also a sympathetic consideration of their perception of national interest. Hasty moves perceived by Pakistanis as "undesirable pressure" would only backfire and create more enemies; the constituency of change will need time to undertake the necessary reforms. While reprogramming robots will take minutes or hours, changing human minds groomed in a certain environment for a particular cause may require years. That is why the best recipe for achieving this objective rests in befriending the institution rather than antagonizing it. Most senior ISI officials are aware that there is no way around reform. The United States and its allies can probably best cultivate these officials through friendly diplomacy rather than imposing demands.

# 12

# Who Funds the Militants?

There is little proof available for the sources of funding for Pakistani militants. The topic has given rise to fertile conspiracy theories. The insurgency is taking place in an area that has become a battlefield for the competing interests of different nations—the United States, Pakistan, India, Russia, Saudi Arabia, and Iran.

Most culprits are thus not surprisingly believed to be foreign governments. Is it the Americans, the Indians, the Iranians, drug lords, the Afghans, or the ISI itself? Or is the Taliban generating financial resources on its own through peace deals, opium production, abductions of important locals and foreigners, and compromises that hinge on huge payments as "compensation" to the victims and those affected by military operations? In addition, indirectly substantial amounts of USAID and donor money that is being routed through the Pakistani authorities ends up with militants—either to ransom the release of hostages held by criminal gangs or to fund agreements aimed at peaceful coexistence.

During the Bajaur operation in 2009, army and intelligence officials found traces of the shoulder-fired Stella missile, which is produced in Russia. In one incident, militants destroyed two Pakistan army tanks with the help of a Milan rocket, a shoulder-fired missile used by the Italian, French, and Indian armies. "That the militants have access to these weapons underscores the fact that they are certainly getting guidance, if not direct support, from elsewhere," Ikram Sehgal, who specializes in security affairs and owns Pakistan's largest private security agency, SMS, told me in Islamabad.

In Peshawar, suspicions run rampant. "We believe the Americans have their fingers in the pie," a very senior intelligence official told me in May 2008. He pointed out that the American drones rarely spared Al Qaeda operatives hiding in the tribal areas, as evidenced by the five dozen missile strikes that year on targets in the Waziristan region that took out people like Abu Lait el Libi, Hamza Rabia, and Abu Khabab al-Masri, but they almost never targeted the Pakistani Taliban. (Libi, who served as the Al Qaeda spokesman, was killed on January 29, 2008. Rabia was Al Qaeda's third in command while al-Masri was considered the top bomb maker and explosives expert and carried a $5 million bounty on his head.)

During an informal discussion at his official residence in Rawalpindi, General Kayani vented his frustration. He admitted that the Americans "embarrass us with precise locations of militants and their movements they obtain via their satellites. . . . They confront us with satellite videos that track militants' movement from our areas into Afghanistan and vice versa, quite precise surveillance."[1] He explained that American troops regularly coordinate with Pakistani forces across the border and usually keep "very close track of things happening here."

Until the death of Baitullah Mehsud in August 2009, many within the Pakistani establishment questioned why the U.S. and NATO troops did not use such "actionable intelligence" against the Pakistani Taliban. They believed the Americans proferred these images only to embarrass Pakistani military top brass in order to extract more cooperation on Al Qaeda. Pakistani security officials had intercepted a number of Afghan and Pakistani informers who were carrying gadgets that look ordinary but are extremely high-tech, able to pinpoint locations, and lead drones to suspects and their hideouts. Why were these tools not employed against Pakistani militants? Was it lack of American will, capability, shortage of resources, or a matter of deliberate design? Did the Americans want to bleed the Pakistan army by ignoring the militants who have given an extremely rough time to the army in Bajaur, Swat, and Mohmand since November 2007? Or were they prevented from acting by the Pakistan government?

## Funding from Poppy Cultivation

Owais Ahmed Ghani, the governor of Khyber Pakhtoonkhwa (the former NWFP), believes that the TTP spends between $31–37 million (PKR 2.5–3 billion) yearly on procurement of weapons, equipment, and vehicles, and to maintain the families of injured or killed militants. Talking to an English daily in May 2008, Ghani opined that "narco-dollars" were feeding the militancy in both Pakistan and Afghanistan.[2]

A report on Afghanistan published by the U.S. Bureau of International Narcotics and Law Enforcement Affairs in March 2008 also concluded that "narcotics traffickers provide revenue and arms to the Taliban, while the Taliban provide protection to growers and traffickers and keep the government from interfering with their activities."[3]

In 2007, the report pointed out, Afghanistan provided 93 percent of the world's opium poppies, the raw material for producing heroin. Despite repeated calls for action against some very prominent figures, part of or indirectly linked with the Karzai government, nothing happened to change this. "Drug lords benefit from chaos and insurgency, whether in Afghanistan or the tribal areas. Why wouldn't they spend part of their income on keeping the conditions volatile?" asked a security official in Peshawar.

Ghani said that continual strife had turned Afghanistan into a narco-state, with even influential people allied with the United States actively supporting and benefiting from the drug trade. He elaborated: "Some sixty percent of its economy is narcotics based, it's supplying ninety-five percent of the world's demand for heroin, valued by the United Nations at over fifty billion dollars per annum. Now that is a huge vested interest there. We think this one factor has totally negated all the gains that have been made. That is why much of the violence in Afghanistan is based on narcotics—their warlords, their drug lords."[4] He said the United States and United Kingdom had ignored his "early warning of serious repercussions if poppy cultivation was not curtailed after the ouster of the Taliban regime."

In his November 4, 2008, meeting with U.S. assistant secretary of state Richard Boucher in Islamabad, Pakistan president Asif Ali Zardari pointed out that Afghan drug traffickers were funding terrorists in Pakistan's tribal areas. Ever since Pakistan had stopped Afghan drug dealers from using its territory for smuggling, the smugglers had leaned on terrorists so that they could continue their trade. "He urged the United States to take action and to stop the infiltration of terrorists from Afghanistan into Pakistan," an official at the president's house told the author. Boucher assured the president of "all possible help."

## The Frontier Corps: Also a Culprit?

It has been suggested that the paramilitary Frontier Corps (FC) has been abetting violence and participating in criminal activities under the cover of the Taliban. "We cannot rely on Pakistan to stop the traffic of terrorists crossing that border despite the strong statements of its leaders," Senator Carl Levin, the Michigan Democrat who chairs the U.S. Senate's Armed Services Committee, told journalists after visits to Afghanistan and Pakistan in the spring of 2008.[5] Levin and other U.S. defense officials suspected that Taliban fighters may be getting assistance from Pakistan's army. They hinted that if those suspicions were true, it might jeopardize a multimillion-dollar U.S. assistance package for the FC. "If that's our intelligence assessment, then there's a real question as to whether or not we should be putting money into strengthening the Frontier Corps on the Pakistan side because if anything, there's some evidence that the Pakistan army is providing support to the Taliban," Levin was quoted as saying.

Because the FC guards important trade routes, it is always possible that its members do make money—at times even letting off criminals, fugitives, or wanted militants. This happened frequently until early 2006, when the salaries and perks of FC soldiers were raised and their strength doubled on main arteries. But endemic corruption within the organization still represents a big challenge. Collusion of some of its personnel with drugs dealers, timber merchants, and mafia gangs involved in robberies and kidnappings for ransom is another.

The United States set up a program in 2007 to train and equip the Frontier Corps, which comprises fifty-seven wings and recruits its manpower largely from within the tribal areas for border security and counterterrorism. Under the program, Washington planned to supply equipment like helmets and flak vests to the Frontier Corps, but would not provide weapons or ammunition.[6] The U.S. Army trainers were to instruct the paramilitary force, for which Washington allocated $52.6 million in 2007. A defense spending authorization bill for the 2009 fiscal year, which starts on October 1, included $75 million for Frontier Corps training at the headquarters of the Swat Scouts in Warsak. The Americans also funded the construction of new quarters for the two dozen U.S. military trainers who would routinely visit the facility as master trainers.

## The Timber Mafia

Hameedullah Jan Afridi, the minister for environment from the Khyber agency, offers his own interesting analysis. The "timber mafia" is responsible for funding militancy in the NWFP and the provincial government is devising a strategy to crack down on the covert industry, the minister told Dawn News TV. The timber mafia is one of the militants' many collaborators because they depend on them for help transporting their goods safely. Yet people familiar with the tribal insurgency say that kidnappings for ransom, collection of transit fees and road taxes in areas under militant control, or money collected in the name of compensation to the areas affected by military operations are all more important sources of income for the militants. "We could discern from our conversations with Baitullah's aides that he received 2.5 million dollars in return for the release of ambassador Tariq Azizuddin," said one journalist who visited Kotkai for a meeting with the militant leader and spent two days with Baitullah Mehsud and his fighters. "Some of the coalition support funds that Pakistan receives in return for the services it provides to the partners of the coalition against terrorism are also used to pay ransom for the release of kidnapped civilian and government officials," said a local journalist, with good access to the FATA secretariat.[7]

## Islamic Charities and the *Hawala* System

Muslims are required by their faith to pay *zakat*—a kind of tax of as much as 2.5 percent of their total earnings—for the needy, either directly or through the state. It is the duty of an Islamic community not just to collect *zakat* but to distribute it fairly.

Dozens of millionaire Arabs from the Gulf countries, including scores of Saudi Arabian nationals, make yearly donations in cash and kind to people and groups they think deserving. Sometimes the consideration is purely humanitarian and sometimes it is ideological, meaning that they would extend financial support to groups and people they believe are serving the cause of Islam.

It is this part of *zakat* that feeds Islamist networks all over the globe. Donations from Saudi Arabia, Qatar, Bangladesh, and Kuwait have all made their way to Pakistani extremists. Donations from Saudi Arabia, in particular, have tended to go to the Salafi-Wahhabite parties such as Jamatud Dawa, Lashkar-e-Taiba, Ahle Hadith, or the Al-Ittehad-al-Islami of Afghan mujahideen leader Ustad Abdul Rabi Rasool Sayyaf. (Sayyaf turned his group into a political party, the Islamic Dawah Organization of Afghanistan.)

I know of one Kashmir group whose funding dried up once the Pakistani intelligence decided to suspend its funding as a result of U.S. pressure in June 2003. The head of the group told me later that year that he went around and mobilized new funds for sustenance. "God is gracious; Pakistan shut the financial window on us and several such windows opened up to us in Saudi Arabia and a couple of other places," he told me.

Part of the network of Muslim nongovernmental organizations (NGOs) that sprouted and prospered during the anti-Soviet jihad in the 1980s still exists in Peshawar and serves as a conduit for funneling money from the Gulf and elsewhere. Most of these NGOs were run by

Arabs or had financial links with like-minded mentors back home. Many went on to be associated with Osama bin Laden's network, working as possible conduits for passing on donations to Al Qaeda and the Taliban. There is no dearth of "God-fearing, kindhearted" Muslim businessmen—and opportunists—who help the Taliban and Al Qaeda in their own way.

Some of the Arab volunteers from the first Afghan jihad still live in Pakistan; some have been questioned by Pakistani and U.S. interrogators about their alleged links with Al Qaeda and Taliban outfits. A British convert who had been living first in Peshawar and then in Islamabad confided to one of my friends that as many as five thousand Taliban had passed through him on the way to jihad in Afghanistan and Waziristan.

Another important source for transactions is the age-old *hawala* system, which moves money informally on an honor system, and is frequently used by tens of thousands of Pakistani expatriates working in the Gulf countries. All together, these workers remit at least $3 billion a year through formal and informal banking, including the *hawala* system. Jihadist organizations used this channel extensively for their transactions, though stricter regulations governing big transactions have made it difficult to transfer significant amounts.

Pakistan army officials told us that during their campaign against the Swat militants in the summer of 2009 they stumbled upon registers that contained records of donations from families who have a member or two working in the Gulf.

"There were entries with names and addresses of the households in the register that we recovered from one of the training centers next to a mosque being run by the TTP leader Mulla Fazlullah," recalled Major General Ejaz Awan, who led the military operation in the area. The total donations came to a staggering $300,000 (PKR 25 million), Awan said. He also quoted locals as saying that most of the donations were coercive and not voluntary.

In testimony on January 29, 2002, before the Senate Banking Committee, Kenneth W. Dam, deputy secretary of the U.S. Treasury, mentioned the *hawala* system as a conduit for funds to Osama bin Laden. Dam's statement underlined how important the system has been for Al Qaeda and its Taliban hosts. One of the companies he targeted was the Al-Barakaat *hawala* network. "When we shut down the Al-Barakaat *hawala* network, we seized $1.9 million in assets," Dam testified. "Our analysts believe that Al-Barakaat's worldwide network channeled as much as $15 to $20 million to Al Qaeda a year."

Al-Barakaat, a Somalia-based *hawala* system founded in 1989 with locations in the United States and forty other countries, was one of more than three dozen foreign organizations designated as terrorist-related financial entities on November 7, 2001, leading to the freezing of its assets. Dam added that since September 11 the United States and other countries had frozen more than $80 million in terrorist-related assets.

Back in 2002, one money changer in Islamabad told me that several Arabs, apparently students of the International Islamic University in Islamabad, and several Afghan Taliban officials, visited the commercial Blue Area district of Islamabad either to change Kuwaiti dinars or Saudi riyals. "Many of them would also use *hawala* to get money from their friends and relatives," he said.

In those days, business peaked in Peshawar, where scores of traders made good money off *hawala* transactions. "The amounts used to be in the thousands, and sometimes in the tens of thousands," a Pakistani intelligence official in Peshawar told me. He found that some of the most active money changers disappeared once the United States announced an all-out war on terrorism.

"There are scores of rich Arab sheikhs who, despite being filthy rich with petro dollars, believe in the causes that the Taliban and Al Qaeda people espoused," said an official working for a pro-Taliban NGO in Pakistan. These Arabs donate the compulsory 2.5 percent Islamic tax to charities, and in many cases those operating in Peshawar and Karachi rank as their favorites.

On a flight from Kandahar to Kabul in June 2001, I bumped into Iqbal Cheema, who claimed to be a senior official of Sarsabz International, a London-based charity affiliated with Islamic Relief. He said his organization had revived a flour mill in Kandahar, another one in the northern town of Mazar-i-Sharif, and was working on a couple of other projects.

Interestingly the man, of Pakistani descent, was clean-shaven—usually an affront to the Taliban, who take issue with almost every visiting Muslim, even journalists and businessmen, for not wearing a beard.

A family I know in North Waziristan told me in December 2005 that they have been compelled to cough up to local extremists part of the remittances that two family members send from Dubai every quarter. This form of extortion is apparently widespread. The arrests of a number of TTP-related commanders and traders, including a police official, in Karachi on December 14, 2009, highlight how these terror networks extend beyond the FATA regions and have little difficulty finding partners in crime and generating funds. The bulk of militant funding comes from these sources, though most Pakistanis favor more colorful explanations.

New rules regulating financial transactions, introduced by the United States and Pakistan to curb terror financing, have been helpful insofar as illegal remittances by over a million Pakistanis in the Gulf countries and elsewhere began flowing through normal banking channels. As a result, Pakistan's official expatriate remittances shot up to more than $6 billion in 2009 as compared to less than $2 billion in 2002. Unlike in the past, all remittances must carry the identity of the sender and receiver, which can help track the end use of the money, although only to a certain extent. Dozens of dubious money exchanges and dealers have shut down in cities such as Karachi, Lahore, Faisalabad, and Islamabad because they could not easily get around the new regulatory regime put in place with the help of the United States.

Since the Americans began monitoring the global financial transactions from early 2002, restricting the upper limits of money transfers for individuals and companies, Islamist NGOs found informal ways of moving money, sending cash through agents or transferring small amounts. *Hawala* is still important but the amounts involved are smaller because regulations are enforced even in the Gulf, which had served as the financial base and source for Al Qaeda and other groups.

## American Designs

Pakistani intelligence officials often hint at nefarious American designs for the region. The conspiracy theory essentially runs along these lines: U.S. forces are in Afghanistan for the long haul. They plan to expand their presence into Pakistan, and to justify that expansion, the U.S. intelligence and security apparatus keeps churning out stories about FATA as the sanctuary of the Taliban and Al Qaeda. This, say officials, would provide them with a justification to physically intrude into Pakistani territory, even if apparently only for surgical operations. Many Pakistanis fear the United States wants to engineer a partition and denuclearization of their country, allowing it to break up along provincial lines.

"A redrawn map of South Asia initially circulated as a theoretical exercise in some American neoconservative circles precipitated these apprehensions because it shows [Pakistan] truncated, reduced to an elongated sliver of land with the big bulk of India to the east, and an enlarged Afghanistan to the west," said a report in the *New York Times* on November 23, 2008. It added, "It has fueled a belief among Pakistanis, including members of the armed forces, that what the United States really wants is the breakup of Pakistan, the only Muslim country with nuclear arms."

This theory is useful as it helps deflect responsibility. "Some commentators suggest that the United States is actually financing some of the Taliban factions. The point is to tie down the Pakistani Army, they say, leaving the way open for the Americans to grab Pakistan's nuclear weapons," the paper said.

Until his targeting in a drone attack in 2009, Baitullah Mehsud was suspected by Pakistani officials and commentators of being used as an instrument of America's Pakistan policy. Officials within the security establishment would sometimes claim that America was providing him with financial resources. "Being responsible for the area, I often know where Baitullah is. Why is it impossible for the Americans to track and take him down?" asked a civilian intelligence official, echoing an oft-repeated line.[8]

These officials also raised questions about the unusually large number of FBI and CIA spies present in Pakistan. By 2009, the number of U.S. expatriates at the embassy in Islamabad had swollen to more than two hundred, with dozens of them popping in and out of Peshawar at frequent intervals.

Suspicions have been flying around ever since U.S. ambassador Anne W. Patterson spoke of the need to at least triple the expatriate embassy staff of more than two hundred and to expedite the construction of a huge complex spread over eighteen acres in Islamabad, begun as part of the embassy expansion plans, ahead of the $1.5 billion-a-year, five-year Kerry-Lugar aid package passed by the Senate in October 2009.

Adding to the suspicion and speculation has been the alleged presence in Pakistan of the notorious private security firm Blackwater, a U.S.-based firm that is the State Department's biggest security contractor, under the new name Xe Services and U.S. Training Center. The company has entered into working agreements with private Pakistani security agencies for guarding U.S. diplomatic missions as well as hundreds of facilities set up by American NGOs and private contractors in Islamabad, Lahore, Peshawar, and Karachi. Another similar American firm, DynCorp International, shot into the spotlight after it struck a cooperation deal with the Pakistani security agency Inter-Risk. The owner of Inter-Risk was arrested in October 2009 after government security agencies intercepted vehicles owned by the company but being driven by American nationals who claimed to be DynCorp personnel. (DynCorp International is a Virginia-based company that offers, according to its Web site, "innovative solutions and relentless performance in support of U.S. national security and foreign policy objectives. [It operates] major programs in law enforcement training and support, security services, base operations, aviation, contingency operations, and logistics support.")

In November, the Pakistan press splashed reports on Blackwater's presence in Pakistan, saying both Blackwater and DynCorp had been commissioned to carry out covert operations in Pakistani territory, such as fixing or taking out militants or opponents of U.S.-Pakistan cooperation in the northwestern border regions. Skeptics also suggested sting operation teams were being readied to secure Pakistan's nuclear weapons in case of political chaos.

Against the backdrop of the enormous controversy, CIA chief Leon Panetta announced in November that he had canceled a deal with Blackwater in June 2009. That program put Blackwater at the epicenter of a U.S. military operation within the borders of a nation against which the United States has not declared war. In 2006, the United States and Pakistan struck a deal that authorized America's Joint Special Operations Command (JSOC) to enter Pakistan to hunt Osama bin Laden with the understanding that Pakistan would deny it had given permission. Writing in the *Nation* on November 23, 2009, Jeremy Scahill, a U.S. journalist, gave a detailed account of Blackwater's presence and mandate in Pakistan. The report, picked up by Pakistani media on November 23 and 24, said:

> [A] former senior executive at Blackwater confirmed the military intelligence source's claim that the company is working in Pakistan for the CIA and JSOC, the premier counterterrorism and covert operations force within the military. He said that Blackwater is also working for the Pakistani government on a subcontract with an Islamabad-based security firm that puts US Blackwater operatives on the ground with Pakistani forces in counter-terrorism operations, including house raids and border interdictions, in the North-West Frontier Province and elsewhere in Pakistan. This arrangement, the former executive said, allows the Pakistani government to utilize former US Special Operations forces who now work for Blackwater while denying an official US military presence in the country.

The U.S. government denies that Blackwater has any involvement in its military and intelligence operations in Pakistan. In the same article, Scahill quotes Patterson's firm statement that "Blackwater is not operating in Pakistan." Secretary of State Hillary Clinton largely evaded the subject during open forums on her visit to Pakistan in

October. On the Pakistani side, Interior Minister Rehman Malik has said that he would step down should evidence of Blackwater's operations there come to light.

Pakistani security officials often speak about the position of Wackenhut, a U.S. private security company, in Pakistan. In late 2007, Wackenhut's parent company, G4S, a mega U.S. security agency, acquired more than a 50 percent stake in SMS, a Karachi-based Pakistani private security company, and an 86 percent shareholding in Wackenhut.

Ikram Sehgal, who now looks after the Wackenhut operations, told me that U.S. law requires its diplomatic missions to be guarded by an American company, hence the SMS and G4S deal. As a result of this deal, most SMS top management, particularly in Peshawar, underwent almost a complete change and a new set of officers took charge. Police sources confirmed that the "new look" SMS-G4S guards man a number of buildings in the Hayatabad and town residential townships, mostly housing U.S. diplomats, USAID workers, and businessmen. "It all shows that the Americans have something up their sleeves and thus are converging in Peshawar," opined Saleem Durrani, a retired ISI colonel, who told me that Blackwater was already in Pakistan, busy training Pakistani paramilitary Scouts at a facility some twenty-two kilometers northwest of Peshawar.

"The current American agenda revolves around two points, that is, preventing a second 9/11 inside the United States and destroying those who possess the will and wherewithal to do so," says Dr. Farrukh Saleem, analyst and former executive director of the Center for Research and Security Studies, Islamabad.[9] To achieve these objectives, says Brigadier Mehmood Shah, a former security secretary for FATA, the Americans are seeking to co-opt some of the militants into their operational strategy and fix Al Qaeda from within.

## The Saudi Connection

Saudi Arabia is largely seen in Pakistan as a country that quietly follows Washington on critical foreign policy matters—partly because the Saudis remain low profile, unlike the Americans, who pop in and out of

Islamabad very regularly. Saudis play an important role by funding and arming religio-political groups such as Ahle Hadith, Lashkar-e-Taiba, and Ittehad Islamic Afghanistan, among others—and by building and funding mosques and madrassas—but their presence is more subtle and hard to pin down.

The Iranian revolution in January 1979 heralded a new phase of rivalry between Tehran and Riad. The Saudi monarchs feared that the Iranian revolution might undermine their authority over their own restive population and weaken their control over neighboring countries. Thus began a funding spree, as the Iranian mullahs began exporting their revolution by setting up cultural centers and supporting like-minded Shia organizations across the region, including Pakistan. The Saudis responded by funneling funds to Sunni and Wahhabi political parties. The Soviet invasion of Afghanistan in December 1979 provided the Saudis with a perfect opportunity to fund and support sympathetic Sunni religio-political parties. The Saudis funded madrassas and helped create political parties such as Sipahe Sahaba Pakistan to counter the (perceived) advancing Iranian Shia influence. The Saudis spent nearly $4 billion supporting the anti-Russian jihad, which largely went to the Sunni and Wahhabi Afghan parties fighting the regime in Kabul. As the factional fighting in Afghanistan raged after the Soviet pullout in April 1992, the Saudi-Iranian rivalry also intensified. The Saudis and Pakistanis joined hands to contain the Iranian influence both in Afghanistan and in Pakistan itself, by funding (and permitting) the mushrooming of Sunni religious seminaries all over the country. Some religio-political parties such as Jamiat Ulema-e-Pakistan (JUP) were major recipients of Saudi funding.

While the Saudi funding flowed for Sunni seminaries in Pakistan, it also triggered a violent sectarian conflict throughout the 1990s, mostly centered in Central Pakistan—in the Punjab, where radical Sunni groups (such as SSP, Lashkar-e-Jhangvi, Jaish-e-Mohammad, Lashkar-e-Taiba, and Jamatud Dawa) and radical Shia organizations (including the defunct Tehreek-e-Jafria Pakistan) are headquartered.

Almost all of these organizations were banned in January 2002 but their sources of funding never really dried up. The money continues to trickle in through various sources, including Saudi Arabia. Today, most of these organizations—from Karachi to Punjab to Waziristan—share objectives and are glued by their overarching adherence to Al Qaeda ideology. At least 75 percent of Pakistan's 175 million people are Sunni Muslims.

Interestingly, the Saudi royal family has often extended help to Pakistan in critical times, offering free oil exports, for instance, immediately after Pakistan's nuclear tests in May 1998. On several other occasions they have offered emergency budgetary support. Saudis brokered a deal with General Musharraf, allowing the former premier Nawaz Sharif to leave the country and settle down in Saudi Arabia for ten years. Such interventions clearly underline the royal family's desire to maintain its clout within Pakistan. Close relations with right wing religio-political parties, and Sunni outfits in particular, provide the Saudis with an important tool of influence.

## An Indian Hand?

Another theory prevalent in Pakistan counterintuitively singles out India as a source of funding for the militancy. The Indian establishment has always viewed Pakistan and its intelligence–security apparatus with great skepticism. It holds Pakistan responsible for supporting the Sikh insurgency in Indian Punjab in the early 1980s and creating the Kashmir insurgency in the late 1980s and believes that the ISI was deeply involved in the hijacking of the Indian passenger aircraft to Kandahar in December 1999, the attack on India's parliament in 2007, on its embassy in Kabul in July 2008, and the Mumbai attack of November 2008. According to this line of argument, the Indian establishment has decided to settle scores with its neighbor. The mounting Indian engagements in Afghanistan—monetary support worth more than $500 million between 2002 and 2007, personnel training, and reconstruction projects—are all held out as manifestations of an Indian desire to undermine Pakistani influence in Afghanistan.

The Pakistani establishment's suspicion of India has a long history and was fueled by the breakup of Pakistan in 1971, when its eastern wing became Bangladesh following months of insurgency and a war with India. Pakistanis at that time accused India of direct support to Bengali secessionists led by the nationalist Sheikh Mujeebur Rahman. "India essentially midwifed the birth of Bangladesh by helping Mujeebur Rahman," says Mushahid Hussain, former editor of the *Muslim* and a syndicated columnist turned politician. Pakistan has sought many times since then to shore up Indian separatist movements and to foment insurgency, most notably in Kashmir.

I happened to be in Kandahar to cover the hijacking of the Indian Airbus as it drew to a close on December 31. Indian Airlines Flight 814 had taken off from Kathmandu's Tribhuvan International Airport for New Delhi's Indira Gandhi International Airport on December 24, 1999. The Airbus 320 with about 156 passengers was hijacked shortly after it entered Indian airspace at about 5:30 p.m., when five Pakistani nationals seized control of the aircraft. Following a refusal by Pakistani and UAE authorities, the aircraft ultimately landed at Kandahar airport, in Afghanistan.

Shortly after successfully negotiating the release of some 150 countrymen onboard the hijacked plane, one of India's senior negotiators wondered where the four militants swapped with the hostages and the hijackers themselves would end up and how this would affect the image of Pakistan. As expected, at least three of the released prisoners ended up in Pakistan, including Omar Saeed Sheikh (who was later convicted of involvement in the execution of the American journalist Daniel Pearl), Maulana Masood Azhar, and Mushtaq Zargar. So did the hijackers, presumably because the deal provided them with about ten hours to leave Afghanistan, and none of them went to the Iranian border.

The hijacking episode severely bruised the Indian ego. Despite agreeing to release militants from Indian jails, the foreign minister, Jaswant Singh, sounded furious when responding to pointed questions by journalists present inside the Kandahar airport. "We will never surrender to terrorists," Singh said. "But sir, you have just surrendered to them by setting four terrorists free," an American journalist pointed out. Singh chose not to respond to this observation and turned to another questioner.

Those were testing times for the entire Indian team of negotiators. They managed the release of the aircraft and its passengers, but at a price. And yet the hijacking opened the way for an Indo-U.S. strategic dialogue, which contained counterterrorism cooperation as one of the key components. "We will absorb what you have done to us," a senior member of the Indian team at Kandahar told me pointing to the aircraft, which was being readied for the flight back. "But you will not be able to absorb what we might do to you." His words clearly implied that he believed Pakistani agencies were behind the hijacking.

When the Taliban was brought down, India focused on building ties with the Karzai administration. The Indian official I had spoken with in Kandahar was also part of the Indian diplomatic offensive to win the hearts and minds of common Afghans. Three Airbus aircraft, four hundred passenger buses, almost a hundred vehicles—trucks, waste disposal trolleys, etc.—were donated to the Kabul municipality, and tens of thousands of tons of edibles were given along with the promise of cooperation in numerous fields. During 2002 and 2006, India was credited with diverting Afghan government telecommunication to Indian satellites. Not only do the governmental communication routes go through Indian satellites now, but so do the official Radio and Television Afghanistan (RTA) and dozens of FM radio stations across Afghanistan. India provides crucial training to certain branches of the Afghan forces and is currently constructing the new parliament building in Kabul.

A civilian Pakistani intelligence official in Kabul[10] says that Indian diplomats have played a crucial role in cultivating Afghan and Pakistani human assets who they believe to be in cahoots with people like Baitullah Mehsud to destabilize Pakistan. Interestingly, some of Baitullah's aides themselves brought up the issue of Indian involvement when thirty-odd journalists traveled to South Waziristan in May 2008 for a meeting with their chief. "The ameer [Baitullah] told us he declined an offer of support from India when his talks for a peace deal in

South Waziristan with the Pakistan authorities hit snags," one of the journalists, requesting anonymity, quoted a masked Mehsud fighter as saying.[11]

The offer, he said, came in March, when his people were in talks for the release of Tariq Azizuddin, the Pakistani ambassador to Kabul, through close associates of Jalaluddin Haqqani. "Baitullah mentioned this to the captive ambassador as well," the TTP fighter told the journalist in question. The veracity of such statements obviously remains suspect until directly confirmed by the people or parties involved. Even Ambassador Azizuddin, during our meeting in Kabul in June, refused to comment on the issue, saying he would not like to add fuel to an already explosive situation. He restricted himself to what has been public knowledge for a couple of years, reiterating the Pakistani government's position that they suspect the Indian diplomatic missions in Afghanistan to be working against Pakistan's interest through militant groups.

Most Pakistanis, civilian and military alike, believe that India, through its diplomats and agencies, has helped mount insurgencies against Pakistan—one in FATA and the other one in Balochistan. They believe the mysterious Balochistan Liberation Army receives financial and technical support from India, and that the Indian consulates in Jalalabad and Kandahar in particular are using anti-Pakistan elements to "settle scores with Pakistan for its involvement with the Kashmir militancy." The Pakistani establishment draws on Indian media reports and expert opinions expressed therein to reinforce its allegations of Indian involvement in FATA and Balochistan.

A cover story in *India Today* magazine on January 19, 2009, is a case in point. "There are lessons that India should learn from the 1971 conflict that was a result of careful strategy and planning," the article argues. "What the current situation calls for is a similar massive effort with a clear end goal in sight. If the 1971 objective was to dismember Pakistan, then the 2009 game plan should be to neutralise Pakistan so that it can no longer pose a threat to India." One of the four points of the action plan the magazine suggests is to "exploit the divisions within Pakistan and expose its weaknesses in Balochistan, FATA and Pakistan Occupied Kashmir." Another is to "drive a wedge between the army and the jihadis. Also win over the moderate democratic forces."

The magazine quotes G. Parthasarthy, a former ambassador to Pakistan who is a hard-liner within the Indian establishment, on how to deal with Pakistan: "We need to build covert capabilities in Pakistan and mount psychological war. We should not shy away from political destabilization and inflicting economic damage to Pakistan. The time has come for us to say that Pakistan's border with Afghanistan is disputed."

Such thoughts, in one of India's most prestigious newsmagazines, obviously work as cannon fodder for those Pakistani institutions and individuals who insist that politically strong and influential lobbies inside India are out to undermine Pakistan. They use these statements and articles to reinforce their argument that India is funding militants in FATA and Balochistan to bleed Pakistan.

## Is the ISI in Cahoots with the Militants?

Among the liberal political elite, one will often encounter the view that the Inter-Services Intelligence and the army sponsor militants to counter the United States and retain their contacts with them for the day when the United States might physically intervene in FATA or the Frontier Province.

"Militants—whether Haji Naamdar or Baitullah Mehsud—still serve as the extensions of a conservative and hawkish Pakistani establishment that keeps knitting alliances with them as and when necessary to pursue its objectives," Afrasiab Khattak, the firebrand central leader of the Awami National Party now ruling the NWFP, wrote in an article distributed over the net by Professor Barnett Rubin, the U.S. expert of Afghan affairs. "The entire world is astounded by our fixation with the cold war mode. We have developed an incredible capacity to live in unreality. This is indeed dangerous for any state system but it can be catastrophic for a state dancing in a minefield."[12]

The ANP will often echo accusations made in Washington and

Kabul: that the Al Qaeda sanctuaries in FATA are a direct source of instability and threat to the entire world, and Pakistan needs to do more to destroy these havens of terrorists.

Both the army chief, General Ashfaq Kayani, and the head of the ISI, General Ahmed Shuja Pasha, have repeatedly spurned these allegations. "I have also heard these perceptions," General Kayani said when I asked him about this during a meeting in January 2009 at his Rawalpindi residence. "My field commanders and civilians keep conveying to me anecdotal evidence about the ISI's contacts and cooperation with militants like Mehsud and Fazlullah in Swat. But let me tell you categorically, we have nothing to do with these people, and there is little I can do about perceptions," said the general. "When I was heading the ISI, I requested a meeting with the civilian security apparatus in the home ministry and also took the military field officers along. In the presence of everyone, I told the secretary of the interior and the entire police high command that if someone from the ISI interferes in your work, call me directly on my cell," Kayani explained.

General Pasha was equally vociferous in his rejection of the ISI's links with militants. "We would obviously like to fix these rogues. They are killing our own people and are certainly not the friends of this country," Pasha told me during a meeting at the general headquarters in Rawalpindi in early October 2008.

In late November 2008, I had an interesting encounter with a FATA journalist. To my repeated queries on possible motives for the ISI to support militants, my journalist friend came up with answers that were premised in the period between 2004 and 2007. He quoted ISI and military officials and referred to the contents of several meetings with them to support his arguments on the involvement of the ISI with militants such as Baitullah Mehsud and Afghan war veterans like Jalaluddin Haqqani.

Time and again during the conversation, I drew his attention to the massive casualties that the Pakistan army has taken, particularly since early 2007, including the abduction of more than 250 soldiers by the TTP in South Waziristan in August of that year. I repeatedly confronted him with more or less the same question: would the ISI and the military still support a force which was striking the very foundation of the country, destroying schools and hospitals, butchering and executing soldiers, killing civilians, and slaughtering tribal elders? I reminded him that more than half the suicide attacks during 2008 had clearly targeted armed forces personnel and government servants. Would the ISI indulge in a force as destructive as the TTP?

When left with no argument, the journalist asked, "What about the possibility of the ISI's being on the payroll of the American CIA? Perhaps the CIA is paying our intelligence to create unrest and turmoil in Pakistan?" Realizing I could not possibly influence deep-seated perceptions grounded in paranoia and conspiracy theory, I thanked my friend for his thoughts and left his office.

## Compensation or Appeasement?

In late May 2008, the print and electronic media highlighted the news of large amounts of money being handed to Baitullah Mehsud's aides following their withdrawal from areas like Makeen, Kotkai, and Spinkai Raghzai; under a new understanding, the Pakistan army and the political administration provided tens of millions of rupees in compensation, albeit through the TTP. Mehsud had insisted that the government distribute the compensation through him. He distributed $125,000 (PKR 10 million) among the affected tribes in Kotkai, which suffered badly during the military operation, with almost half the buildings in the town destroyed.

A Pashtoon journalist who spent a few days in Wana quoted a Pakistani official who wanted to remain anonymous as saying that the government had paid some $2.5 million (PKR 200 million) to the Taliban to compensate for the dead and wounded in the Zalzala operation. Only half the amount, he told me, was ultimately used for compensation. Sources in Wana claim that Mulla Nazir, who drove out Uzbek militants wary of the Pakistan army in a fierce battle in March 2007, also received several million rupees in recognition of his services.

Personal friends and sources in the region have confirmed that

Baitullah Mehsud received several inducements from the authorities, including a big piece of land in Dera Ismail Khan and several development schemes through his cover men, who also act as interlocutors in talks with the government, which prompts one to ask whether these are bribes to the militants or an indirect funding of their activities.

A lot of foreign development funds for FATA are being routed either through the FATA secretariat or through various security outfits, including the FC. "And this is the money that is usually used as payouts to the militants as part of deals or unwritten understanding," insisted a friend privy to how the Taliban has been extracting money from government officials. He believes that donor agencies do not know where some of their funding ends up. But the "burden of circumstances" makes them accept this.

All negotiations or undeclared deals for "peaceful existence" between the government and militants usually encompass hefty payments to the Taliban and their leaders. While some of the "schemes approved by the government" might be under execution, most existed only on paper, says a source from Wana and Makeen, in South Waziristan. Here are some examples, drawn from interviews with friends and relatives of the militants in question, and with intelligence officers and members of the civilian administration:

· In November 2007, Baitullah Mehsud received $600,000 (PKR 50 million) for the release of about 280 soldiers whom he had ambushed in late August. Twenty-five of his associates charged with various crimes were also released.

· In early 2008, Malik Amir Mohammad, a close aide to Baitullah Mehsud, received funds in the name of several development schemes including for animal husbandry and the construction of schools and roads in his area.

· Noor Wali, in charge of the TTP's vice and virtue department in the Gurgury village (South Waziristan), received $110,000 (PKR 9 million) for a water development scheme.

- Azmatullah, the TTP commander at Spinkai village, received $125,000 (PKR 10 million) for a water supply scheme.

- Ikramuddin, considered a trusted aide to Baitullah Mehsud, was given several million rupees for the installation of a tube well, the construction of a road, and a school in the area. He was also promised a job for any of his nominees in the local militia force called Khassadars.

- Malik Masood Mehsud Khan, another close aide to Baitullah Mehsud, was rewarded with funds for animal husbandry and a hospital.

- Malik Roman Malikshahi, also a Baitullah Mehsud associate, was given funds for a medical dispensary and a water channel in his village, Danga.

- Malik Saifurrehman, another trusted aide to Baitullah Mehsud, got funds for a middle school and a tube well.

- Sangeen Zadran, an Afghan aide to Baitullah Mehsud, got a road construction contract worth $10 million (PKR 800 million).

As for other militants, Mulla Nazir, head of his own Tehreek-e-Taliban, receives a $600 (PKR 50,000) monthly stipend from the administration. For his drive against the Uzbeks in March 2007, Nazir received $62,500 (PKR 5 million) as a personal reward from the authorities. One of Nazir's allies, Mulla Sharif, gets $300 (PKR 25,000) monthly while the authorities gave him $250,000 (PKR 20 million) for constructing a hospital in his hamlet, Sheen Warsak near Wana.

"A good part of these payments usually end up with Baitullah Mehsud and constitute an important source of funding for him," said a journalist from the area, now settled in Peshawar and requesting anonymity. It is certainly appeasement, if not a direct source of financing for the TTP, he said.[13]

The Pakistan military spokesman Major General Athar Abbas denied any connection with the payments to the militants. "As far as I know, the FATA secretariat and political administration are not involved in the process of compensating people affected by the conflict," Abbas told a daily.[14] Officials at the FATA secretariat, which functions under the direct supervision of the provincial governor in Peshawar, also rebutted media reports that TTP and other Taliban militants were paid huge sums as "appeasement." Even if this has happened, it would hardly go into the books because these payments are done from discretionary funds or from the secret funds available to intelligence agencies.[15]

Journalists and intelligence officials based in Peshawar and other NWFP districts such as Kohat, Dera Ismail Khan, and Bannu insist that narcotics and abductions for ransom remain a big source of funding for the militants.

"Smaller kidnapping gangs sell their hostages to bigger ones if they fear they have kidnapped someone too high profile for them to hold. This is what happened to Tariq Azizuddin [the Pakistani ambassador to Kabul]," wrote Zahir Shah Shirazi in the monthly magazine *Herald*, published from Karachi, in its October 2008 issue. Shah quoted a Taliban commander on how drug money was used for the jihad: "A Taliban leader based in Mohmand agency tells the *Herald* that the use and sale of drugs for serving the cause of 'jihad' is not *haram* [forbidden]. He claims that this cash crop is god's gift to fight the infidels. Protection has also been provided to timber and trucking mafia involved in transporting smuggled goods."

Official confusion regarding terrorist financing notwithstanding, most civilian and military intelligence institutions know that the average abduction a day from inside the city of Peshawar feeds into the terror networks. Most of the kidnappings are targeted and in almost all cases involve affluent people or traders, who are released against huge amounts of ransom. I know families in Peshawar, friends of friends and relatives, who had to pay through their noses to secure the release of their family members.

To cap it all, Islamist networks operating in Afghanistan and the border regions of Pakistan and the North West Frontier Province have built capacities in- and outside the region that keep them afloat. They project their financial strength through complex and lethal acts of terror and have struck alliances with criminal gangs. Convergence of commercial interests and of vaguely defined ideologies have helped these alliances to harness means such as *zakat*, donations in mosques and seminaries, drugs, guns, smuggling, and external interference within the region to finance and pursue their violent agendas.

As a whole, the presence of American and international troops in Afghanistan, the massive deployment of Pakistani troops on the 2,560-kilometer border with Afghanistan, the increasing desire on India's part to assert itself as a major regional player, Iran's proximity to an American-dominated Afghanistan, and the omnipresent narcotics trade have all turned the entire tribal region into a battlefield of competing interests, with many players fighting for their piece of the pie. This war of interests obscures the view, making it difficult to pinpoint who is working for whom and at what cost. What is indisputable is Al Qaeda's presence in FATA, which it has turned into a hunting and training ground for the recruits it deploys against the United States and other NATO members. Western governments ostracize Al Qaeda for its "global anti-Western campaign" and project it as the single largest threat to world peace. Al Qaeda, meanwhile, curses the entire West as "evil and a threat to the Muslim world."

During several meetings on the nature and components of the insurgency in FATA, I confronted one of my friends in the security establishment with a number of probing questions. At the end of our last session, he admitted in frustration, "I am probably as confused as you are. . . . It is murky and obscure . . . sorry."

# Epilogue

I n late February of 2010, residents of Miranshah, in North Waziristan, stumbled upon three beheaded bodies. A note placed near the decapitated men said: "They were U.S. spies. Anybody found engaged in espionage will meet the same fate."

Before these brutal murders, several hundred tribesmen had been killed on these same grounds—espionage for the United States and the Pakistan army. These incidents are a reminder of the dangers for noncombatants in the areas that have been hit hardest by the insurgency now raging inside Pakistan. They are also an illustration of the cost to Pakistan of its support for America's war in Afghanistan.

With the fall of the Taliban regime in December 2001 and the subsequent pressure on General Musharraf to stop supporting violent jihadi groups, all shades of militants took refuge in Pakistan's tribal areas. The convergence of foreign and Pakistani militants, bolstered by local support, turned this region into a hotbed of Al Qaeda-inspired militancy. In 2007, Baitullah Mehsud unified many of the disparate groups that had made their way to the tribal areas under his command and formed a new and more lethal Pakistani Taliban. His group, Tehreek-e-Taliban Pakistan (the TTP), brought suicide bombing on a massive scale to Pakistan as a lethal tool to pin down the state. Attacks climaxed with 87 suicide strikes in 2009, claiming more than 3,000 lives. Analysts estimate that there have been more than 32,000 casualties in Pakistan since the war on terror began.

Pakistan has lost more than 2,300 army and paramilitary soldiers, including 3 generals, 5 brigadiers, and as many as 73 senior intelligence operatives in its recent counterinsurgency campaigns in FATA. In all, the army has conducted 211 major military operations in the tribal areas and Swat since 2007, with almost 150,000 of Pakistan's 550,000-strong armed forces now busy scouring for militants and criminal bands in the border regions.

Despite this clear indication of Islamabad's new determination to hunt down and neutralize the militants who have been wreaking havoc in the country, the U.S. intelligence community remains wary of its Pakistani interlocutors because of their long-standing complicity with Afghanistan's Taliban factions. It has continued to criticize the ISI for allegedly protecting Afghan Taliban leaders such as Mullah Omar, Gulbuddin Hekmetyar, and Sirajuddin Haqqani, the eldest son of veteran jihadist leader Jalaluddin Haqqani, all of whom are staging operations from Pakistani soil against American and NATO troops in Afghanistan.

The first quarter of 2010 saw a sudden surge in Pakistan's crackdown on the Afghan Taliban. The arrest in February of Mullah Baradar, known as the Taliban's master strategist, followed by a dozen or so more catches—including Ameer Muawiya, an associate of Osama bin Laden's responsible for foreign militants, and Akhunzada Popalzai, also known as Mohammad Younis, a former Taliban shadow governor of Afghanistan's southern Zabul province and ex-Kabul police chief—suggested a new resolve. In early March, Motasim Agha Jan, a former head of political affairs for the Afghan Taliban, was arrested in Karachi. A few weeks later, the Pakistani police picked up Maulvi Kabir, a former governor of Afghanistan's Nangarhar province.

Baradar was the latest and most prominent in a long string of Taliban stalwarts captured by Pakistani and U.S. authorities in joint operations. The ISI chipped in by using local influentials—the usual go-betweens—and was in all probability aware of these men's presence in Pakistan for some time. The 2007 arrest of Mullah Obaidullah, the former Taliban defense minister and Baradar's predecessor, was also apparently the result of a joint operation—not so different from the one that resulted in the arrest in 2003 of alleged 9/11 mastermind Khalid Sheikh Mohammad.

One factor that appears to have prompted Pakistan to move against the members of the Afghan Taliban operating on its soil was the suggestion, at the London conference on January 28, 2010, by British and NATO officials that they intended to move forward with a policy of reconciliation and dialogue with elements of the Taliban. Sensing the possibility of a greater role in the reconciliation process, Islamabad might have recalibrated its policy to position itself accordingly, in the hope of persuading the United States and its allies that it could be trusted to act as a key intermediary in the negotiations. With their families now ensconced in Pakistan, most Afghan Taliban leaders sneak in and out of the country, posing as family men on their way to meet relatives or as visiting doctors.

Within days of Baradar's arrest, news began flowing out of Kabul and Washington, largely from intelligence sources, suggesting that Pakistan had nabbed him to scuttle his talks with the Afghan government. But when I met with Daniel Benjamin, the State Department's coordinator for counterterrorism, in Islamabad a few weeks later he told me that Baradar's arrest was a joint Pakistan-U.S. sting operation. "We had been tracking him for quite some time," he said.

I got confirmation of Benjamin's account in early October from a Pakistan army general who was directly involved in the operation. "Baradar had come to Karachi to collect a huge cash consignment that Taliban financiers had sent through a courier from Dubai," the general said. "We had offered to hand him over to Kabul in return for Brahamdagh Bugti." A grandson of Baloch nationalist leader and tribal chieftain Nawab Akbar Bugti, who was killed in August 2006, Brahamdagh Bugti had fled to Afghanistan and vowed to revenge his grandfather's death, which has widely been attributed to Musharraf's government. Pakistani authorities wanted him back for trial but the Afghan government denied that he was in Kabul.

Another senior military official who now occupies a top position in the GHQ told me earlier in Quetta that the army had offered to undertake joint action if U.S. intelligence could identify Baradar's location. Other army officials admitted that they were aware of the movement of various prominent members of the Afghan Taliban to and from Quetta but said it was difficult to get hold of them if they were traveling with their families. No one evinced much enthusiasm for the notion of hunting them down.

It seems unlikely that Pakistan will go after the most wanted leaders of Al Qaeda or the Afghan Taliban, such as Mullah Omar or Gulbuddin Hekmetyar. Any reconciliation attempt minus Mullah Omar would likely be shorn of credibility. Alive and outside the fold, Mullah Omar would remain a major stumbling block to peace. That Pakistan, mindful of its relations with the dozens of Pashtoon tribes that live across the border, would risk eliminating him altogether does not seem probable. Pakistan will most likely continue to put pressure on Omar by picking up more of his top leaders, inducing a leadership paralysis, and thus with any luck persuading him to give up the path of confrontation. It is possible that he may give in to negotiations if convinced that that the U.S.-led forces are on their way out and that Pakistan will no longer accommodate him and his Al Qaeda friends and provide them with shelter.

On the domestic front, while it continued its operations in Mohmand, Orakzai, and Khyber, the army declared on March first that it had cleared the Bajaur region, where it had launched a campaign in August 2008. Police in Karachi arrested several militants, including Ismail Mehsud, a police inspector who happened to be a cousin of Baitullah Mehsud's, and Alam Mehsud, both of them wanted TTP commanders who were busy offering covert support and mobilizing resources for the Pakistani Taliban. The army also claimed in early March that it had killed Maulvi Faqir Muhammad, the TTP leader in Bajaur, Afghan Taliban commander Qari Ziaur Rahman, and twenty-eight others in an aerial strike on their hideout in the Mohmand tribal area. No independent confirmation of Faqir Muhammad's death was available. Earlier, CIA-operated drones had rocked the TTP to the core, first by taking out Baitullah Mehsud on August 5, 2009, and then his vicious successor, Hakimullah Mehsud, in a similar strike in January 2010. Two former TTP spokesmen, Muslim Khan and Maulvi Mohammad Omar, were already in jail, and their ferocious partner in Swat, Maulvi Fazlullah, is reportedly paralyzed and hiding in Afghanistan.

A decapitated TTP, without Baitullah Mehsud, Hakimullah Mehsud, and several of their top deputies, represented a golden opportunity for the Pakistan army to consolidate its gains in Waziristan and elsewhere in FATA through a military-intelligence campaign, supplemented by U.S. drone strikes. Military operations in 2009 reversed the TTP's campaign of carnage by wresting territories back in Swat and South Waziristan; these advances stopped the retreat that the state had slipped into since May 2004, when it signed its first peace deal with the Taliban of South Waziristan, followed by several others, the most recent of which was on February 17, 2008.

## Drone Strikes

Since the first strike by an unmanned vehicle flying over Pakistan in June 2004, which killed the Waziri Taliban leader Nek Mohammad, CIA-operated Predators and Reapers have conducted over 210 drone strikes, killing some two thousand people. The exact number of casualties remains controversial. In 2010 alone, roughly 118 drones took out high-value targets, mostly in North Waziristan. Largely uncommented on by the world press, the Obama administration has quietly turned drone strikes into a key part of its strategy in the region, targeting the militants operating in Pakistan's tribal areas with unprecedented intensity. In a February 24, 2010, report titled "The Year of the Drone," Peter Bergen and Katherine Tiedemann of the New America Foundation wrote that "under the Obama administration, there were 51 reported strikes in Pakistan's tribal areas, compared with 45 during the entire administration of George W. Bush." According to Bergen and Tiedemann's report, "The White House reportedly authorized an expansion of the drone program in Pakistan to reinforce the efforts of the 30,000 new U.S. troops being sent to Afghanistan, even before the December attack on the CIA post in Khost," though they conceded that "the flurry of 12 missile attacks in less than three weeks after the suicide attack on the CIA officers was unparalleled." Interestingly, the report points out that none of the Obama administration's strikes has targeted Osama bin Laden or Ayman al-Zawahiri.

The report also touched on the killing of civilians in drone attacks, a subject that has generated massive resentment and anti-American sentiment. Most Pakistanis, including members of the media and mainstream political leaders, view these attacks as a violation of their national sovereignty. But privately even top generals support drone strikes. In a recent meeting with a handful of Pakistani journalists, a very senior general told us, "As long as they take out the guys who are a threat to us all, why crib about it?" Leading government officials, including Prime Minister Gilani, will agree even if publicly they condemn the drone strikes. Most Pakistanis believe that if the United States allowed the Pakistan army to operate drones, it would be much better, but top military leaders will concede that the Pakistan army doesn't have the satellite technology that is required to operate the drones, and no one really expects this to happen.

U.S.-Pakistan military cooperation appears to be headed in a new direction. Both military establishments are now managing to coordinate drone attacks and army campaigns better than ever before (the United States largely stopped drone strikes in South Waziristan at the Pakistan army's request while the latter was carrying out its latest campaign).

Drone strikes are increasingly precise, and intelligence is improving. With several Al Qaeda-linked leaders killed by drones in February 2010, including Qari Zafar, a rabidly anti-Shia member of Lashar-e-Jhangvi wanted in connection with the deadly 2006 bombing of the U.S. consulate in Karachi, and Muhammad Haqqani, the thirty-year-old younger brother of Sirajuddin Haqqani, who has been leading the Haqqani network in and around North Waziristan and Afghanistan's Paktia province, it became clear that the United States and Pakistan are coordinating their actions more closely than ever.

## Paradigm Shift?

Most Pakistani observers believe that Musharraf's successor as chief of army staff, Lieutenant General Ashfaq Kayani, has played a central role in turning the tide on the insurgents and in bringing about a fundamental strategic shift in Pakistan's security paradigm, which for decades has looked to militant groups as crucial allies. He has also significantly improved relations between Pakistan and America. Some attribute the new cooperation to the personal rapport that the U.S. chairman of the Joint Chiefs of Staff, Admiral Mike Mullen, and Centcom chief, General David Petraeus, have cultivated with General Kayani and the head of the ISI, General Ahmed Shuja Pasha. It may also be a fruit of President Obama's less confrontational, less absolutist, and less offensive approach to diplomacy.

Since taking over from Musharraf in November 2007, Kayani has gradually distanced himself from his predecessor, relieving Musharraf's allies of sensitive duties and charting a new course in the army's relationship with the United States. He has increasingly provided U.S. military commanders with operational details and critical information concerning regional developments. In return, Kayani has attempted to convince his American counterparts that a truly effective partnership must be built on mutual trust.

"I have been telling Mullen and Petraeus, as well as others in NATO, that if you keep suspecting and insinuating against us publicly, we will find it difficult to motivate our rank and file," Kayani told me during a briefing at his office in Rawalpindi. "With doubts as to our intentions and allegations of inaction against militants being hurled at us, our room for maneuvering and motivating our officers and soldiers shrinks." He seems to have convinced the U.S. administration of the sincerity of Pakistan's military establishment and of the fact that more and more Pakistanis realize that the stakes in this conflict are greater for Pakistan than for any other country.

This augurs well for a complicated bilateral relationship that continues to be strained by allegations that General Musharraf played a "double game" between 2001 and November 2007, when he finally stepped down from his army position. During these years, Pakistan received more than $12 billion in U.S. aid, but the security establishment was slow to break ties with the militants it had supported in Afghanistan and Kashmir.

In October 2009, President Obama's administration agreed to a

further $7.5 billion aid package—known as the Kerry–Lugar Act—
that the U.S. government believes will pave the way for a long-term
strategic partnership between the two countries. Initially the army
reacted extremely negatively to the Kerry–Lugar Act because of the
self-defeating conditions that Congress had insisted on attaching to
the bill. The entire high command voiced its displeasure by issuing a
press release after a corps commanders' meeting in early October, saying that aid would not be accepted at the cost of national sovereignty.
The debate in Congress also upset the civilian government. Within
twenty-four hours of this statement, Foreign Minister Shah Mehmood
Qureshi flew to Washington to seek assurances that the act would not
be used to arm-twist the armed forces of Pakistan. The result was an
annex to the Kerry–Lugar Act containing some assurances, following
which the army toned down its criticism. In October 2010, President
Obama announced yet another financial incentive, a $2 billion assis-
tance package for the Pakistan army, pushed through Congress by
Richard Holbrooke and his team and supposed to start some time
after 2012.

While the U.S. government decided early in 2010 to establish a
Quick Reaction Force for the protection of its ever-expanding diplomatic and development personnel in Pakistan, it hoped the new $1.5
billion annual aid package under the Kerry–Lugar Act would address
some of Pakistan's pressing financial and energy needs and improve
America's dismal image among Pakistanis. This package was to be administered independently of the security-related assistance and the sale
of military hardware, which included F-16 fighter planes, guns, military
cargo planes and helicopters, APCs, and surveillance equipment.

The proximity of the arrest of so many members of the Afghan
Taliban to this infusion of American dollars prompted many within the
administration and outside the United States to ask whether President
Obama's incentives to Pakistan had begun bearing fruit. But many
observers in the United States remain skeptical of Pakistan's long-
term motives and play down its recent roundup of the Afghan Taliban
as, in the words of one of the Western diplomats based in Islamabad,
"window dressing." Some American skeptics in Kabul will go so far as

to suggest that the arrests were designed to undermine peace talks with the Taliban or to put Islamabad in the center of those talks. But most observers have greeted recent developments with guarded enthusiasm. "Of course, we planned it together and executed it jointly," said a top American official in charge of counterterrorism, taking some credit for Mullah Baradar's arrest. He brushed aside criticism by Karzai, former UN representative Kai Eide, and some U.S. intelligence sources, saying, "Some people thrive on such negative talk without knowing the inside story."

While the U.S. media has been relatively slow to respond to the shifts in Islamabad, a new appreciation for Pakistan's drive against its militants has been growing outside the administration as well. David Ignatius, an op-ed columnist for the *Washington Post,* recently pleaded with his readers, in a March 4, 2010, article entitled "To Pakistan, Almost with Love," to take a sympathetic view of Pakistan's gradual turnaround:

> In the upbeat White House version, the first big success for the Obama administration's new Afghanistan policy has come not in the battle of Marja in Helmand province but in Islamabad. Officials cite Pakistan's cooperation with the CIA in capturing and interrogating top leaders of the Afghan Taliban, and Pakistan's new dialogue with India [begun in February 2010, after a break of over fifteen months]. . . . Military and intelligence officials on both sides appear wary of overpromising what this new partnership can deliver. There's greater confidence, they say, because officials know each other better. One U.S. official counts 25 high-level American visits to Pakistan since President Obama took office.

The article recounted "several little-noticed steps" that the Obama administration has taken: One is to implicitly accept Pakistan's status as a declared nuclear weapons state and thereby counter conspiracy theories that the United States is secretly plotting to seize Pakistani nukes. The United States is also trying to combat Pakistani fears about covert U.S. military or intelligence activities. And the administration has repeated Obama's assurance last June that "we have no intention of sending United States troops into Pakistan."

One can discern a greater realization within the top echelons in Pakistan and the United States that both countries need each other, despite the widespread anti-United States sentiment in Pakistan. To mitigate Pakistani concerns and improve its image, the United States will have to balance its expanding corporate and strategic relationship with India with the need to engage Pakistan for the long haul. Blinded by an obscurantist ideology, pampered by vested interests, and bulging with a skewed sense of power, the militants are drunk on their own elixir and more vulnerable than they realize.

A trust-based, long-term engagement with Pakistan is the primary prerequisite for America's success in the region. Only time will tell whether and how long it will take to defeat what has now become a global challenge, this vicious ideology, influenced by Al Qaeda, that cuts across national borders and attracts zealous followers ready to die and kill. These militants' contempt for societies governed by universal democratic values undoubtedly represents a common threat to us all.

To take on these threats, Pakistan will also have to look inward and to engage in the kind of overdue introspection that its civilian and military ruling elite have long avoided to fix the country's pressing problems. Rather than externalize their internal issues and seek to blame America, or India, or any other handy scapegoat, the leadership will have to address issues such as good governance and the rule of law. It will also have to integrate FATA properly into Pakistan. No state can afford to have pockets of land being ruled by nonstate actors. The country has already paid heavily for the politics of expedience, corruption, and denial. Without addressing these challenges, the dangerous ideological drift that has gripped Pakistan will be hard to contain.

Americans like to say that Pakistan is the most dangerous place in the world because of its combination of nuclear weapons and a murderous insurgency. But however vulnerable its government may appear

to be at any moment, the state of Pakistan, its military and civil bureaucracy, is stronger than people realize. The real challenge lies in
addressing the subversion of minds that is taking place daily among
the millions of Pakistanis across the country. Radical Islamist ideology
seems to cut across all sections of society, albeit with varying degrees
of success. Real believers and followers may be few in number, but
these small numbers in a country of more than 175 million inhabitants
do translate into a few million. This militant outlook, blended with a
conservative sociopolitical environment precipitated by poor governance and a lack of quality education, makes for a lethal combination.

It is not the few thousand armed militants and criminals who
make FATA the most dangerous place, but those silent millions who
look up to these militants as daring followers of God and Islam, out
to challenge the wayward and corrupt Western world. That is why the
chattering classes in Islamabad, and in the upscale neighborhoods
of Karachi, Lahore, Multan, and Faisalabad, are apprehensive. They
perceive a creeping danger, not from FATA but from within their
own cities, where religio-political organizations are lobbying their
cause, attracting and inviting the vulnerable youth into their ranks.
Unless adequately addressed, this trend over the long run will spell
ever greater dangers not only for Pakistan but for the entire region and
the world.

# Acknowledgments

Much of the content of this book comes from my own experience—from firsthand information on the tribal areas gathered through scores of interviews during trips made to the area as well as several visits to Afghanistan dating back to 1988. I have also drawn on more than three hundred articles I wrote on the subject for the Pakistani weekly *Friday Times*, the Peshawar daily the *Frontier Post*, and the national daily *News*. I have drawn on material from my book *The Unholy Nexus: Pak-Afghan Relations under the Taliban* (Vanguard Books, 2002) and several papers on the subject. My work between 1988 and 2006 for the German Press Agency dpa and for Deutsche Welle Radio, in Germany, helped tremendously in allowing me to make friends and acquaintances in the tribal areas on both sides of the Durand Line as well as in Pakistan, all of whom were valuable sources of information.

I must acknowledge that for reference and while compiling this book, I drew on the following published works:

- *Some Major Pukhtoon Tribes along the Pak-Afghan Border*, S. Iftikhar Hussain, Areas Study Center, Peshawar, 2000.

- *The True Face of Jehadis: Inside Pakistan's Network of Terror*, Amir Mir, Roli Books, Lahore, 2006.

- *A to Z of Jihadi Organizations in Pakistan*, Muhammad Amir Rana, Mashal Books, Lahore, 2004.

- *Tribal Areas of Pakistan: Challenges and Responses*, edited by Pervaiz Iqbal Cheema, Islamabad Policy Research Institute, Islamabad, 2005.

Finally, a survey the Center for Research and Security Studies (CRSS) conducted in all seven tribal agencies of FATA provided extremely valuable information and insights about the area and its people. The CRSS, a think tank based in Islamabad, has permitted me to use the results of the FATA survey in this book.

I would like to thank my original publisher, Penguin Books India, and especially Jaishree Ram Mohan and Ranjana Sengupta, who published a different version of this book as *The Al Qaeda Connection*. I am also very grateful to my

American publisher, Viking, and to my editor there, Joy de Menil, and her assistant, Chris Russell. Joy and Chris worked overtime and kept me engaged with their queries. Joy's deep involvement with the text—corrections, additions, and also observations—has lent the book an entirely different character and added linguistic and stylistic value to it.

My heartiest thanks go to a number of very good friends— journalists, retired and serving army officers, and intelligence officials—who have been very helpful in this compilation, particularly those who provided valuable input on the subject but who would not like to be named for obvious reasons.

I am also indebted to my friends Dr. Farrukh Saleem and Mubashir Akram, and especially to Aarish Khan, whose critical review provided extremely useful help in correcting and fine-tuning the contents of the book.

My special thanks to Alamgir Bhittani, Ehsanullah Dawar, Noor Mohammad Wazir, Shaukat Khattak, Khitab Gul Orakzai, and Sailab Mehsud, who served as a compass on the basics of FATA and kept correcting me where I erred.

I must also thank Hafeez Khan, whose meticulously collected FATA Press Review, a monitoring report maintained by CRSS, kept the contents of the book as updated as possible.

I also owe a debt of gratitude to Mohammad Anwar Durrani, who on behalf of the CRSS risked his life and toured some of the most risky areas inside FATA and helped to conduct the survey for the center.

Thanks also go to all friends within the Inter-Services Public Relations, the Pakistani armed forces' media wing, who always extended support and enabled me to visit some of the remotest and embattled areas inside FATA ever since I began reporting from out of Islamabad in 1988.

I also owe thanks to the following:

Khalid Aziz, ex-chief secretary (North West Frontier Province); Shamim Shahid, Peshawar; Manzoor Khan Wazir, Wana; Mehfoozullah, Miranshah; Khan Zaman Dawar; Malik Azhar Khan, Wana; Noor Ahmed Wazir, Wana; Shahjehan Khan, Swat; General (Retired) Ali Mohammad Jan Orakzai (ex-governor, North West Frontier Province), and Owais Ghani (governor, North West Frontier Province).

# Appendix 1

# A Profile of Pakistani Militants

While reliable material on militant leaders is hard to come by, over the years, through personal contacts with intelligence officials, journalists, and from occasional reports in the press, I have put together this Who's Who of Pakistani militants in FATA. These profiles explore how young tribesmen, driven by Islamist jihadi rhetoric echoing from across the Durand Line and exploited by external and internal forces, became instrumental in an insurgency that is threatening the very foundations of a state that once used militants as tools of its foreign policy. While many Afghan and Arab militants have taken shelter in the tribal area, they are not included here, with the notable exception of Jalaluddin Haqqani.

## Leaders of the TTP

**Baitullah Mehsud:** In its early May 2008 issue, *Time* magazine listed Baitullah Mehsud among its one hundred most influential individuals. The other luminary from Pakistan was the chief of army staff General Ashfaq Pervez Kayani. Both made it to the list of "Leaders and Revolutionaries," a reflection of how much the military and militants have come to dominate international perceptions of Pakistan. On August 5, 2009, an hour past midnight Pakistan time, a Hellfire missile fired from a CIA-operated drone tore Baitullah Mehsud's body into two pieces. He was said to have been on a glucose drip—dispensed by a local paramedic named Saeedullah (Mehsud was a diabetic suffering from dehydration)—on the rooftop of his in-laws' house in Zangara, South Waziristan, when hell rained down and took several lives, including that of his second wife. With this missile attack, the icon of Al Qaeda-inspired militants in Pakistan was gone.

"Our main aim is to finish Britain and the United States and to crush the pride of the non-Muslims. We pray to God to give us the ability to destroy the White House, New York, and London. Very soon, we will be witnessing jihad's miracles," the diminutive militant told the Doha-based Al Jazeera satellite channel in December 2007. That January, a cell of Pakistanis was arrested in Barcelona for allegedly planning suicide operations in Spain and elsewhere in Europe on his behest.[1]

Mehsud carried a $5 million bounty after the U.S. State Department described him as a clear threat to American interests in the region. He stunned many in and outside the country on March 31, 2009, when he owned up to a commando raid and the ensuing bloody siege of a police training academy a day earlier on the outskirts of Lahore.

Early in January 2008, Pakistan's security officials and the CIA named Mehsud as the prime suspect behind the December 2007 assassination of former prime minister Benazir Bhutto. On May 24, 2008, in a meeting with journalists in South Waziristan, Mehsud denied his involvement. "We didn't kill Benazir Bhutto. We are not involved. She had not taken any action against us, so there was no need to harm such a person," he told the group visiting him.[2] Yet the two men accused of killing her are associated with Mehsud's TTP, according to investigators and other sources.

Mehsud shot into international headlines for his suicide bomber training camps, led by his deputy Qari Hussain and located mostly in and around the Shawaal area between North and South Waziristan. Stocky and barely five feet two inches tall, Mehsud, at thirty-six, was less than swashbuckling, but he radiated a certain charisma that appealed to people much stronger in physique. Born into a poor ethnic Pashtoon family in the Makeen village of South Waziristan, he participated in the anti-Soviet Afghan jihad as a young man and later assisted the Afghan Taliban in their fight against the Northern Alliance. During his years fighting in Afghanistan, he drew inspiration from Mulla Omar, the Afghan Taliban chief, and from Osama bin Laden and his deputy Ayman al-Zawahiri. Mehsud embraced their vision of an Islamic state based on sharia (as they interpret it).

Mehsud formed the Tehreek-e-Taliban Pakistan (TTP) in December 2007, when several tribal commanders agreed to join up under his leadership. The TTP originated in South Waziristan; all its component groups called themselves Taliban, as do militants in the Ahmadzai Wazir areas of South Waziristan, though they do not share the same leadership structure. As Pakistan's most influential Taliban leader, he trained and lined up a new cadre of die-hard commanders, ready to take on Pakistani security forces. Before his death, the TTP comprised about forty militant commanders with a collective strength of about twenty-five thousand men and was the most lethal of the militant outfits in Pakistan's tribal regions bordering Afghanistan.

In May 2007, the group caused great embarrassment to the Pakistan army when it ambushed and took at least 250 officers and soldiers hostage before releasing them in August after arduous talks and, most probably, the payment of a heavy ransom. In July 2009, Mehsud's men again caused great embarrassment to Pakistani security forces when they sniped at a military convoy, killing about a dozen soldiers, including two officers. Pakistani security forces, the police, and the paramilitary are the TTP's special targets; since 2006, Mehsud and his allies have killed close to 3,000 policemen and paramilitary security personnel.

Baitullah Mehsud's assassination shocked his followers, although no panic ensued after his death. Most analysts following Al Qaeda–inspired militancy in the region agree that the TTP was united and much better networked than previous militant organizations, and thus posed a bigger threat to the region and the world. Mehsud's group was accused of involvement in kidnappings for ransom. They used these abductions to bargain for the release of alleged TTP militants. The group held Pakistan's former ambassador to Kabul, Tariq Azizuddin, for ninety-seven days.

In September 2008, Mehsud married for the second time after his first marriage failed to produce any children. He married a third wife before he was killed. Waziristani journalists and supporters referred to him as the "governor" of the region because of his influence over the Mehsud tribe's areas of the rugged and inhospitable terrain.

Until Mehsud's death, the Pakistan army establishment had accused the United States of sparing him by design. Defense and intelligence officials claimed that since Mehsud was inflicting damage on the Pakistani security apparatus, the Americans were refraining from a conclusive action against him. The United States in turn accused Pakistan of using him as a bogeyman. In this way, Baitullah Mehsud remained a source of friction and distrust between the American and Pakistani security establishments. The August 5 drone strike put an end to this irritant, but not to the vicious corps of the TTP, who continue to sow terror and fear all over Pakistan by targeting the security establishment in particular.

"The real war is the media war," Mehsud told the journalists who came to see him in May 2008. "It is our desire to learn also how one should fight the media war." He aimed to do this by acquiring the ability to upload videos on Web sites such as YouTube,[3] demonstrating how mindful the militants are of the necessity of "outreach," and of keeping up with of modern technologies, especially those that reach the young.

The Taliban media cell has released videos and CDs showing horrific images, apparently with different aims. One such video shows a boy as young as ten firing shots at the head of a blindfolded man and beheading another.

The Pakistani government struck a peace accord with Baitullah Mehsud weeks after his militants swept though Sararogha and the Laddha forts in South Waziristan, which until then had been jointly manned by the FC and Pakistan army. The attack, in January 2007, invited a military operation that lasted for a couple of weeks. The military operation failed to weaken his base, though it recaptured the main towns under his control.

**Qari Hussain Mehsud:** Qari Hussain Mehsud is in charge of Tehreek-e-Taliban Pakistan's suicide squads. Its training camps, including those run by the Haqqani family, are mostly in and around Shawal, in North Waziristan, but some can be found in Spinkai Raghzai and Kotkai. Hussain heads the anti-Shia operation in the Kurram agency, which is plagued by Sunni-Shia conflict. He was a member of the now defunct anti-Shia outfit Sipahe Sahaba Pakistan, based in the central Pakistani town of Jhang, a hotbed of Shia-Sunni rivalry. He announced the formation of the TTP, and is often the contact person for media organizations.

Hussain, in his early thirties, was essentially Baitullah Mehsud's deputy. He belongs to the Eshangi subclan of the Mehsud tribe and he was raised in Kotkai, near Spinkai Raghzai in South Waziristan. He was allegedly involved in the killing of a local bigwig, Amiruddin Khan, the political agent of the Khyber agency, and his family on May 31, 2007. He was also involved in the kidnapping of twenty FC personnel and the beheading of one in August 2007.

In late September 2009, a series of drone attacks on targets in South Waziristan triggered speculation that Hussain had been killed. But on December 3, a day after President Obama's speech to the United States Military Academy at West Point, Hussain called up a couple of trusted journalists from an undisclosed location, vowing to continue the "jihad" against the United States. He was later injured in the attack that killed Hakimullah Mehsud.

Qari Hussain studied in the madrassa Jamia Farooqia Karachi, in Jhang, for four years. He returned to his hometown in South Waziristan in 2003, when a military operation was launched there against non-Pakistani militants. During his stay at Jamia Farooqia in Jhang, he joined the Sipahe Sahaba Pakistan. He commands the loyalty of four to five hundred personnel, slightly more than the force of two to three hundred that midlevel commanders usually maintain.

During their May 2008 visit to Baitullah Mehsud, journalists also met with Qari Hussain, who told them that he had "by the grace of God" survived the Pakistan army cleanup Operation Zalzala in January. "I am born to live and serve the Taliban," said the gray-haired zealot whose house was destroyed. Asked if he was still training suicide bombers, he did not respond directly and instead looked at the Talib standing beside him. Hussain hedged when asked if he was still a member of the banned militant organization Sipahe Sahaba Pakistan. "I am with every Muslim group," he said.[4]

**Hakimullah Mehsud:** Following Baitullah Mehsud's death on August 5, 2009, and after more than two weeks of speculation over the succession, Hakimullah Mehsud became the head of the TTP. Until his promotion, he had been in charge of the TTP in the Kurram, Orakzai, and Khyber agencies. In his early thirties, the well-built five-foot-nine-inch Hakimullah had his brush with journalists in late November 2008, when he invited them to the rugged Orakzai agency to demonstrate his hold over the area. He vowed to continue the "jihad" against foreign forces in Afghanistan, and said the TTP would target all the allies of the United States as well.

Some of the journalists who met him discerned a charisma in Hakimullah and tipped him as Mehsud's successor. The battle-hardened Hakimullah's real name is believed to be Jamshed. He first rose to prominence by the name of Zulfiqar Mehsud as a spokesman for the TTP in 2007. Born and raised in the Kotki village of the Sarwaki subdivision, South Waziristan, Hakimullah briefly studied at a madrassa in southern Hangu district.

A Pakistani journalist who met him quoted Ajmal Mehsud, a close associate of Hakimullah's, as saying, "Hakimullah is the best shooter and driver in the entire tribal area and no one except Shaheed Nek Mohammad could have matched him." (Nek Mohammad was one of the Taliban leaders in South Waziristan, killed in a predator strike in June 2004 in his village, Sheen Warsak.)

"If the Pakistan government continues with its policy of following American dictates, (some day) we can even try to capture Peshawar, Hangu, and even Islamabad," Hakimullah told Pakistani journalists. In an interview with *Dawn News*, he openly praised Al Qaeda. "We are Al Qaeda's friends as both us the Taliban and the Arab fighters have shown our allegiance to Amir-ul-Momineen Mullah Omar of Afghanistan, but there is no Al Qaeda in South Waziristan. It's only the U.S. and the Pakistan government's propaganda. They don't have any proof," he told the journalist Zahir Shah Shirazi, on camera for the private English-language Dawn TV.

A close confidant of Baitullah Mehsud, Hakimullah Mehsud was caught by the coalition forces in Afghanistan during a raid inside Pakistani territory in Lowara Mandi, Shawal area of North Waziristan, on March 8, 2007, and later released. He has said his targets include President Asif Ali Zardari and his allies for their "pro-American" policies. He accused members of the ruling alliance and in the NWFP of "working to break up Pakistan in collaboration with the U.S." and in November 2009, he threatened to "cut off" supplies to American forces in Afghanistan if U.S. drone attacks continued. He was widely reported to have died in a mid-January 2010 drone attack but Taliban sources insisted he was still alive and in April 2010 produced a video to prove it. The video was apparently filmed in North Waziristan, where he is reportedly hiding under the protection of Sirajuddin Haqqani.

**Noor Said:** The leader of the local Taliban in the Barwand area of South Waziristan and a close confidant of Baitullah Mehsud, Noor Said led the eight-member Taliban group for negotiations with the family of Amiruddin Khan, a tribal elder whom militants suspected of maintaining contact with the military and government officials, after TTP activists murdered members of the Khan clan. Several rounds of negotiations between the Khans and the Taliban for a peace deal remained inconclusive and it seems that rather than asking for compensation or going for retribution, the Khans have accepted the killing. Noor Said participated in the jirga that secured the release of the fifteen Frontier Corps men and a local politician from Laddha on August 28, 2007. Noor Said was one of Baitullah Mehsud's most trusted aides, in effect his front man for wheeling and dealing with the government and other groups. He is an influential commander and is respected within the TTP ranks.

**Wali ur-Rehman:** After growing up in a middle-class family in the Mal Khel branch of the Mehsud tribe in South Waziristan, Rehman graduated from Jamia Islamia Imdadia madrassa in Faisalabad. Before joining the Taliban movement in 2004, he was affiliated with Jamiat Ulema-e-Islam (JUI). Rehman is reputed to be humble, cool-minded, and intelligent. Despite earlier disagreements with Hakimullah Mehsud over ending the war with the army, Rehman now serves as chief of the TTP in South Waziristan, as well as the organization's primary military strategist.

**Maulvi Shamim:** This young commander ran a suicide training camp at Laddha, in South Waziristan, after capturing the paramilitary fort there. The TTP also set up a seminary called Jamia Farooqia, supervised by Shamim, which was destroyed in aerial bombardment by the Pakistan air force in advance of their military operation in the region in November 2009. When we visited the area on November 17, the only sign left of the seminary were the stone walls and a sign board that said: Madrassa Jamia Farooqia, Administrator: Maulvi Shamim. In his midtwenties, Shamim is a Shaman Khel tribesman. He comes from a family of carpenters, and is reportedly quite unpredictable in his behavior. His men briefly held hostage a Frontier Corps delegation that went to negotiate the control of a paramilitary check post.[5] The colonel who led the delegation and his soldiers were later released on the intervention of local tribal elders.

**Asmatullah Shaheen:** A former aide of Baitullah Mehsud, Shaheen, who also goes by the name Bhittani, was injured during one of the campaigns in Afghanistan but is still very active. He was also injured in a clash between local tribesmen of Jandola and his men when the latter tried to blow up a British-era bridge in the area on October 5, 2007. He is among the twenty most wanted Taliban commanders operating in South Waziristan and has enforced his writ in several areas in Tank and Dera Ismail Khan. His deputy, Jahanzeb, a Bhittani tribesman, runs the TTP's offices in Jandola, the headquarters of Tank. He claimed responsibility for the December 29, 2009, bombing in Karachi and the Pakistani government has put a $120,000 (PKR 10 million) bounty on his head.

**Shah Faisal Barki:** The Taliban commander in Saam, in Kanigoram, South Waziristan, Shah Faisal Barki kidnapped three Frontier Corps personnel, including a colonel, on August 25, 2007. He released them on August 28, after a jirga brokered a deal between the militants and the government of Pakistan.

**Khan Gul Bhittani:** A resident of Bubbakhel, Bhittani is a notorious criminal and known to be involved in kidnapping for ransom. He is a self-proclaimed Taliban member, having declared allegiance to militant commanders in South Waziristan.

## Non-TTP Taliban Leaders in South Waziristan

**Mulla Nazir:** In his forties, Mulla Nazir is the head of the Taliban in the Ahmadzai Wazir areas of South Waziristan, having replaced Haji Omar in 2006. He belongs to the Karokhel Wazir clan of the Zillikhel subtribe of the Ahmadzai Wazirs. He earlier fought against the Afghan Northern Alliance alongside the Taliban in Kunduz and Takhar (in northern Afghanistan). He led a fierce campaign against Uzbek militants in the surrounding areas of Wana in March–April 2007, after they started kidnapping locals, attacking Pakistan military, and forcing locals to live according to their dictates. The TTP's hold in the Ahmadzai Wazir areas is practically nonexistent, and pro-Uzbek militant leaders had to flee from the area. Some observers contest that Mulla Nazir was actually part of a front started by Tojikhel tribesmen, and that he hijacked the leadership halfway through the fight. (All its components call themselves "Taliban." But so do militants in the Ahmadzai Wazir areas of South Waziristan who did not join the TTP. They all call themselves Taliban but have different leaders.)

Following his anti-Uzbek operation, Nazir was considered suspect by TTP militants for his alleged contacts with the Pakistani government, and rivals twice sent suicide bombers his way. Fortunately, Nazir's guards overpowered the first attacker before he could blow himself up near Nazir. The would-be assailant was arrested with explosives.[6] The second was shot dead by Nazir's guards.

Nazir heads the five-member Taliban shura of South Waziristan that was reconstituted after the ouster of Uzbeks from the area.

**Khanan Wazir:** Khanan Wazir was the emir of the Taliban in South Waziristan's Shakai valley. He opposed the presence of Uzbeks in South Waziristan, and was killed in an ambush by Uzbek militants in early June 2008.[7] In September 2006, he survived an ambush by his Uzbek detractors. So it was only natural that he extended support to Mulla Nazir's anti-Uzbek operation. Khanan's supporters were attacked by Uzbek militants again in January 2008, after which tensions grew between Ahmadzai Wazir and Mehsud tribesmen because the latter are believed to be sheltering Uzbek militants. Khanan was part of the five-member Taliban shura of South Waziristan that was reconstituted after the ouster of Uzbeks from the area.

Khanan's murder was a severe blow to Mulla Nazir, as he had established his control over the difficult Shakai valley, where the government had signed its first peace accord in May 2004. An aide to Qari Hussain admitted to his group's involvement in the killing for his "association with the government."

"All those acting for or on behalf of the U.S. or its allies—whether the Afghan or Pakistan army—are our target. They are damaging the cause of the Muslims in Afghanistan and other parts of the world. We will spare none," Qari Mudassir, an aide to Qari Hussain, said in a phone conversation recorded on June 6, 2008. A friend, whom Hussain himself had called, recorded the conversation and he played the audiotape for me during one of our meetings in Peshawar.

**Haji Omar:** Haji Omar, forty-eight, is a cousin and successor of the slain militant leader Nek Mohammad. He belongs to the Ahmadzai (Yargulkhel) Wazir tribe and is a resident of the village of Kaloosha near Azam Warsak in South Waziristan. A battle-hardened jihadi who fought alongside the Taliban in Afghanistan, he sided with the Uzbek militants during Mulla Nazir's attack in March–April 2007. Subsequently, he moved to North Waziristan and then took refuge in the Mehsud areas of South Waziristan. He was killed in the first drone attack of 2010.

**Haji Sharif:** Haji Sharif is Haji Omar's brother, also from the village of Kaloosha. In his midfifties, he sided with Mulla Nazir after initially opposing him. The exact circumstances surrounding the differences between the brothers are not clear, but ideological affinity seemed to have played a key role in keeping the majority of the brothers on the side of the Central Asians.

**Noorul Islam:** Noorul Islam is another brother of Haji Omar and Haji Sharif. He fought alongside the Taliban in Afghanistan in the past and spent a lot of time in the United Arab Emirates. He is believed to be very close to Uzbek militants and to shelter them and their families. Noorul Islam fiercely supported the Uzbek militants during their clashes with Mulla Nazir in March–April 2007.

**Zawal Khan:** A Zillikhel Wazir by tribe, Zawal Khan belongs to Khanghi village near Angoor Adda. He is believed to be a supporter of Uzbek militants.

**Maulvi Abdul Aziz:** A Yargulkhel Wazir by tribe, Maulvi Abdul Aziz is a resident of the village of Ghwakha in South Waziristan. Besides being the administrator of a madrassa at Azam Warsak, he is also a schoolteacher at the Government Middle School, Ghwakha. He got his religious education from the madrassa of Maulana Noor Mohammad, a former member of the National Assembly from South Waziristan. A strong supporter of the Taliban in the area, Maulvi Aziz led a procession on March 31, 1999, in favor of the Afghan Taliban and their Pakistani supporters in Waziristan. He is a cousin of Haji Omar and Haji Sharif and he was affiliated once with the Tehreek-e-Nifaze Shariate Mohammadi. He had to leave Kaloosha along with Abbas, Omar, and Sharif because they had all supported and sheltered activists of the Islamic Movement of Uzbekistan. Aziz had maintained close contacts with Arab militants, and he took refuge somewhere in North Waziristan.

**Maulvi Abbas:** A veteran Taliban commander who controlled the Ahmadzai Wazir areas of South Waziristan alongside Nek Mohammad, Maulvi Abbas belongs to the Malik Khel Wazir tribe and resides in the Kaloosha area. He is believed to be in his midforties. He got his religious education from Darul Uloom Haqqania in Akora Khattak, one of the largest seminaries in the NWFP, established in 1947 by Maulvi Abdul Haq.

Interestingly, the current head of the Darul Uloom Haqqania, Senator Maulana Sami ul-Haq, is believed to have immensely benefited from money the CIA and ISI funneled into the anti-Soviet-Russian resistance; during the 1980s this seminary kept churning out fighters for the CIA-sponsored jihad. Several mujahideen commanders, including Jalaluddin Haqqani, studied in the seminary. Many Afghan Taliban leaders also received their degrees from this institution.

Maulvi Abbas is a supporter of Haji Sharif. He fell out with Al Qaeda after differences over the Uzbek militants' raid on the Pakistan military at Zari Noor on January 8–9, 2004.

**Maulvi Javed Karmazkhel:** Maulvi Javed is an Ahmadzai Wazir Taliban commander and he supported the Uzbeks in 2007. In February 2007 a group of Lashkar-e-Jhangvi–associated suicide bombers reportedly confessed to being trained in a training camp run by Maulvi Javed and Maulvi Abbas.

**Mittha Khan:** A member of the reconstituted Ahmadzai Wazir shura after the ouster of the Uzbeks, Mittha Khan was seriously injured in a bomb blast on September 2, 2007. He was reportedly treated in an FC hospital for his injuries, and later on in the Combined Military Hospital, Peshawar. He fought alongside Mulla Nazir to oust Uzbeks from the Ahmadzai Wazir areas of South Waziristan.

**Halimullah:** Halimullah belongs to the Tojikhel subtribe of the Ahmadzai Wazir tribe. He was formerly associated with Haji Nazir but now has an independent command in the Tojikhel area of Kirkot. He is still a member of the Mulla Nazir–led Taliban shura of South Waziristan.

**Ghulam Khan:** An Ahmadzai Wazir tribesman believed to be very close to Uzbek militants in the area, Ghulam Khan sided with the Uzbeks during their clashes with locals in Azam Warsak, Shin Warsak, and Kaloosha in March–April 2007.

**Younas:** A part-time journalist turned Taliban, Younas used to call the Online news agency to offer coverage from the area. He is now close to Uzbek militants, and largely out of the news for security reasons.

**Abdullah Mehsud:** Hailing from Nano, in the Makin area, Abdullah Mehsud was a Guantánamo Bay detainee who rose to prominence after he abducted two Chinese engineers and killed one of them. He blew himself up to avoid capture by Pakistani forces in July 2007. According to a Pakistani government official, Mehsud directed a suicide attack in April 2007 that killed thirty-one people. After being transferred to Afghanistan in March 2004, he sought several media interviews and became well known for his attacks in Pakistan. In October 2004, his men kidnapped two Chinese engineers from the Gomal Zam Dam site.

## Militants in North Waziristan

**Jalaluddin Haqqani:** Jalaluddin Haqqani, believed to be in his early seventies, is a veteran of the Afghan jihad against the Soviet Union in the 1980s. He received considerable support during this time from Saudi Arabian intelligence and the CIA. He joined the Taliban and was made supreme commander of Paktia and Paktika, where he had commanded mujahideen troops, and defense minister. After the fall of the Taliban, Haqqani went underground. He is known to have visited Islamabad and Peshawar after the U.S.-led coalition began bombing Taliban targets in Afghanistan in October 2001. After this he retreated into the tribal area of North Waziristan, from where he declared jihad against Pakistan and became a mentor to scores of Pakistani jihadists.

Haqqani's current whereabouts are not known but a video CD dispatched to Pakistani newspaper offices in Peshawar in March 2007 showed him in poor health. Looking pale and frail, he reiterated his commitment to the anti-American jihad in Afghanistan and urged people to support the mujahideen.

Four Guantánamo detainees were captured and held because U.S. intelligence officers received a report that one of them had briefly hosted Haqqani after the fall of the Taliban. Some say that Haqqani has since been offered positions of authority in President Karzai's government, including the post of prime minister, which he turned down.

Today, his eldest son, Sirajuddin Haqqani, is actively pursuing the goals that he set forth under the banner of his group, Amarate Islami Afghanistan, an umbrella organization that maintains good relations with a cross section of Taliban and Al Qaeda operatives, including the TTP, Mullah Nazir, Harkatul Mujahideen, Jaish-e-Muhammad, Uzbekistan's IMU, the Arab Jaish-e-Mehdi, and a Turkish militant organization. All these groups operate independently, but close consultations are carried out whenever a contingency arises. Amarate Islami Afghanistan is considered a shelter and cover for many militant groups active and hiding in Waziristan.

Like his father, Sirajuddin Haqqani is suspected of having close relations with Pakistan's intelligence agencies, which have provided his group with financial support. A report, compiled by the Pentagon's Defense Intelligence Agency entitled "Defense Intelligence Assessment; Osama bin Laden/Al-Qaeda Information Operations" described Jalaluddin Haqqani as "the Afghan tribal leader most exploited by Pakistan's prime intelligence agency, the ISI, during the Soviet-Afghan war, to facilitate the introduction of Arab mercenaries."

Bin Laden hooked up with Jalaluddin Haqqani when he went to Khost, in eastern Afghanistan, in early 1998 to set up a Zawar training camp, which was destroyed by American Tomahawk missiles in August the same year.

Haqqani is counted as one of the Taliban's most influential and conservative commanders. He was a client of the CIA in his days as a mujahideen leader in eastern Afghanistan, fighting with the help of weapons and money that the CIA funneled to him through Maulvi Younus Khalis, the head of his own faction of the fundamentalist Hez-be-Islami.

The Haqqani group serves as the most important battlefield partner for many of the insurgents fighting American and NATO troops in Afghanistan. It is believed to have introduced the use of suicide bombings to Afghanistan. The network operates out of havens on both sides of the porous Afghanistan-Pakistan border and is believed to maintain close ties to Al Qaeda.

United States military officials told the *Wall Street Journal* and the *New York Times* on January 1, 2001, that the Haqqani network was in fact the primary target of the CIA team stationed at the Chapman base, located in the violent and lawless southeastern province of Khost, close to the Pakistani border. Following a suicide bombing at Chapman base on December 30, 2009, that killed seven officers, CIA-operated drone flights over North Waziristan increased manifold. The *Wall Street Journal* quoted intelligence and military officials familiar with the base's operations as saying that the CIA personnel at Chapman used the facility to recruit and pay informants as well as to pass along information about high-value targets and other intelligence to Special Operations forces.

In the first three months of 2010, U.S. forces and the CIA escalated their shadow war against the Haqqani group, dispatching contingents of elite American Special Operations troops to develop more detailed intelligence and to kill or capture specific commanders.

**Maulana Sadiq Noor:** Maulana Sadiq Noor is in his midforties and hails from Khati-Kelay, a small village in the suburbs of Miranshah along the Tochi River in North Waziristan. He belongs to the Daur tribe of North Waziristan. An experienced warrior who fought on the Bagram front in Afghanistan against the Northern Alliance, he is believed to support anti-U.S. entities in Khost, Afghanistan. For the past fifteen years, Sadiq Noor has operated a seminary in Khati-Kelay. He hit the headlines in 2006 when Pakistani troops conducted an operation against his compound to flush out foreign terrorists (Uzbeks and Arabs). After the military operation in North Waziristan in July–October 2007, Sadiq Noor reportedly ceased to support foreign militants and began cooperating with the security forces. His supporters patrol the streets to keep militants away. Probably because of his close links with the security forces, he is reportedly no longer a member of the local Taliban shura of North Waziristan.

**Maulvi Abdul Khaliq Haqqani:** A Daur by tribe and mulla of a mosque in Miranshah Bazaar, Maulvi Abdul Khaliq Haqqani thrived in the past on delivering fiery speeches against President Pervez Musharraf and President George W. Bush. His anti-U.S. rhetoric continues to date, but Zardari has replaced Musharraf and Obama has taken the center stage in his speeches, delivered usually during Friday congregations. He came into the limelight in March 2006, when his men captured the telephone exchange and other government buildings. In the cross fire that ensued, his mosque and seminary were pounded with heavy artillery, causing substantial damage. By May 2008, the complex had been repaired and restored to its preoperation condition.

**Haji Gul Bahadur:** A Madakhel Wazir from the southern part of North Waziristan, Hafiz Gul Bahadur is a very powerful local Taliban commander and is the main leader of the local Taliban shura in North Waziristan. He entered into a peace deal with the Pakistan army after the military operation in North Waziristan in July–October 2007. His commitment not to attack Pakistani security forces was tested when Baitullah Mehsud asked him in January 2008 for help against the Pakistan army, which was scouring and bombing the area to cleanse it of TTP militants.

Bahadur refused to cooperate with Mehsud, ostensibly to keep his commitment to the Pakistan army, but also to keep North Waziristan out of the conflict. During the army operation in South Waziristan in January 2008, Baitullah kept requesting help through emissaries. He urged Bahadur to attack military targets to ease pressure on him, but Bahadur refused and advised Mehsud to avoid the Shawal area of North Waziristan, which he considered his territory.

In early July 2008, Bahadur forged an alliance with Mulla Nazir of South Waziristan. They named the alliance Taliban Ittehad and vowed to keep up their anti-U.S. campaign, triggering speculation that they might have acted to facilitate the government's isolation of Baitullah Mehsud. In late July, Bahadur was reelected as the chief of the Taliban in North Waziristan. More than eight hundred Taliban attended the meeting held at Razmak, seventy-five kilometers south of Miranshah. By August 2008, Bahadur had forged an alliance with Maulvi Abdul Khaliq Haqqani, further isolating Mehsud.

Bahadur condemned the U.S. missile attack of Zyara Leeta, South Waziristan, on July 28, 2008, which killed six people, and called it "a gift of the Pakistani prime minister for the Americans during his visit to the U.S." But by then, Bahadur and Maulvi Abdul Khaliq had cemented their alliance and maintained good relations with Mulla Nazir. This meant Baitullah Mehsud stood isolated.

The following leaders are independent power brokers in North Waziristan, many of them fence-sitters, sometimes siding with one group or the other and at other times opposing them. This way they maintain their nuisance value.

**Sangeen Khan Zadran:** An Afghan belonging to Khost's Jadran tribe, now based in Shawal, Sangeen Khan Zadran claimed in late November 2006 that his group had provided forty suicide bombers for attacks in Afghanistan.

**Maulana Siddique Darpakhel:** Hails from the Darpakhel area of North Waziristan and is a prominent militant leader.

**Waheedullah:** The Taliban shura member assigned the responsibility of administering Miranshah on behalf of the Taliban, college-educated Waheedullah was killed in a CIA-operated drone attack in South Waziristan (where he had gone on a visit) in October 2008.

**Haleem Khan:** A militant known to have links with foreigners, especially Uzbeks, and believed to be involved in targeted killings in the area.

**Abu Okash:** An Iraqi Arab militant, who has gained considerable influence in parts of North Waziristan, like Mirali and Miranshah. His name, according to some sources, is Abu Kashif but he has gained fame locally with the name Abu Okash. There were reports that he had been injured in an extensive aerial bombardment on villages around Mirali in October 2007. In early 2008, he released his first videotape calling for jihad against the infidels.

## Bajaur Agency

**Maulvi Sufi Mohammad:** The founder of the defunct Tehreek-e-Nifaze Shariate Mohammadi (TNSM), which launched a campaign in 1994 to bring sharia law to Bajaur, Mohammad was released from Dera Ismail Khan prison on April 21, 2008, to facilitate a deal between the Taliban and the administration. He had been jailed in late 2001 for sending several thousand armed fighters for jihad to Afghanistan. There are conflicting reports about his native village, with some claiming it is Kumbar, in Bajaur, and others the Maidan area of Dir. Though Sufi Mohammad's influence waned over the years, he is expected to play a role in calming the situation in the Swat/Malakand division, where the followers of his estranged son-in-law, Maulana Fazlullah, ran amok in the latter part of 2008, triggering a vicious army reaction.

**Maulvi Faqir Mohammad:** Sufi Mohammad's former deputy eventually grew out of his shadow and become the deputy to Baitullah Mehsud for the Bajaur agency, with several thousand militants at his disposal. Now in his early forties, Faqir Mohammad was born in Changai Bala village in the Damadola area of the Bajaur agency, about nine kilometers north of Khar, the agency's headquarters. He is a graduate of the strict Wahhabist Punj Pir seminary near Swabi. He fought against the Soviets alongside the mujahideen in Afghanistan in the 1980s and is now one of the most wanted men in Bajaur, but he can still be seen in public addressing rallies, etc. He has been outspoken in his resolve to wage jihad against the coalition forces in Afghanistan and the Musharraf administration in Pakistan, and to establish sharia in Bajaur and adjacent districts. He was among the first few of the FATA militants to pledge support to the Red Mosque, condemning the military operation and holding President Musharraf personally responsible. "If Musharraf doesn't stop promoting the U.S. agenda, peace may return to Kashmir and Afghanistan but the situation in Pakistan will worsen," he said. "The government is trying to divide the Taliban and is backtracking on its commitments."[8] Faqir Mohammad is believed to be behind most terrorist incidents in Bajaur and the adjacent districts, including attacks on security forces.

He is currently underground, reportedly either badly injured or partially paralyzed from Pakistan army rocket fire on his cavalcade in June 2009. A few of his bodyguards and a son were killed in the attack by a Cobra gunship helicopter, but his whereabouts remain a mystery.

A source in Bajaur told me recently that Mohammad had been removed from the leadership of the TTP when the central Shura grew suspicious of him for alleged links with the security forces. He was replaced by Maulvi Dadullah.

## Khyber Agency

**Mufti Munir Shakir:** The founder of the strictly Wahhabist organization Lashkar-e-Islam, Mufti Munir Shakir originally belonged to the Kurram agency. He left his home after a family feud which left his mother dead. Some say he killed his mother, while others are of the view that she was killed while trying to save him from his father, with whom he had a strong relationship. He moved to another city (most probably Karachi) and eventually to Bara. Some accounts also suggest that he is actually from Hangu but that his family had settled in Lower Kurram.

In late 2005, Lashkar-e-Islam developed serious differences with Ansarul Islam, a Barelvi organization led by Pir Saifurrehman. Both groups incited hatred against each other through their illegal FM radio stations. Their differences were often violent, and remain so. Mufti Munir Shakir left the Khyber agency in the last week of February 2006, after the political administration conveyed a stern warning to him through a tribal jirga after grueling negotiations between the tribesmen and government authorities. He was arrested soon after by Pakistani intelligence agents and was sentenced to an indefinite jail term.

**Mangal Bagh Afridi:** Mangal Bagh Afridi succeeded Mufti Munir Shakir as leader of Lashkar-e-Islam. He comes from a humble background, and officials often deride him as a "trucker's helper." Afridi is an independent, sometimes high-handed ultraconservative cleric considered close to the administration. He enjoys considerable support of the people because of his daring religious decrees against criminals; when the government fails, Afridi steps in to maintain law and order or deliver justice. He has administered public punishments to people he declares to be criminals for dealing in liquor and drugs, running murderous gangs, committing adultery, etc. In the process he has gained formidable clout among local tribes. His illegal FM radio station delivers sermons and urges people to take the right path, that is, join Lashkar-e-Islam to serve God and Islam.

In the absence of effective government control, Afridi has grown enormously powerful. In June 2006, Lashkar-e-Islam ran into trouble when the administration disagreed with the peace committees that Afridi had set up to maintain law and order in the area. The disagreement resulted in the closure of local markets for a few weeks. Some locals suggest that the government sometimes ignores Afridi's militant activities and indirectly supports him whenever the state machinery is unable to fix a problem.

Under Afridi's leadership, Lashkar-e-Islam has occasionally picked battles with some of the local subtribes. In April 2008, his men had a skirmish with the powerful Kukikhel tribesmen of Jamrud because the Kukikhels wanted to indulge in businesses that Afridi considered un-Islamic. And on March 3, 2008, Lashkar-e-Islam militants attacked a controversial shrine in the Bara Sheikhan village on the outskirts of the provincial capital Peshawar and killed about eighteen locals; it claimed that the shrine was being used by drug peddlers and addicts.

Afridi's group has some connection with the Taliban movement in Afghanistan, but contacts with Al Qaeda cannot be established. Publicly, Lashkar-e-Islam expresses solidarity with the Afghan Taliban and Osama bin Laden, but it is difficult to ascertain whether this relationship extends beyond verbal expressions of support. Afridi did maintain good contacts with Haji Naamdar, an avowed opponent of the TTP and of Al Qaeda in the area who was killed in a TTP attack.

In November 2007, Afghan Taliban leaders mediated a dispute between Lashkar-e-Islam and their rival Ansarul Islam. Even if Mangal Bagh is not sending his men to fight in Afghanistan, his state within the state does provide safe haven for like-minded Taliban.

**Pir Saifurrehman:** An Afghan who lived in the Khyber agency from 1977 to 2006, Pir Saifurrehman is the founder of the religious-cum-militant group Ansarul Islam. Since late 2005, Ansarul Islam has been involved in hate mongering through illegal FM radio stations and in violent clashes with its main rival, Lashkar-e-Islam.

Pir Saifurrehman was forced to leave the tribal area after the authorities detained some forty of his supporters in the first week of February 2006 because his verbal attacks on Mufti Munir Shakir had led to violence in the Khyber agency. For shelter, he reportedly moved to central Punjab, where he is thought to be staying with the like-minded Pirs of Jamaat-e-Ahle Sunnat, an anti-Taliban religious group.

**Haji Naamdar:** Haji Naamdar founded Amar bil Maroof wa Nahi Analmunkir (Promotion of Virtue and Prevention of Vice). Inspired by Mulla Omar, Naamdar aspired to the enforcement of Islamic sharia in Pakistan. The TTP claimed responsibility for killing Naamdar, who was shot dead by an assassin on August 13, 2008, alleging he was collaborating with the army. He was in his midthirties.

Although Naamdar launched his organization to cleanse the society of infidels and criminals, he often talked of the "foreign occupation of Afghanistan." A senior government official told me in Peshawar in April 2008: "Naamdar does nothing inside Pakistan and is interested only in Afghanistan. He runs his own prisons, and his utterances are treated as final, like that of Mulla Omar."[9]

Naamdar opposed suicide attacks inside Pakistan, but justified them as the "best weapon" to use against the enemy in Afghanistan. "We have to finish our enemy in Afghanistan by any means and suicide bombing is the best weapon," he said. Naamdar acknowledged the presence of Taliban militants in the Khyber agency and their "active participation" in cross-border anti-U.S. jihad.

A day after surviving a suicide attack, Naamdar told the media that he was helping to "detoxify" militants staying with him through "Islamic classes," which teach them that attacking Pakistani forces, people, or state installations "is no jihad at all" and that rather, by "doing so, we are strengthening anti-Islamic forces."[10]

"I am reforming these mujahideen as Islam does not allow jihad against Muslims," he said. "These [mujahideen] leaders brainwash teenagers, telling them that each and every Pakistani is their enemy and his or her killing is justified. Are they not killing innocent Pakistanis?"[11]

"We will never wage jihad inside Pakistan. Afghanistan needs mujahideen to liberate that country from United States-led foreign occupation. We do attack the US forces across the border and that is what real jihad is all about," he said. "The way President Bush is waging a crusade against Islam, we will hit the US wherever and whenever it is possible. Our jihad against the US in Afghanistan goes on. . . . Why should mujahideen target Pakistan when this country provides everything for jihad in Afghanistan?"[12]

Naamdar's influence was restricted to the Bara Kambarkhel tribe, but he played host to various tribal and foreign militants, and that made him a potentially influential commander in a region through which food and fuel supplies flow to the U.S. and NATO forces based in Afghanistan.

**Mehbubul Haq:** The successor to Pir Saifurrehman as head of Ansarul Islam, Mehbubul Haq lives a low-profile life in the remote Tirah valley. He graduated from a madrassa and is inspired by the philosophy of Mulla Omar.

**Tariq Afridi:** A native of Darra Adamkhel, Afridi is fiercely antigovernment and one of the top TTP commanders in the Khyber agency, though he is apparently headquartered in Orakzai. He was allegedly behind the execution of a Polish engineer, Piotr Stanczak, who was kidnapped in September 2008 and killed on February 7, 2009. His followers also claimed responsibility for a number of suicide bombings and other attacks in different parts of the country in recent years, including a deadly attack on a mosque in Darra Adamkhel in October 2010.

**Adnan Afridi:** A militant commander from the Tirah valley of the Khyber agency and an aide to Tariq Afridi, Adnan Afridi was wanted by the government for his involvement in attacks on security forces and the 2008 kidnapping of Pakistan's ambassador to Afghanistan, Tariq Azizuddin, an Iranian diplomat and the Afghan ambassador-designate. During 2010, he operated from a base in Nikkah Ziarat, Kurram Agency, and was reportedly at odds with Mullah Toofan, the head of TTP Taliban in Orakzai agency and Kurram agency. Their political differences resulted in frequent bloody clashes between their followers.

Afridi suffers from kidney ailments and is said to have visited hospitals in Rawalpindi for treatment. He was reportedly murdered on a visit to Rawalpindi in late October 2010, but Taliban sources in Peshawar refused to confirm or deny his death.

## Mohmand Agency

**Abdul Wali Raghib:** In his early forties, Abdul Wali Raghib is the top Taliban commander in the Mohmand agency, and is the deputy emir of the TTP for the Mohmand area. Raghib, known as Omar Khalid, is a resident of Kared. His father is known as Haji Sahib. He was affiliated with Harkatul Mujahideen in 1990–91 and was involved in jihadi activities in Kashmir and Afghanistan. He used to sit in Mianmundi as a local commander of the Mohmand agency and was famous among his colleagues for reciting revolutionary poetry. Close associates describe him as a born jihadi who glorifies the fight against "infidels" through his poetry, which is all about jihad.[13]

Formerly a journalist, Khalid worked for the projihad publications *Zarb-e-Momin* and the daily *Islam* in the 1990s before he joined the "freedom struggle" of the Kashmiri people. Local journalists said his membership in the Ghalanai Press Club was revoked after he became involved in militant activities.

Ghalanai administration officials maintain that Khalid and his people usually engage American forces in the eastern Afghan province of Kunar and closely coordinate their actions with Maulvi Faqir Mohammad of the Bajaur agency, though unlike the latter, Khalid "does not host foreign militants" in Mohmand. He reportedly commands at least twenty-five thousand trained militants, though figures are difficult to verify.

**Sangeen Khan Kandahari:** On September 2, 2007, young Talibs associated with Kandahari abducted ten Frontier Corps men, including a major, carrying $3,500 (PKR 260,000) in cash, the salaries of those deployed in the Mohammad Gat area. He made certain demands but then apparently released them unconditionally two days later.

**Abu Nuhman Sungri:** Also known as Dr. Assad, Sungri is one of TTP's strongmen in Mohmand. He liaises with the media, but few people know him by face.

### Orakzai and Kurram Agencies

**Maulvi Said Khan:** Said Khan is the most influential commander operating in the Orakzai agency. About thirty-eight years of age, Khan belongs to the Mamoozai subtribe of the Orakzai. He follows the Panjpeer brand of Deobandi Islam and does not disguise his deep contempt for Shias. He has actively participated in the sectarian clashes in the Kurram agency and Hangu. The TTP appointed him to the Amir Orakzai agency after the death of Baitullah Mehsud.

He is notorious for the kidnapping of people from Hangu and the Kurram agency, especially Shias and wealthy political leaders. In fact, he even orchestrated the abduction of the son-in-law of his former employer, a known political figure. He effectively countered the revolt of the Alikhel tribe against the TTP in the Orakzai agency in late 2008, and he was the main culprit behind the suicide attack on a jirga of the Alikhel tribe in Khadezai that left 160 people dead and scores injured in October 2008.

**Maulana Mohammad Nabi Orakzai:** Nabi, in his late thirties, is a powerful TTP commander in the Orakzai agency. He was once the general secretary of Jamiat

Ulema-e-Islami (JUI) in the Hangu district. He has an old association with the Afghan Taliban and thus became a popular Taliban figure in Hangu, Orakzai, and parts of the Kurram agency. He had been hosting TTP commanders in the Orakzai agency since 2006, but in 2008, he developed some personal differences with the TTP. Mullah Toofan was close to Hakimullah because of his influence in the important geographic high grounds of the Kurram agency, and Nabi couldn't digest Toofan's influence with the TTP. As a result, Nabi left the TTP and was seen for some time with his own group of militants in the Orakzai agency. Later on Hakimullah brought him back to the TTP, but this time Nabi didn't perform as a zealous operative. Soon he detached himself again from the central TTP outfit in the Kurram agency and essentially remained a powerful militant commander operating independently.

Shah Nawaz, a young militant commander from the Orakzai agency, was brutally murdered by Mullah Toofan's group because of his association with Mr. Nabi. In retaliation Nabi killed two of Toofan's men in the Spin Waam area of the Kurram agency.

**Maulvi Noor Jamal (Mullah Toofan):** Noor Jamal is known as Mullah Toofan (Toofan means "storm") because of his viciousness and brutality. He belonged to a poor family from Mamoozai and in 2004 he left Mamoozai for Qurat in the Kurram agency to serve as a professional mullah in a mosque owned by a local tribal malik (elder). He received two thousand rupees as a monthly stipend for his services. He told the local malik he was moving out of the area because of a feud between the families of his two wives. He apparently migrated to another mosque in Togh Sarai, a village of the Hangu district, but then he was spotted a few months later, in the summer of 2008, in his native village. He told friends a Pakistani intelligence agency had arrested him and he was taken to Quetta for interrogation. He claimed that during one of the journeys, when a vehicle of the security forces capsized and caught fire, he found an opportunity to escape.

As early as 2005, Toofan started visiting South Waziristan before joining the list of the top TTP commanders in the Kurram agency. He remains involved in many cases of kidnapping and murder.

**Mir Salam:** A Mamozai commander of the TTP known for his commitment and unquestionable loyalty to the TTP movement. Two of Mir Salam's brothers have committed suicide attacks, one of them during Jumma prayer at a mosque in the Khyber agency in March 2009. Mir Salam, who is thirty-five, is a close friend of Mullah Toofan and Maulvi Said Khan.

**Daulat Hafiz:** Daulat Hafiz, thirty-five, belongs to Khuidad Khel, a subtribe of the Orakzai tribe in the Kurram agency. His close friends say that Baitullah Mehsud considered him to be his right hand because of his loyalty. He is a proud commander of the TTP operating in central Kurram and parts of Hangu. His home in Sparkate, Kurram agency, remains a station of TTP commanders and militants.

He fought in Afghanistan in 2005 but didn't cross the Durand Line after joining the TTP.

**Maulana Fazal Saeed:** A member of the Watizai tribe in the Kurram agency, Maulana Saeed owns and operates a petrol pump in Bagan, a village on the main road in Kurram. Due to the Taliban's frequent visits to the petrol pump for refueling, many Taliban militants befriended him. He joined the TTP formally in 2007.

Saeed had imposed taxes on the "flour smugglers" who were using the routes from the Kurram agency to Afghanistan. He received $38 (PKR 3,000) per vehicle loaded with flour illegally bound for Afghanistan. Local people claim that he provided millions of rupees to the TTP out of these taxes. He is an active TTP operative in Lower Kurram and involved in planning sectarian attacks. Both Hakimullah Mehsud and Qari Hussain were reportedly at the forefront of the anti-Shia campaign in the area that left hundreds of tribesmen dead in dozens of direct clashes and gory incidents of slaughter since 2008.

## Swat and Malakand

**Maulana Fazlullah:** Born on March 1, 1975, in the small village of Imam Derai near Kanjoo, Maulana Fazlullah, the son-in-law of Maulvi Sufi Mohammad, has emerged as the new face of Al Qaeda in the Swat region. Militants from other regions, particularly from areas like Waziristan, and some foreigners rallied around him because of his charisma. Locals and outsiders alike must establish contact with him or his people for a clear passage through the areas outside Mingora. He enjoyed support within the security establishment of Pakistan because of his role in the Afghan Taliban movement. In Bajaur and Malakand, he was considered as dangerous as Baitullah Mehsud.

He used the mosque in Imam Derai and Sufi Mohammad's mosques to deliver jihadist sermons, condemning the "liberal and pro-Western government in Pakistan" and urged people to join him in the jihad inside Afghanistan. Unlike Sufi, Fazlullah radiated charisma and appealed to the largely illiterate and dispossessed poor masses. He was reported to be very popular among women because of his emotional speeches aired over his illegal FM radio station. In January 2007, he collected a large amount of money (approximately $19,000) for the construction of a seminary in Imam Derai in lower Swat from the residents of Mingora. Many people volunteered to help construct his madrassa, a sprawling fifty-acre compound with a hundred-square-foot hall for a mosque.

A number of friends and journalists used to tell stories about how people in Swat and its periphery would fall over one another to donate to the TNSM's cause. Cash, gold jewelry, and anything that they thought would help Fazlullah would find its way to his centers and mosques. When Fazlullah's people would set up camp to collect donations, men and women would throng the spot to part with their valuables. Support, sympathy, or silence were the three major options as long as Fazlullah's thugs ruled the streets in Swat and other areas of Malakand.

Maulana Fazlullah was arrested with Sufi Mohammad and scores of others late in 2001 for their daring attempts to help the Taliban against the U.S.-led coalition and spent seventeen months in Dera Ismail Khan jail before being released. He essentially resurrected the once forgotten TNSM and used TNSM cadres to raise his own army, provoking some members to disown him, particularly after he began spewing hatred against the government and the army through his FM radio station. He is now a full-fledged member of the TTP and has made his affiliation evident on many an occasion by linking peace in Swat to peace in Waziristan.

Fazlullah made international headlines in October 2007, when the government of Pakistan took military action against his supporters to restore the writ of the state in Swat. The confrontation continued for a couple of months, and claimed the lives of many of his supporters, including his brother Fazle Ahad, as well as many security-forces personnel. Controversy surrounds Fazlullah. One report says he escaped to Afghanistan, but others say he is disabled as a result of wounds from an aerial attack on his hideout in the summer of 2009. I was told by a high-ranking officer that he was in Afghanistan, though some suspect he may be in army custody.

One of his younger brothers, Fazle Wahid, was killed along with eighty-three others in the Pakistani military's strike on a seminary at Chenagai, in the Bajaur agency, on October 30, 2006. After the Red Mosque operation in July 2007, Maulana Fazlullah used his illegal FM radio station to incite violence against security forces in the area, which eventually prompted a military operation in October 2007, restoring the government partially. Following elections on February 18, 2008, the provincial government signed a peace deal with Fazlullah's militants to buy some time, though these Taliban continued to impose sharia justice in the Peochar, Janikhel, and Imam Derai areas, still considered to be out of bounds for government officials.[14]

Maulana Fazlullah defended his FM radio station in Swat as a tool to reform society, and until he went underground during the military onslaught, his followers viciously campaigned against TVs, VCRs, CDs, and music shops, which Fazlullah condemned as "sources of evil that promote obscenity and vulgarity." On a number of occasions during 2007 following his appeal, hundreds of people burned their TV sets and VCRs publicly all over Swat. He has given Islamic names to villages and turned against female education, urging people not to send their daughters and sisters to schools, an action that he termed "un-Islamic." His appeal prompted parents in Swat to remove about 1,700 girl students from schools within two to three months. As many as 67 girls' schools were destroyed or damaged by unknown attackers between November 2007 and July 2008.

Maulana Fazlullah went as far as declaring polio drops an "un-Islamic practice" and asked people in his area not to get their children vaccinated, saying that it was a conspiracy by the West to make them infertile. Interestingly, the maulana also argued that there was no concept of a cure for the disease in Islam. Sociopolitical pressures forced Fazlullah to allow a three-day antipolio vaccination drive in Swat in July 2008, though he kept threatening suicide attacks if the army did not pull out of the area. In late July, when the army mounted attacks on the TTP militants and their hideouts, Fazlullah again disappeared to guide the militancy from underground. Today, Fazlullah is a fugitive along with his hard-line supporters, many of whom have surrendered to military forces or been captured.

Fazlullah reportedly sustained serious injuries between July and August 2009, when the military operation was in full swing. A spokesman indirectly confirmed that the cleric was incapacitated. Speculation abounded that Fazlullah might be in the custody of the security forces. Military officials denied it.

Following months of silence, Fazlullah's mother, Aamna Bibi, appeared before the media on January 9, 2010, and appealed to her son to renounce violence and surrender to the security forces. "I don't know where my son is at the moment but I urge him to surrender to the government," she said at a press conference organized by the security forces in Swat. Waliullah Kabulgrami, a former teacher of Fazlullah's, sat by her side. She said that she had last seen her son in September and that he had been unable to speak. The family has been under the army's protective custody since April 19, 2009, when Maulana Sufi Mohammad unleashed a scathing attack on Pakistan's constitution, the parliament, and the Supreme Court, ridiculing them as un-Islamic.

Interestingly, only two days after the army announced the arrest of Muslim Khan, a spokesman for Fazlullah, in September 2009, Fazlullah sent an audio message. The message, in Pashto, reads as follows: "The Taliban movement is presently in a state of illness. When you are ill, your activities are curtailed. That is what has happened to the Taliban organization, but it will bounce back." Salman, who took over as the spokesman for the Swat Taliban after the arrest of Muslim Khan, said the brief recording was delivered to him on Friday. Maulana Fazlullah mentioned the TTP founder Baitullah Mehsud in his message and stressed that all Pakistani Taliban wished to die like him. "Like Baitullah Mehsud, all Taliban fighters want to embrace martyrdom. Getting arrested while fighting for a cause is no big deal for the Taliban," he maintained. He said the Taliban in Swat and Malakand would continue their struggle for the enforcement of real sharia and offer every sacrifice to achieve this goal. Maulana Fazlullah made it clear that he and his men had lost trust in the Pakistan army after it allegedly invited his organization to peace talks and arrested the five negotiators. He said a need may arise again for the government and the military to talk to the Taliban, but the Swat Taliban had decided once and for all not to hold any negotiations with the government.

**Maulana Shah Dauran:** Dauran was from Qambar, in Swat. He was the deputy head of the Swat Taliban led by Maulana Fazlullah. In the summer of 2008, Dauran went on evening shows on Fazlullah's FM radio station, ridiculing Pakistani leaders as well as the army and issuing harsh pronouncements on common citizens and welfare workers associated with NGOs.

Shah Dauran disappeared from the scene in late April 2009, after the government decided to launch a military campaign against the Swat militants. On December 26, 2009, following months of mystery, the Swat Taliban announced his death from cancer. He had been in hiding despite his serious illness and breathed his last somewhere in the Bajaur agency.

**Sirajuddin:** A cousin of Fazlullah's and a resident of Imam Deray, Sirajuddin was once a member of a leftist student group, the Demoratic Students' Organization (DSO). Now in his early thirties, he champions Fazlullah's hard-line Islam, and is ready to kill and die for the Taliban cause. He is in charge of areas that were once prime tourist attractions, such as the skiing resort of Malam Jabba.

**Muslim Khan:** In his midforties, Muslim Khan served as a brutal spokesman for the TTP in Swat until his dramatic capture along with four other Taliban militants in a military intelligence sting operation in the village of Mangalore on September 3, 2009. The operation became possible only after Kamal Khan, an old acquaintance settled in the United States, agreed to cooperate with the authorities, creating a façade of negotiations and trapping the militants, who had been publicly vowing more attacks on the Pakistani government institutions.

As a student in Peshawar, Muslim Khan had been a member of the progressive Pakistan People's Party before heading to the United States, where he took up menial jobs, including driving cabs, before returning to Pakistan immediately after the 9/11 terror attacks in the United States. Once in Swat, he hooked up with Fazlullah and soon rose to become his spokesman.

Besides his mother tongue, Pashto, Khan is conversant in Urdu and English. He defends the TTP as an alliance of mujahideen struggling against the "cruel policies of America and Pakistan," and vows to continue the jihad.

In February 2009, Muslim Khan released a list—also mentioned on Shah Dauran's radio program—of forty-five people and their family members, eighty-six in all, who he said were wanted for their opposition to the Taliban. He offered these people an opportunity to clear their names by appearing in one of the forty shariat courts, which he calls a "forum for dispute settlement."

Muslim Khan was arrested by military intelligence on September 3, 2009, along with a senior commander and three others, from the outskirts of Mingora. He and another senior Taliban commander, Mehmood, carried a reward of $125,000 (PKR 10 million) each on their heads. It was the third major setback to the militant outfit since August 5, when a drone-fired missile took out Baitullah Mehsud, the TTP founder. (Only a few days after Mehsud's elimination, the TTP spokesman Maulvi Mohammad Omar was captured in the Mohmand tribal region.)

Under a façade of negotiations, the militants, who had been publicly vowing attacks on Pakistani government institutions, were trapped in a raid involving some six dozen commandos. Khan and others were immediately dispatched to the Peshawar jail under extremely elaborate security arrangements.

As the TTP Swat's spokesman, Muslim Khan had owned up to scores of suicide bombings on the security forces and admitted to blowing up dozens of girls' schools in the Swat region. Khan also claimed responsibility for sending two suicide bombers to weapons-manufacturing complexes—the Pakistan Ordnance Factories near Islamabad—where about ninety people were blown to pieces in April 2008 in one of the deadliest attacks in Pakistan. According to a rough estimate, Muslim Khan accepted responsibility for more than one hundred acts of sabotage, including the burning of schools, attacks on security forces, and the slaughtering of government officials, mostly policemen.

**Said Rahman, alias Fateh:** Fateh became the Taliban's field operations commander after Hussain Ali, alias Tor Mullah, was killed during a raid by the security forces. In his midthirties, he is a graduate of a madrassa.

**Ibn-e-Amin:** An emerging Taliban commander in his late twenties, Amin has injected terror in the residents of the Matta subdistrict of Swat by decreeing harsh punishments to rivals and government functionaries.

**Mohammad Alam Khan:** Known as Mullah Binori because he headed a mosque in the Binori village near the Khwaza Khela subdistrict, Alam Khan uses FM radio to spread his message of fear and terror.

**Maulana Saifullah:** Maulana Saifullah is the emir of TNSM in Malakand. Addressing TNSM workers in Matta on March 25, 2007, he set a seventy-two-hour deadline for the government to release Sufi Mohammad and warned that one hundred suicide bombers were ready to strike targets inside Pakistan if he was not released. The suicide bombers never materialized and Sufi Mohammad was eventually released in April 2008.

Two Taliban militants belonging to North Waziristan and caught in Afghanistan testified that they were sent to Afghanistan by Maulana Saifullah after the signing of the peace deal in September 2006.

# Appendix 2

# A Profile of Militant Organizations in Pakistan

Many of Pakistan's militant outfits took seed during the anti-Soviet jihad but subsequently evolved into lethal sectarian entities. Harkatul Mujahideen, Lashkar-e-Taiba, and Jaish-e-Mohammad became heavily involved in the so-called "jihad" in Kashmir and developed close ties with the Afghan Taliban. Most of these groups represent an obscurantist, pan-Islamist worldview and are rabidly opposed to the Western style of life as well as to India.

Events since 9/11 changed the rules of the game for militants and militant organizations, some of whom had traditionally enjoyed the support of the Pakistani establishment for their strategic objectives both in Afghanistan and the Indian part of Kashmir. Most of these groups originated in central Pakistan, in the most populous province of the Punjab, and sprouted from the Jamiat Ulema-e-Pakistan, a Deobandi movement. They were known as "guest organizations" in Kashmir, while in Afghanistan they owed allegiance to Taliban chief Mulla Omar and Osama bin Laden. These organizations drew people predominantly from their province and were thus known as the Punjabi factor in FATA.*

## Harkatul Mujahideen (Harkatul Ansar)

Harkatul Mujahideen emerged as Harkatul Ansar in the 1980s with a mission to fight the Soviet Union in Afghanistan (harkat means "movement"). The organization believes that an Islamic system of justice should be promulgated inside Pakistan, and that those who are insincere to Islam and Pakistan must be killed. Its cadre received basic training inside Afghanistan and fought alongside the Afghan mujahideen. Though not directly involved in sectarian violence, Harkatul Ansar

---

* Note: Besides my own research and book *The Unholy Nexus*, the information here is based on three other sources: the weekly *Friday Times*, Amir Mir's *The True Face of Jehadis*, and Muhammad Amir Rana's *A to Z of Jihadi Organizations in Pakistan*.

strongly supported Sipahe Sahaba Pakistan's move against the Shia community. After the Soviet withdrawal from Afghanistan, the group reorganized its basic cadres and moved them into Kashmir under the patronage of members of the Pakistani intelligence service.

Its erstwhile chief, Maulana Fazlurrehman Khalil, appeared on the Kashmir scene in 1993–94. He is a big fan of Osama bin Laden and the Taliban. "I saw him with an American Stinger missile in his hands," he said when I asked him about his last encounter with Osama bin Laden during a meeting in Rawalpindi's lower-middle-class residential neighborhood Khayaban-e-Sir Syed, in April 2000. "Yes, Osama is a great Muslim mujahid. We fought together in Afghanistan against the Soviet-Russian troops but then I moved on to help Kashmir's Muslim liberation movement after the Russians left Afghanistan this month eleven years ago," Khalil said. "We have nothing in common anymore," he quickly added. The denial had a hollow ring to it.

On May 24, 1998, one of his deputies, a trusted longtime aide and veteran of the Afghan war, code-named Allah Wasaya, arranged a trip for a few Pakistani journalists to Khost, in eastern Afghanistan, for a meeting with the sheikh, a title they used for Bin Laden. I was invited, but backed out the day before the trip because I sensed the next couple of days were going to be crucial as Pakistan's preparations for nuclear tests were almost complete. Sources in one of the nuclear organizations had asked me to stay on for the "big moment." Pakistan exploded its nuclear devices on May 28 and 29, 1998, while my colleagues were in Afghanistan.

Khalil, along with thousands of his zealots who idolize Osama bin Laden as their role model, vowed revenge on the United States after its Tomahawk missiles destroyed Bin Laden's camp on the outskirts of Khost in August 1998, killing at least twenty-five people. The ostensible reason for this action was the terror strike on U.S. diplomatic missions in Kenya and Tanzania a few days earlier, which the American establishment believed had been masterminded at Bin Laden's camp in Khost. Nine of those killed were members of Khalil's Harkatul Mujahideen. Harkatul Ansar had changed its name after the U.S. State Department banned it as a terrorist organization in October 1999, along with twenty-eight others.

Harkatul Mujahideen was rated as the most lethal of the militant groups operating in the Indian-administered Kashmir. India insists the group acted in Kashmir with a mission from Pakistan's intelligence agency, the ISI. The ISI backed Harkatul and other parties because this was a cost-effective way of keeping India bogged down in Kashmir, an approach that brought criticism and scorn on Pakistan. During 1999 alone, the group claimed to have killed 43 officers and 1,825 soldiers of the Indian army in attacks on convoys or military posts. They also killed 10 alleged Indian spies and lost 96 of their own fighters during skirmishes with the Indian forces.

"They are all martyrs; we are proud of them because they gave their lives for a sacred cause," Khalil said, rejecting Western allegations that his was a terrorist organization. "I think this is the Indian propaganda that makes the world view us as terrorists. We condemn terrorism but we do believe in jihad for the liberation of

Kashmir," said the soft-spoken Khalil. He took exception to the Western definition of terrorism.

"Not a single person was declared a terrorist during the Afghan war against the Soviets. Instead, the Americans and other Western nations welcomed and celebrated them as Islamic warriors. Osama bin Laden was one of these heroes of the West," Khalil pointed out.

Harkatul Mujahideen continued to train its fighters at the Rishkor camp on the outskirts of Kabul even after the 1998 missile attacks on its facilities in eastern Afghanistan. The proof came when one of the bombs dropped by the coalition jets hit a residential complex close to the Rishkor camp and killed at least thirty-five Harkatul people in late October 2001.

Harkatul Mujahideen currently lies extremely low. Its leader, Khalil, lives practically underground, with little contact with the media. Most of its members were disbanded after the government decision in 2003 not to tolerate any infiltration into Indian Kashmir. Many Harkatul fighters, however, are believed to have joined the TTP or the Afghan Taliban.

## Jaish-e-Mohammad (JeM)

When Maulana Masood Azhar was freed from an Indian jail and returned to Kandahar on December 31, 1999, in exchange for the release of hostages aboard a hijacked Indian passenger jet, few in Pakistan or elsewhere had any inkling as to what the stocky fellow was up to. Soon afterward, he emerged in Pakistan to a rousing reception. He announced his intention to raise an anti-India force—Jaish-e-Mohammad, or the Army of Mohammad—to liberate Kashmir. This was yet another Deobandi Sunni–militant organization created in the name of jihad against infidels. It enjoyed the blessings of Mufti Nizamuddin Shamzai, the spiritual head of Banoria, a mosque and madrassa based in Karachi. Shamzai had in 1998 declared that the killing of any American was "legal and Islamic." Azhar's agenda endeared him to Mulla Omar, who eventually declared Azhar his deputy for Pakistan. Until the rout of the Taliban regime, Azhar spent most of his time in Kandahar and Zabul, where he ran training camps for his Kashmir operations.

Interviews with intelligence officials, including Pakistani operatives based in Kandahar, yielded interesting revelations.

"I think we should also keep in mind our interests in Kashmir. These fighters have made the job much easier for us and they need our support," a senior official of the ISI observed when confronted with hard questions on the ISI's support for militancy. Jaish-e-Mohammad was one of sixteen organizations united under the umbrella of the United Jihad Council (UJC) to battle Indian troops in Kashmir.

Two factors may have influenced Azhar's decision to go his own way; first, he had become more radical and rigid during his captivity in the Tihar jail in India. Second, one of his associates told me in Rawalpindi shortly after the creation of

Jaish-e-Mohammad that Azhar thought he could provide a fresh impetus to the insurgency in Kashmir with the help of the Afghan Taliban. Azhar's oratory and his close relations with the inner circle of the Afghan Taliban quickly won him scores of new members, and within a year or so Jaish-e-Mohammad gradually outnumbered Harkatul Mujahideen.

But the creation of Jaish-e-Mohammad led to another complication: apparently while the Pakistani establishment supported the move, it also suspected Azhar of playing a double game. It thought Azhar might be acting on behalf of his former Indian captors because, while his jihadi outfit appeared more radical and motivated, it further divided the Kashmiri militant movement. His zealots openly admitted, and frequently at that, to acts of terrorism in Kashmir and India, including the attack on the Kashmiri legislative assembly. These admissions were seen as suspect as they provided ammunition for the Indian government to lash out at Pakistan.

The emergence of Jaish-e-Mohammad marked virtually the fourth division within Harkatul Mujahideen. In the initial years of jihad, Harkatul Mujahideen and Harkatul Jihad-e-Islami (HJI) had merged into Harkatul Ansar. But the bond did not last and both resumed their original identities. This development encouraged Ilyas Kashmiri, who was leading the 313 Brigade of the Harkatul Mujahideen in Kotli, to go independent in 1999. The launch of Jaish-e-Mohammad in early 2000 was the most severe blow.

Azhar had been jailed in India for overstaying his visa. It was believed that the Indian Airlines passenger plane had been hijacked primarily to secure his release and that of two other militants.

Just a few days after his release, Azhar emerged in his hometown of Bahawalpur, in southern Punjab, and received a hero's welcome from his followers. Soon after announcing his intention to raise tens of thousands of dollars for Jaish-e-Mohammad, Azhar undertook a whirlwind tour of the country, including Islamabad, where he received special attention from the intelligence agency's personnel, who could be easily identified at public meetings by their appearance, especially their stiff bearing. Jaish-e-Mohammad drew away hundreds of Harkatul Mujahideen activists. Once the party structure was in place, scores of new mosques and madrassas sprouted within months in the NWFP, where they attracted hundreds of jihad-oriented students. That Azhar had been in an Indian jail worked as a special pull; his top-tier leaders used this fact to portray him as a great mujahid, whom "we snatched from the jaws of India."

Some observers believe that the Pakistani backers of the Kashmiri militancy had found in Masood Azhar a new tool to reinforce the jihad in Kashmir after the setback in Kargil in the summer of 1999, when Pakistani special troops were forced to vacate positions they had occupied in the winter after crossing the Line of Control that separates the Indian and Pakistani parts of Kashmir.

Pakistan was still recovering from the Kargil humiliation when the hijacking took place. With the release of Azhar, the establishment hoped it could inject a new vigor in the demoralized mujahideen as well as the regular forces. Azhar moved to

Afghanistan, received the blessings of the Taliban supreme commander Mulla Omar and began establishing camps there to train fighters.

By the end of 2000, he had managed to entrench his group in the NWFP and in southern Punjab. He turned Hangu, considered the most sensitive part of the border region with a history of Sunni-Shia hostilities, into his virtual headquarters. Sipahe Sahaba Pakistan (SSP), headed by the firebrand Maulana Azam Tariq, assisted Jaish-e-Mohammad in establishing new mosques and recruitment centers for those desirous of fighting in Kashmir. The SSP helped out Azhar in this region for two reasons. Both idolized the Afghan Taliban for their "commitment to Islam" and the SSP was focused on Pakistan's internal politics and essentially thrived on its radical anti-Shia outlook whereas Azhar dreamed of "liberating Kashmir"; hence there was no conflict of interest.

Hangu has a volatile mix of Shia and Sunni populations. The town is also a gateway to the Kurram and Orakzai agencies. Jamia Taleem-ul-Quran, a seminary set up by Maulana Masood Azhar's followers in Hangu, became the nucleus for his followers. It stands out as a landmark for those approaching the town. Sprawling over more than five acres, the complex attracts money and people and substantial support and sympathy from officialdom.

From Kohat up to Bagato, in Hangu, one could observe highly provocative anti-Shia slogans and invitations to join the jihad by Jaish-e-Mohammad, Al-Badr, Harkatul Mujahideen, and Hezbul Mujahideen, all of which are ideologically and radically anti-Shia, and given to jihad in Kashmir. These organizations offered military training to youngsters eager to participate in jihad. The invitations were painted on hilltops, roadsides, and walls of private homes.

The expanding influence of the militants' outfits generally aroused concern among the people of Pakistan. "It is not going to be without consequences for our society either," said Dr. Rasool Bakhsh Raees, an Islamabad-based expert on Afghanistan and international affairs. "Religious indoctrination and the zeal of jihad inculcated a sense of self-righteousness, of being on the right path," Dr. Raees argued and, like many others, he was unequivocal in maintaining that the mushrooming of dozens of training camps and madrassas across Pakistan and Afghanistan in the 1980s was directly related to the proxy war against the Soviet Union in Afghanistan.

Until it was banned in January 2002, the Jaish-e-Mohammad network was spread over seventy-eight districts in Pakistan. The biggest center, Karachi, oversaw about a hundred subordinate offices. Bahawalpur and Multan centers followed in size, with fifty-five offices functioning in Bahawalpur and forty in Multan. Jaish-e-Mohammad also maintained large centers in the NWFP's Waziristan agency, Malakand, Kohat, Bannu, and Dera Ismail, while Muzaffarabad used to be the largest Jaish-e-Mohammad establishment for Pakistan-administered Kashmir.

## Lashkar-e-Taiba

Lashkar-e-Taiba (LeT), widely believed by Indian intelligence agencies to be behind the Mumbai attacks of November 26, 2008, is the armed wing of the Pakistan-based religious organization Markaz-al-Daawatul Ershad, a Sunni anti-U.S. missionary organization formed in 1989. LeT is one of the four largest and best-trained groups fighting in Kashmir, besides Jaish-e-Mohammad, Harkatul Mujahideen, and Hezbul Mujahideen, and is not connected to a political party. The organization has conducted a number of operations against Indian troops and civilian targets in Kashmir since 1993, and was suspected of eight separate attacks in Kashmir in August 2001 that killed nearly a hundred, mostly Hindu, Indians. LeT militants were suspected of kidnapping six persons in Akhala, India, in November 2000 and killing five of them. The organization collects donations from the Pakistani community in the Persian Gulf and United Kingdom, Islamic NGOs, and Pakistani and Kashmiri businessmen. The amount of LeT funding is unknown. The Lashkar-e-Taiba maintains ties to religious/military groups around the world, ranging from the Philippines to the Middle East and Chechnya through the Markaz-al-Daawatul Ershad.

The man who has made most of the headlines on the Kashmir front is the unassuming, slightly stocky Hafiz Mohammad Saeed, fifty-eight, who headed LeT until December 24, 2002, when the ban on his organization and international pressure forced him to take a backseat within the organization. He had been a staunch ally of the Afghan Taliban and like them considers music and photography un-Islamic. Vociferous and unmoved by what his opponents say in public, Hafiz Saeed is a different man at home or in meetings with guests. The father of a son and a daughter, he appears down to earth in person, with his eyes mostly fixed on the floor, and interjects his answers with "my brother," "my son," "my dear."

His soft demeanor hardly betrays the hyperactive, militant character of the organization he heads; even former prime minister Benazir Bhutto once took exception to LeT's activities when she accused it of "muddying waters" in the Indian subcontinent. Western intelligence sources see the LeT as an arm of the Pakistani intelligence agencies, and credible ties have been established with the ISI. Top Pakistani civilian and military leaders deny these linkages, but quite a lot of documentation is available on the nexus that existed between the LeT and the Pakistani intelligence and security agencies. Most military officials claim these links were severed after the Musharraf ban in January 2002, but there are strong indications that a working relationship, or at least tolerance of LeT by the authorities, does exist even today. Hafiz Saeed brushes aside the allegation as "mere Indian propaganda," saying the Indian establishment sees Pakistan's involvement "even in accidental deaths in India."

The organization's headquarters is in Muridke near Lahore. It is a sprawling complex spread over two hundred acres, and has a mujahideen colony with fifty houses, six fish farms, and a rabbit farm that caters to the residents. Since religious education forms an important element of LeT's work, the complex boasts two model schools—one each for girls and boys—and the university Al-Dawat-al-Irshad. The students attending the university also learn horseback riding. Hundreds of them graduate every year, and hundreds more are swelling its ranks, new recruits driven by LeT's ideology of living for God.

On November 3, 2000, Saeed thundered in the presence of tens of thousands of zealots that "jihad is not about Kashmir only. About fifteen years ago people might have found it ridiculous if someone had told them about the disintegration of the USSR. Today, I announce the breakup of India, inshallah. We will not rest until the whole (of) India is dissolved into Pakistan." Saeed promises a new war that will "encompass all of India including Junagarh and Hyderabad," and his organization cites the bomb attack on Indian army soldiers at New Delhi's Mughal Red Fort in early 2001 as proof of that vow.

Many retired Pakistan army officers say LeT's terror tactics were quite effective in engaging the Indian army on several fronts inside Kashmir. Until the January 12, 2002, ban on LeT and five other organizations, many within the Pakistani security establishment considered the Lashkar-e-Taiba a very valuable asset because of its superior professionally trained and ideologically driven cadres.

One of the consequences of the ISI's active disengagement was the creation of at least three LeT splinter groups, who continue to sow terror in Indian Kashmir. Some of them might well be in the service of Al Qaeda or other external anti-Pakistan forces. Some officials say that LeT turned many of its activists to charity primarily because of the pressure from the government. The overwhelming work conducted by Jamatud Dawa, the successor to LeT in Pakistan, in the post–October 2005 earthquake was also a result of the demobilization of many units, according to a former ISI officer.

Following the ban on Lashkar-e-Taiba in January 2002, Saeed has been mostly under house arrest. Twice one of the higher courts ordered his release on the grounds that he could not be detained in the absence of evidence. He shot into international spotlight again after the terrorist attacks in Mumbai in November 2008. Indians demanded his arrest and extradition for trial. Pakistan asked for the evidence, saying Saeed is a Pakistan national and should thus be tried in a Pakistani court if evidence connected him to any act of terrorism. At times, Saeed does speak to the media clandestinely, but his movements and access to outsiders are quite restricted by the authorities, who don't want to hand New Delhi an excuse to ask for his head.

## Sipahe Sahaba Pakistan

Sipahe Sahaba Pakistan (SSP) came into being in September 1984 in the deeply conservative district of Jhang in Pakistan's Punjab province. Its founder, Maulana Haq Nawaz Jhangvi, a Deobandi cleric, had been an active member of Jamiat Ulema-e-Islam (Fazalur Rahman's group) before he went his own radical way. He had made an unsuccessful bid to become a member of the National Assembly, losing to a woman rival, Syeda Abida Hussain, from a powerful Shia family. He would not soon forget the slight. His successor, Maulana Azam Tariq, was elected several times to the National Assembly, or Lower House of Parliament. He took over after Jhangvi was gunned down in an ambush by Shia rivals in 1990, triggering a wave of tit-for-tat violence in Jhang that lasted several years.

Sipahe Sahaba has espoused the goal of restoring the caliphate, or the system of a pan-Islamic rule of governance uniting all Muslim states under a single ruler, a system that followed the demise of Prophet Muhammad and that lapsed under the last Ottoman sultan. Rabidly anti-Shia, the SSP offers membership to any Muslim who regards Shia Muslims as "infidels."

Its anti-Shia campaign has had a terrible impact on Jhang and Faisalabad, a prosperous, industrial district in the Punjab and adjacent areas. Many subdistricts became battlegrounds for militants of the SSP and its Shia counterpart, Sipahe Mohammad. During the mid-1990s, these areas witnessed numerous sniper and terrorist attacks on Shia and Sunni mosques and other religious centers, leaving more than a thousand people dead in three years, including two Iranian diplomats. The rivalry between Sipahe Sahaba and Sipahe Mohammad turned the Punjab, Pakistan's most populous and politically influential province, into a hotbed of sectarian violence until President Pervez Musharraf banned the two organizations in 2002.

Authorities would often declare curfew in Jhang to stop the movement of SSP and SM militants. Provocative graffiti against Shiites and other propaganda tactics were part of the SSP's activities. All members of the SSP were barred from joining any other movement or party and were required to always be ready for the holy war. Maulana Azam Tariq used to claim on the floor of the National Assembly that SSP fighters had directly participated in the Afghan jihad and had trained on Afghan soil. "Those acting against us must know that we have fought a jihad against the Russians, and know how to deal with our enemies," Azam Tariq warned while discussing a motion on sectarian terrorism in the National Assembly in 1991. He himself fell to a barrage of bullets fired by unknown attackers in October 2003 near Islamabad, plunging Jhang into weeks of violent riots.

The SSP, characterized as a terrorist organization by the country's intelligence agencies, received huge financial assistance from Saudi Arabia. Ziaurrehman Farooqi, Azam Tariq's predecessor, stated in an interview that he had received funds from abroad but not from governments. "It is just our sympathizers who donate to our cause," Farooqi said, shortly before he was assassinated in a bomb attack in Lahore in 1994, along with more than a dozen followers. Pakistani intelligence sources used to consider the Saudi embassy in Islamabad a major conduit for Saudi and American funding to the Afghan mujahideen between 1981 and 1998, but when insulted by the Taliban chief Mulla Omar over the handling of Osama bin Laden (the Saudis asked Mulla Omar to hand him over but Omar refused), the Saudis terminated the funding. They recount secret visits to the embassy by SSP leaders, as well as indirect contact between them.

The overriding objective of Saudi cooperation with SSP and other radical Sunni groups in Pakistan has been to undermine Iranian influence and attempts by Tehran to reinforce its supporters both in Pakistan and in Afghanistan. In 1992, there was an unprecedented increase in the circulation of anti-Shia pamphlets, justifying the killing of Shias. Six of these pamphlets obtained by the *Friday Times* from the SSP's central distribution officer in Lahore outlined the reasons for waging jihad against Shias. One pamphlet warns that "if you are not a member of the SSP, then you should be a very worried person." The pamphlet also urges all "Ahle Sunnah" or Sunni Muslims to unite against their common enemy, which by implication is a reference to the Shias. A pamphlet titled "Why Shias Are Not Muslims" calls for a social boycott of the Shias as a religious duty for Sunnis because "they are kafirs (infidels)." Another pamphlet ends in a particularly vicious fatwa from Darul Uloom Deoband, one of the oldest Sunni seminaries in the town of Deoband, which says that anyone who marries a Shia, eats an animal slaughtered by a Shia, participates in their nimaz-e-janaza (funeral prayers) or their annual Eid sacrifices, makes them witnesses to one's marriage, eats with them, offers prayers in their mosques, or has any kind of social contact with them is an infidel. A postscript asserted that even voting for a Shia turns a Sunni into an infidel. A fourth pamphlet warned that Shias were an "alarm bell for the entire Muslim Ummah," or Muslim brotherhood, saying Shias have been the greatest threat to Islam throughout Islamic history. It portrayed the Iranian revolution under Ayatollah Khomeini as the first major attempt by the Shias to spread their brand of Islam throughout Europe, Turkey, and Russia and Central Asian Muslim states, all the way down to Sri Lanka through Pakistan. It appealed to the government to declare Pakistan a Sunni state and Shias as non-Muslims, a favorite theme with the SSP.

## Lashkar-e-Jhangvi

Lashkar-e-Jhangvi (LJ) was created in 1996 by Riaz Basra, the head of Sipahe Sahaba's broadcast and publishing wing. Basra believed in using force to further Maulana Haq Nawaz Jhangvi's mission. His complaint against SSP leadership was that they had abandoned the path of Maulana Jhangvi. Some say that Lashkar-e-Jhangvi was created by the SSP leadership to wash off the label of terrorism.

The SSP claims that it has nothing to do with Lashkar-e-Jhangvi but the two share similar goals and views, and differences between them are largely organizational. Many believe that Lashkar-e-Jhangvi was created as a cover for the more violent activities of the SSP and began its life as the SSP's militant arm. As evidence, it is pointed out that Lashkar-e-Jhangvi activists often stay in the mosques and madrassas that are considered hubs of SSP activities. Visits by SSP leaders to Lashkar-e-Jhangvi activists in jail are no secret either. When a Lashkar-e-Jhangvi terrorist was about to be hanged for the murder of the Iranian counsel Sadiq Ganji in March 2001, Maulana Azam Tariq, the leader of the SSP, offered to pay qisas (blood money) to Iran and threatened dire consequences if the hanging took place. A number of Iranian officials working in Pakistan were targeted in the 1990s and Ganji was thought by the SSP to have been responsible for the assassination of its leader, Haq Nawaz Jhangvi, though there is no evidence of this.

Lashkar-e-Jhangvi began its activities in 1996 and started targeting important Shia leaders and government officials. Its organizational network was strong and extremely complex. Its leader was given the title of Salar-e-A'ala, chief commander, with twelve salars or junior commanders under him and a shura (council) was formed to run the organization. Every activist of Lashkar-e-Jhangvi adopted aliases and had fake identity cards made under these names. An important leader of the Sipahe Sahaba Pakistan based in Jhang claims that Riaz Basra alone possessed twelve national identity cards under different names. A strong network was set up for the supply of arms from Afghanistan to Punjab and from there to Karachi. An official of the civilian Intelligence Bureau told me in Lahore that the number of hard-core Lashkar-e-Jhangvi activists would not be more than a thousand. Yet, from the mid-1980s through to the late 1990s, they kept most of the security agencies on their heels.

Lashkar-e-Jhangvi activists are limited in number because it is mandatory to take a vow until death to complete the organization's mission and to break contact with all family and friends. Pakistan was divided into different regional units for the purpose of terrorist activities. Under this scheme, Gujranwala, Rawalpindi, and Sargodha were under Riaz Basra's command; Faisalabad, Multan, the Bahawalpur division, and the Bhakkar district were under Malik Ishaq; and Karachi was under Qari Abdul Hai's control.

By 2001, Lashkar-e-Jhangvi had been involved in 350 incidents of terrorism. The organization suffered its most difficult time during the second government of Nawaz Sharif when dozens of activists were killed during confrontations with the police between 1998 and 1999. There were reports at that time that Lashkar-e-Jhangvi had received 135 million rupees to assassinate Prime Minister Nawaz Sharif; his brother the chief minister of Punjab Shahbaz Sharif; and the federal minister of information, Mushahid Hussain Syed. The attempt on Nawaz Sharif's life by exploding a bomb on Raiwind Road in Lahore on January 2, 1999, is thought to have been part of this plan.

Riaz Basra remained a challenge for law enforcement authorities for twelve years. He was wanted in three hundred cases of murder and carried a bounty of about $60,000 on his head. That is why Basra's presence in Afghanistan was a source of friction between Afghanistan and Pakistan when Afghanistan was controlled by the Taliban. He kept in touch with newspapers by phone and even gave media interviews while in hiding and on the run from law enforcement agencies. He was a dreaded figure, and at times, because of threats, journalists saw to it that his messages were put across in newspapers. Basra was known to use ten aliases that included Shah Ji, Abdul Rehman, Ashraf Butt, Sajjad, Pir Sahib, Bawa Ji, Chaudhry Sahib, and Asif and Haji Sahib.

Former interior minister Moinuddin Haider told me he and his officials raised the issue of Basra's criminal activities several times with Mulla Omar and his ministers. "We had solid intelligence that suggested Basra's presence in Afghanistan and his close links with the Taliban. But every time we would raise the issue, Taliban ministers would either ignore it or brush it aside," Haider told me. Finally, on May 14, 2002, Basra was killed in a police encounter in Mailsi, in southern Punjab. He was accused of killing Sadiq Ganji; Sikander Shah, chairman of the Shia political party, and Syed Tajamul Hussain, commissioner of Sargodha. He was held responsible for the murder of twenty-five Shias at Mominpura, as well as the explosion near Raiwind, both located near Lahore.

Many Lashkar-e-Jhangvi activists reportedly joined Tehreek-e-Taliban Pakistan and similar outfits in the tribal areas after increased intelligence surveillance made their operations in central Pakistan's urban centers difficult. Its cadre's strength is no more than three hundred, with hundreds of others either under arrest in Pakistan or based in various training camps in Afghanistan, from where they regularly come to Pakistan to carry out terrorist activities, acting both as hired assassins as well as extremely charged religious zealots. Isolation at home also gradually pushed LeJ followers into the Al Qaeda ranks.

Akram Lahori, currently in jail on multiple terror charges, was the commander in chief of Lashkar-e-Jhangvi until his arrest in 2005. Lahori, according to senior police reports of July 2, 2002, was involved in thirty-eight cases of sectarian killings in Sindh. Lashkar-e-Jhangvi also maintains links with another Pakistan-based terrorist outfit, the Jaish-e-Mohammed. Jaish chief Maulana Masood Azhar reportedly wanted to name his outfit Lashkar-e-Mohammad but was "advised" to avoid the association with the Lashkar-e-Jhangvi.

Unconfirmed reports say that the LeJ has been securing financial assistance from Saudi Arabia. Evidence of private Arab funding was disclosed with the arrest of several LeJ cadres responsible for the May 1997 killing of Ashraf Marth, a senior police officer who had arrested the killers of Agha Mohammed Ali Rahimi, the Iranian cultural attaché in Multan. A substantial portion of LeJ's funding is reportedly derived from wealthy benefactors in Karachi.

In recent years, LeJ has moved away from the SSP and joined forces with the Afghan Taliban. Many of its cadres moved to the tribal areas after the group was banned by Musharraf in 2002. Some Lashkar-e-Jhangvi members were reportedly involved in the abduction and execution of the American journalist Daniel Pearl in 2002 and carried out numerous attacks against Iranian interests and Iranian nationals in Pakistan. The outfit uses terror tactics with the aim of forcing the Pakistani state into accepting its narrow interpretations of Sunni sectarian doctrine as official law. The victims of its terror tactics have been leaders and workers of rival Shia outfits, bureaucrats, policemen, doctors, and worshippers of other sects.

According to senior intelligence sources, the Al Qaeda network is suspected of having worked with LeJ cadres to plant car bombs in Karachi and strike at targets in Pakistan. Akram Lahori's successor, Qari Mohammad Zafar, had been operating out of Waziristan until his death in a drone strike around February 25, 2010. Akram Lahori himself remains in jail. Some of his colleagues have been charged with plotting to kill Musharraf, his prime minister Shaukat Aziz, and various high-profile military officials.

# Notes

*Abbreviations*
CRSS: Center for Research and Security Studies
ISPR: Inter-Services Public Relations

## 1. Pakistan's Dangerous Game

1. Cohen, Stephen P., *The Idea of Pakistan*, Brookings Institution Press, 2004.
2. Todd, Paul, and Jonathan Bloch, *Global Intelligence: The World's Secret Services Today*, Zed Books, 2003.

## 2. A Cauldron of Militancy

1. Gul, Imtiaz, www.thefridaytimes.com, September 9-15, 2005.
2. Rana, Muhammad Amir, analysis in South Asianet, Pakistan Institute of Peace Studies, August 2006.
3. Also see A Profile of Pakistani Militants (p. 225) and A Profile of Militant Organizations in Pakistan (p. 249).
4. Rana, Muhammad Amir, *Daily Times*, April 12, 2003.
5. *Daily Times*, August 4, 2007.
6. CRSS interviews with locals in Wana.
7. CRSS interviews during the FATA survey, April/May 2008.
8. Gul, Imtiaz, *The Unholy Nexus: Pak-Afghan Relations under the Taliban*, Vanguard Books, 2002.

## 3. The Kaloosha Operation

1. As told to the author in June 2004 during interviews with Mohammad Noor Wazir and several other Wana residents.
2. As told to the author in an interview with an ex-militiaman at Shakai who eventually moved out of Waziristan in search of security and employment.

## 4. The Taliban in North and South Waziristan

1. The profiles of the seven agencies are based on Hassan Abbas, "Profiles of Pakistan's Seven Tribal Agencies," *Global Terrorism Analysis*, Volume 4, Issue 20, October 2006.
2. Also see Taliban in Orakzai Agency (pp. 241–243).
3. Interview with a FATA journalist who met Baitullah Mehsud on May 24, 2008.
4. Personal interviews at Peshawar. For security reasons, the journalist cannot be identified.
5. Personal interview at Peshawar.
6. Author's interview at Peshawar, July 28, 2008.

## 5. A Question of Justice: An Administrative Profile of FATA

Note: Much of the information in this chapter comes from official briefs prepared for successive governors and presidents.

1. FATA Secretariat documents.
2. FATA Development Strategy, FATA secretariat.
3. Khalid, Aziz, *Reasons of Failure*, article for the Regional Institute of Policy Research, Peshawar, 2006.
4. Khalid, Aziz, *Tribal Areas of Pakistan, Challenges and Responses*, paper for the Regional Institute of Policy Research, Peshawar, September 2005.
5. Shah, S. Iftikhar Hussain, *Some Major Pukhtoon Tribes Along the Pak-Afghan Border*, Areas Study Center, 2000.

## 6. The Al Qaeda Connection: Arabs, Uzbeks, and the Haqqani Network

1. CRSS interviews.
2. Press briefing near Wana, South Waziristan, April 1, 2007.
3. CRSS interview at Rawalpindi, April 10, 2008.
4. Speech at National University of Defense, April 12, 2007.
5. *Friday Times*, April 2007.
6. *Dawn*, April 12, 2007.
7. *Dawn*, March 29, 2007.
8. CRSS interviews.
9. Gul, Imtiaz, *The Unholy Nexus: Pak-Afghan Relations under the Taliban*, Vanguard Books, 2002; and Mir, Amir, *The True Face of Jehadis: Inside Pakistan's Network of Terror*, Roli Books, 2006.
10. Author's interview at Peshawar, July 27, 2008.
11. Voice of America, Urdu and Pashto broadcasts, August 6, 2008.
12. *News*, July 21, 2008.
13. Ibid.
14. NNI news agency, July 22, 2007.
15. *New York Times*, June 17, 2008.
16. *Dawn*, May 7, 2007.

### 7. Crime and Corruption in Khyber and Bajaur

1. *Pulse*, November 23, 2007.
2. Author's interviews with intelligence and security officials in Torkham, May 3, 2008.
3. Associated Press, May 21, 2008.
4. CRSS interview at Hayatabad Market, Peshawar, May 2008.
5. *Friday Times*, March 31, 2006.
6. Sources in Bara, and *Daily Times*, May 20, 2007.
7. Author's interviews with senior intelligence officials responsible for FATA, May 2008.
8. Interviews with officials and locals in Peshawar.
9. *Daily Times*, May 4, 2008.
10. *News*, May 3, 2008.
11. I. Kukikhel, a resident of Jamrud in interview for CRSS.
12. *Daily Times*, May 4, 2008.
13. Author's article in the weekly *Pulse*, August 1, 2008.
14. Interview at Peshawar, July 20, 2008.
15. Associated Press, January 14, 2006.
16. *New York Times*, January 15, 2006.
17. Gul, Imtiaz, and Jason Burke, *Observer*, January 15, 2006.
18. ABC-News, October 30, 2006.
19. Gul, Imtiaz, *Telegraph*, November 9, 2006.
20. *Washington Post*, November 12, 2006.
21. *Dawn*, May 7, 2007.
22. NNI news agency, May 5, 2008.
23. CRSS interview.
24. *Daily Times*, July 29, 2008.
25. Ibid.

### 8. Mohmand, Kurram, and Orakzai

1. CRSS interview with intelligence official, Peshawar.
2. *News*, July 21, 2008.
3. CRSS interviews in Ghalanai.
4. *News*, May 27, 2008.
5. Ibid.
6. Geo TV, May 27, 2008.
7. Interviews/views obtained through Ghalanai based contacts, July 24/25, 2008.
8. Telephone interview on July 29, 2008.
9. *Daily Times*, July 24, 2008.
10. Discussion took place during a meeting at Peshawar, July 20, 2008.
11. *Aaj*, July 27, 2008.
12. CRSS report from Ghalanai.
13. *Dawn, Daily Times*, May 27, 2008.
14. Compiled from various sources including *Aaj*.

15. Author's interview in Rawalpindi, July 25, 2008.
16. Peshawar newspaper, APP reports, July 26/27, 2008.
17. BBC Urdu broadcast, July 27, 2008.
18. *News*, May 10, 2008; Online news agency, May 9, 2008.
19. CRSS source interview.


## 9. Swat Is Burning

1. Gul, Imtiaz, *Pulse*, November 1, 2007.
2. *Daily Times*, July 29, 2008.
3. Author's meeting with the official at Peshawar, December 2006.
4. *Daily Times*, May 4, 2008.
5. Media/Online news agency reports, May 24, 2008.
6. *News*, July 28, 2008.
7. Online news agency, August 5, 2008.
8. Based on CRSS discussions with Swat residents.


## 10. Al Qaeda Brings Suicide Bombing to Pakistan

1. *News*, June 1, 2008.
2. *Guardian*, May 20, 2008.
3. *Dawn*, May 20, 2008.
4. CBSNews.com, May 20, 2008.
5. *Ilhaq, Aaj*, November 4, 2008.
6. Rahimullah Yusufzai in *News*, August 5, 2007.
7. Geo TV, July 22, 2008.
8. NBC News Online, March 28, 2007.
9. Ibid.
10. http://www.longwarjournal.org report on November 13, 2006.
11. Based on the author's interview with his friend from Miranshah who had interviewed the would-be suicide bomber in Peshawar in February 2008.
12. Rahimullah Yusufzai in *News*, August 5, 2007.
13. Author's interview at Dera Ismail Khan, December 2007.


## 11. The ISI Factor

1. Gul, Imtiaz, *The Unholy Nexus: Pak-Afghan Relations Under the Taliban*, Vanguard Books, 2002.
2. DIA Assessment, September 24, 1999.
3. Human Rights Watch annual report, 2002.
4. Author's interviews in Kabul, Kandahar, and Islamabad with diplomats who served in Afghanistan between 1995 and 2002.
5. Author's interviews with a militant at Muzaffarabad, capital of Pakistani Kashmir.

6. Interview with a Kashmiri militant leader who quoted his officer friend as narrating this incident, Islamabad, June 2003.
7. Bruce Riedel Paper on Kargil, April 2000.
8. Author's interviews with Kashmiri leaders in Muzaffarabad, Rawalpindi and Islamabad in 2002 and 2003.
9. Amir, Mohammad, *A to Z of Jihadi Organizations in Pakistan*, Mashal Books, 2004.
10. Mazzetti, Mark, and Eric Schmitt, "CIA Outlines Pakistan Links with Militants," *New York Times*, July 30, 2008.
11. Interview with ABC-News, August 1, 2008.
12. CRSS interview at Peshawar, June 13, 2008.
13. Press release ISPR, July 28, 2008.
14. *New York Times*, July 30, 2008.
15. *Los Angeles Times*, July 30, 2008.
16. Interviews with Pakistan army officials in Rawalpindi, January 2008.
17. *New York Times*, August 1, 2008.
18. Author's interview at Rawalpindi, August 1, 2008.
19. *News*, August 5, 2008.
20. Author's meeting with Azizuddin in Kabul, June 2008.
21. Author's interview with ISPR head General Athar Abbas.
22. STRATFOR, April 22, 2007.
23. CRSS interview, June 16, 2008.
24. Tim McGirk in *Time*, May 6, 2002, Vol. 159, No. 17.
25. News agency AFP, June 16, 2008.
26. CRSS interview, May 2008.
27. Council on Foreign Relations, October 10, 2006.
28. NBC interview in late September 2006.
29. Todd, Paul, and Jonathan Bloch, *Global Intelligence: The World's Secret Services Today*, Zed Books, 2003.
30. *New York Times*, July 21, 2008.
31. *Friday Times*, January 26, 2001.
32. Author's interview with Ansar Abassi at Islamabad, August 1, 2008.
33. *Friday Times*, August 1, 2008.

## 12. Who Funds the Militants?

1. General Kayani's meeting with a select group of journalists at his residence in Rawalpindi, July 12, 2008.
2. Khattak, Iqbal, *Daily Times*, May 30, 2008.
3. U.S. government official Web site, March 2008.
4. Ghani's interview with Voice of America, August 2, 2008.
5. *Dawn*, May 31, 2008.
6. Ibid.
7. Author's interview in Peshawar, December 2007.

8. Author's interview in Islamabad, July 2008.
9. Author's interview in Islamabad, August 7, 2008.
10. Author's interview in Kabul, April 2005.
11. Peshawar meeting after the visit, early June 2008.
12. Khattak, Afrasiab, *Dawn*, July 31, 2008.
13. Author's interviews in Peshawar between February and July 2008.
14. *News*, May 31, 2008.
15. Author's interview with a senior FATA secretariat official at Peshawar, August 5, 2008.

## Appendix 1: A Profile of Pakistani Militants

1. *Time*, April 28, 2008.
2. NNI News Agency, BBC Online, Samaa TV, May 24, 2008.
3. *Daily Times*, May 2008.
4. Accounts of members of the journalists' group that met Mehsud and his colleagues in May 2008.
5. *News*, August 25, 2007.
6. NNI News Agency, July 17, 2007.
7. *Daily Times*, May 4, 2008.
8. Urdu *Jang*, July 19, 2007.
9. Author's meetings with the officials in Peshawar.
10. *Daily Times*, May 3, 2008.
11. Ibid.
12. Ibid.
13. Interview with Mohmand journalist Mukarran Khan, June 2008.
14. *News*, June 6, 2008.

# Index

Page numbers in *italics* refer to maps.